Remaking
Society

Dedication

**For Art and Libera Bartell,
who have fought for freedom all their lives.**

Acknowledgements

This book could not have been written without the suggestions, encouragement, and assistance of several dear friends. I owe my deepest debts to Dimitri Roussopoulos of Black Rose Books and to Rosella Di Leo and Amadeo Bertolo of Eleutheria Books who literally suggested that it be written and supervised its writing over the past two years. Abiding thanks are also due my dear friend and comrade Karl-Ludwig Schibel for our long and rich intellectual association. Important contributions to this project were also made by Janet Biehl, Beatrice Bookchin, Debby Bookchin, and Joseph Bookchin; my friends in the Burlington Greens who are much to numerous to name; and my colleagues at the Institute for Social Ecology in Plainsfield, Vermont, most particularly Dan Chodorkoff. Finally, I would like to thank Steve Chase of South End Press for his personal interest and assistence in preparing the U.S. edition of *Remaking Society* for publication.

Remaking Society

Pathways to a Green Future

Murray Bookchin

South End Press
Boston, MA

Cover design by Steve Chase and Loie Hayes
Cover photo by Sipa Press
Text design and typesetting by Black Rose Books
Manufactured in the U.S.A.
First edition, first printing

Library of Congress Cataloging-in-Publication Data
Bookchin, Murray, 1921-
Remaking society: pathways to a green future/Murray Bookchin.
p. cm.
Includes bibliographical references.
1. Social policy. 2. Human ecology. 3. Social structure.
4. Radicalism. I. Title.
HN18.B635 1989   361.6'1—dc20   89-21990
ISBN 0-89608-373-X $25.00 (cloth)
ISBN 0-89608-372-1 $10.00 (pbk)

South End Press, 116 Saint Botolph Street, Boston, MA 02115
98 97 96 95 94 93 92 91 90   1 2 3 4 5 6 7 8 9

Contents

WHY THIS BOOK WAS WRITTEN

I had long thought of writing a compact book that would clearly summarize my views on "remaking society" from an ecological viewpoint. It seemed to me (as it did to many of my friends) that a need existed to bring the ideas I have developed over several large books into a work of some two hundred pages; one that would not be too demanding for intelligent readers who are interested in social ecology.

But what finally made me decide to write this book was a rather chilling incident. Early in June, 1987, I was privileged to be a feature speaker in a six-day National Gathering of American Greens in Amherst, Massachusetts. The event received a surprising amount of national press coverage — and rightly so. About two thousand people from at least forty-two states came to Amherst to debate the theoretical and practical problems of a Green movement in the United States. This was the biggest gathering of independent American radicals in many years. Largely anti-capitalist and activist, these Greens were deeply involved in their neighbourhoods, communities, and workplaces. They reflected a wide spectrum of radicalism in America — giving expression to its promise and its problems, its hopes and limitations.

The gathering was marked by over a dozen plenary sessions of five hundred to a thousand people and by an astonishing number of workshops on issues as exotic as ecological ethics and as timely as feminism, racism, imperialism, and economic democracy; indeed, almost every practical social problem that could be of interest to the rapidly growing Green movement in America. There were heated disputes over electoral versus non-electoral politics, independent versus coalition politics, revolutionary versus reformist politics, and, in short, all the debates that have echoed over the years in major radical gatherings.

But something fairly new surfaced in these debates. A number of tendencies, indeed, ways of thinking, appeared that may seem uniquely American, but which I think have already emerged or will emerge in Green movements, and perhaps radical movements generally, outside the United States.

I can best describe at least one of these tendencies by giving an account of the incident that troubled me. It occurred in an after-dinner conversation when people relaxed in small groups on the broad lawn of our meeting place to discuss the events of the day. A young, tall, rather robust man from California began to talk in a vague way about the need to "obey" the "laws of nature," to "humbly subjugate ourselves" (if I recall his words correctly) "to nature's commands." Rhetorical as his words seemed at first utterance, I began to find his increasingly strident monologue very disturbing.

His use of words like "obey," "laws of nature," "subjugate," and "commands" reminded me of the very same language I have heard from anti-ecological people who believe that nature must "obey" *our* commands and *its* "laws" must be used to "subjugate" the natural world itself. Whether I was thinking of the young California Green who was bombarding me with his seemingly "ecological" verbiage, or of modern acolytes of the cold deities of science who believe that "man" must ruthlessly control nature in "his" own interest, it was clear to me that these two seemingly opposed views had a basic thing in common. They jointly shared the vocabulary of domination and subjugation. Just as my California Green believes that human beings should be dominated by nature, so the acolytes of scientism believe that nature should be dominated by "man."

My California Green, in effect, had merely reversed this unsavoury relationship between human beings and nature by turning people into objects of domination, just as his scientistic opponents (usually big industrialists, financiers, and entrepreneurs in our modern corporate society) turn the world of life, including human beings, into objects of domination. The fact that humanity, together with nature, were being locked into a common destiny based on domination by a hierarchical mentality and society, seemed to elude my California Green with his simplistic message of "surrendering" to nature and its "laws."

Already deeply disturbed by the fact that a self-professed Green could think so much like his ecological opponents, I decided to ask him a blunt question: "What do you think is the cause of the present ecological crisis?" His answer was very emphatic: "Human beings! *People* are responsible for the ecological crisis!"

"Do you mean that people such as blacks, women, and the oppressed are causing ecological imbalances — not corporations, agribusiness, ruling elites, and the State?" I asked with complete astonishment.

"Yes, people!" he answered even more heatedly. "*Everyone!* They overpopulate the earth, they pollute the planet, they devour its resources, they are greedy. That's why corporations exist — to give people the things they want."

I suspect our discussion would have become explosive if my California Green had not been distracted by a nearby game of volley-ball and leaped up to join it.

I could not forget this conversation. Indeed, it haunts me to the present day because of the extent, as I have since learned, to which it reflects the thinking of many environmentalists, some of whom would militantly call themselves "radicals."

The most striking feature of such a way of thinking is not only that it closely parallels the way of thinking that is found in the corporate world. What is more serious is that it serves to deflect our attention from the role society plays in producing ecological breakdown. If "people" as a *species* are responsible for environmental dislocations, these dislocations cease to be the result of *social* dislocations. A mythic "Humanity" is created — irrespective of whether we are talking about oppressed ethnic minorities, women, Third World people, or people in the First World — in which everyone is brought into complicity with powerful corporate elites in producing environmental dislocations. In this way, the social roots of ecological problems are shrewdly obscured. A new kind of biological "original sin" is created in which a vague group of animals called "Humanity" is turned into a destructive force that threatens the survival of the living world.

Reduced to a mere species, human beings can now be treated as a simple zoological phenomenon subject to the "biological laws" that presumably determine the "struggle for existence" in the the natural world. If there is a famine, for example, it can be "explained" by simple biological notions like a "shortage of food," presumably caused by "excess population." If there is a war, it can be explained by the "stresses" produced by "overcrowding" or the need for "living space."

In a like manner, we can dismiss or explain away hunger, misery, or illness as "natural checks" that are imposed on human beings to retain the "balance of nature." We can comfortably forget that much of the poverty and hunger that afflicts the world has its origin in the corporate exploitation of human beings and nature — in agribusiness and social oppression. Human beings, you see, are merely a species like rabbits, lemmings, and the like, who are inexorably subject to relentless "natural laws."

If one views the human condition this way, such that all life-forms are "biocentrically" interchangeable despite their unique qualities, people, too, become interchangeable with locusts or, for that matter, viruses — as has been seriously suggested in a debate by advocates of this viewpoint — and are equally expendable in the interplay of so-called natural laws.[1]

The young Californian who presented these views expressed only the crudest notions that make up this growing ideology. He may very well have been one of those people I have recently encountered in the United States who believes that African children — presumably like other "animals" — should be permitted to starve because they are "overpopulating" the continent and burdening the biological "carrying capacity" of their respective countries. Or, what is equally vicious, that the AIDS epidemic should be welcomed as a means of reducing "excessive" population. Or, more chauvinistically, that "immigrants" to the United States from Latin America (often Indians whose ancestors came to the Americas thousands of years ago) should be kept out because they threaten "our" resources.

Presented in so crude and racist a form, with the use of words like "our" to designate an America whose resources are actually owned by a handful of giant corporations, this viewpoint is likely to be repugnant to most Americans. Nevertheless, as simple-minded, purely zoological answers to highly complex social questions, the viewpoint tends to gain a growing following, particularly among the more macho, authoritarian, and reactionary types who have always used "nature" and "natural laws" as substitutes for a study of real social issues and concerns.

The temptation to equate human beings who live in complex, highly institutionalized, and bitterly divided societies with ordinary animals, is finding its voice in seemingly sophisticated arguments that often parade under the guise of "radical" ecological philosophies. The resurgence of a new Malthusianism that contends that growth rates in population tend to exceed growth rates in food production is the most sinister ideological development of all.

The myth that population increases in places like the Sudan, for example, result in famine (not the notorious fact that the Sudanese could easily feed themselves if they were not forced by the American-controlled World Bank and International Monetary Fund to grow cotton instead of grains) typically represents the kind of arguments that are gaining popularity among many environmentalists. "Nature," we are arrogantly told by privileged Euro-Americans who parade as "natural law" theorists, "must be permitted to take its course" — as though the profits of corporations, banks, and agribusiness have anything to do with the "course" of nature.

What renders this new "biocentrism," with its antihumanistic image of human beings as interchangeable with rodents or ants, so insidious is that it now forms the premise of a growing movement called "deep ecology."[2] "Deep ecology" was spawned among well-to-do people who have been raised on a spiritual diet of Eastern cults mixed with Hollywood and Disneyland fantasies. The American mind is formless enough without burdening it with "biocentric" myths of a Buddhist and Taoist belief in a universal "oneness" so cosmic that human beings with all their distinctiveness dissolve into an all-encompassing form of "biocentric equality." Reduced to merely one life-form among many, the poor and the impoverished either become fair game for outright extermination if they are socially expendable, or they become objects of brutal exploitation if they can be used to aggrandize the corporate world. Accordingly, terms like "oneness" and a "biocentric democracy" go hand-in-hand with a pious formula for human oppression, misery, and even extermination.

Finally, ecological thinking is not enriched by recklessly blending such disparate religions as Buddhism and Taoism with Christianity, much less philosophers like the Jewish thinker Spinoza with a Nazi apologist like Heidegger. To declare, as Arne Naess, the pontiff of "deep ecology," has done, that the "basic principles of the deep ecology movement lie in religion or philosophy," is to make a conclusion notable for its absence of reference to social theory.[3]

There is enough in this mix of "biocentrism," antihumanism, mysticism, and religion with its "natural law" ethos to feed extremely reactionary and atavistic tendencies, all well-meaning references in deep ecology about "decentralization" and "nonhierarchy" aside. This raises the question of still another exotic tendency that is percolating through the ecology movements. I refer to the paradoxical need for a new theistic ecological "spirituality." That the word "spirituality" may often mean a decent, indeed, a wholesome sensitivity to nature and its subtle interconnections, is a very substantial reason to guard ourselves against its degeneration into an atavistic, simple-minded form of nature religion peopled by gods, goddesses, and eventually a new hierarchy of priests and priestesses. Mystical versions of feminism, as well as the ecology movement as a whole, alas, have sometimes proved themselves to be all too vulnerable to this tendency. The clear-sighted *naturalism* to which ecology so vividly lends itself is now in danger of being supplanted by a *super*natural outlook that is inherently alien to nature's own fecundity and self-creativity.

May we not reasonably ask why the natural world has to be peopled with earth gods and goddesses when natural evolution exhibits a marvelous power of its own to generate such a rich and wondrous variety of living beings? Is this alone not enough to fill the human mind with admiration and respect? Is it not the crudest form of "anthropocentrism" (to use a word for the projection of the human into the natural that evokes so much disdain in ecology movements) to introduce deified forms created by the human imagination into the natural world in the name of ecological "spirituality?"

To worship or revere *any* being, natural or supernatural, will always be a form of self-subjugation and servitude that ultimately yields social domination, be it in the name of nature, society, gender, or religion. More than one civilization was riddled by "nature deities" that were cynically used by ruling elites to support the most rigid, oppressive, and dehumanizing of social hierarchies. The moment human beings fall to their knees before *any* thing that is "higher" than themselves, hierarchy will have made its first triumph over freedom, and human backs will be exposed to all the burdens that can be inflicted on them by social domination.

I have raised some of the problems posed by the misanthropic, antihuman tendencies in the ecology movement not to defame the movement as a whole. Quite to the contrary: my purpose in surveying these tendencies is to peel away the fungus that has accumulated around the movement and look at the promising fruit ecology can yield for the future. The reason why this book has been written is to show as clearly as possible that ecology alone, firmly rooted in *social* criticism and a vision of *social* reconstruction, can provide us with the means for remaking society in a way that will benefit nature *and* humanity.

However, we cannot achieve such a criticism and vision by swinging mindlessly from one extreme that advocates the complete "domination of nature" by "man" to another, rather confused "biocentric" or antihumanist extreme that essentially reduces humanity to a parasitic swarm of mosquitoes in a mystified swamp called "Nature." We must remove ourselves from an ideological catapult that periodically flings us from fad to fad and absurdity to absurdity.

It is tempting to return to the radicalism of the past where assured dogmas were socially inspirational and had the aura of romantic rebellion around them. Having been raised in that era of a half-century ago, I find it emotionally congenial — but intellectually very inadequate. Traditional radical theory is now in debris. Much that passes for socialism and communism, today, acts as a crucial support for the prevailing market society. Archaic slogans like the "nationalization of property" and a "planned economy" reinforce the growing centralization and rationalization of the corporate economy and the State. Marx's almost reverential attitude toward technological innovation and growth threatens to express the most malignant goals of a technocratic ideology and a technocratic bureaucracy. Even the strategic political goals of orthodox radicalism, with its vision of the proletariat as a hegemonic class, are fading away with the displacement of industrial workers by automation. No great movements are gathering under the banner of the red flag — only the ghostly rebels of the past who perished in the failed insurrections of a bygone era and the leaders who guided them into a historic limbo.

By the same token, liberal environmentalism has become a balm for soothing the bad consciences of rapacious industrialists who engage in a tasteless ballet with environmental lobbyists, lawyers, and public officials. For this crew, nature is essentially a collection of natural resources. Their environmental ballets have the goal of soothing consciences according to an ethics of lesser evils, not an ethics of the greater good and virtue. Typically, a huge forest is usually "traded off" for a small stand of trees and a large stretch of wetlands for a small, presumably "improved," wildlife sanctuary.

In the meantime, the overall deterioration of the environment occurs at a madcap pace. Basic planetary cycles, like the ratio of atmospheric gases and the factors which determine it, are undermined, increasing the proportion of carbon dioxide to oxygen in the air. Ecologically fragile rain forests, that have been on earth for sixty million years or more and whose role in maintaining the integrity of the air we breathe is indeterminable, are recklessly removed. Chemical pollutants like chlorofluoro-carbons threaten to thin out and open vast holes in the ozone layer that protects all complex life-forms from the sun's harmful ultra-violet radiation. These are the major insults that are being inflicted on the planet. They do not include the daily diet of chemical pollutants, acid rain, harmful food additives, and agricultural poisons that may be changing the whole spectrum of diseases that claim human and non-human life today.

The control of these potentially disastrous alterations of the earth's ecological balance has virtually collapsed before the "compromises" and "trade-offs" engineered by liberal environmentalists. Indeed, what renders the liberal approach so hopelessly ineffectual is the fact that it takes the present social order for granted, like the air we breathe and the water we drink. All of these "compromises" and "trade-offs" rest on the paralysing belief that a market society, privately owned property, and the present-day bureaucratic nation-state cannot be changed in any basic sense. Thus, it is the prevailing order that sets the terms of any "compromise" or "trade-off," just like the rules of a chess game and the grid of a chess board determine in advance what the players can do — not the dictates of reason and morality.

To "play by the rules" of the environmental game means that the natural world, including oppressed people, always loses something piece by piece until everything is lost in the end. As long as liberal environmentalism is structured around the social status quo, property rights always prevail over public rights and power always prevails over powerlessness. Be it a forest, wetlands, or good agricultural soil, a "developer" who owns any of these "resources" usually sets the terms on which every negotiation occurs and ultimately succeeds in achieving the triumph of wealth over ecological consideration.

Finally, liberal environmentalism suffers from a consistent refusal to see that a capitalistic society based on competition and growth for its own sake must ultimately devour the natural world, just like an untreated cancer must ultimately devour its host. Personal intentions, be they good or bad, have little to do with this unrelenting process. An economy that is structured around the maxim, "Grow or Die," must *necessarily* pit itself against the natural world and leave ecological ruin in its wake as it works its way through the biosphere. I need hardly add that the growth-oriented, bureaucratic, and highly stratified "socialist" world offers no alternatives to the failure of liberalism. Totalitarian countries are equally culpable in the plundering of the planet. The most important difference between them and their Western counterparts is that a "planned economy" renders their efforts more systematic. Any opposition — be it liberal or radical — is more easily silenced by the institutions of a police state.

The narrowing choices that seem to confront us — notably, an unfeeling misanthropic kind of "ecologism" and a queasy liberal environmentalism — require that we look for another way. Is the only response to liberal environmentalism and its diet of failures a "deep ecology" that mystifies "wild" nature and wildlife, important as remaining areas of pristine nature may be? Are we obliged to choose between lobbying, "compromises," and "trade-offs" and a "biocentric," antihumanist mentality that tends to reduce humanity to nothing more than a mere animal species and the human mind to blight on the natural world? Is the only response to a technology gone wild a return to a hunting and gathering way of life in which chipped flints are our principal materials for acting on the natural world? And is the only response to the logic of modern science and engineering a celebration of irrationality, instinct, and religiosity?

Admittedly, I have simplified the alternatives. But I have done so only to reveal their logic and implications. For one thing, I do not wish to deny that even liberal environmentalism and the value of an instinctive sensibility have their roles in resisting a powerful technology that has been placed in the service of mindless growth, accumulation, and consumption. A stand against the construction of a nuclear reactor, a new highway, an effort to clear-cut a mountainside, or a new condo development that threatens to deface an urban landscape — all represent important acts, however limited, to prevent further environmental deterioration. Land, wildlife, scenic natural beauty, and ecological variety that is preserved from the bulldozer and profit-oriented predators, are important enclaves of nature and aesthetics that must be preserved wherever we can do so. It requires no great theoretical or ideological wisdom to recognize that almost everything of wonder and beauty, from a statuesque tree to a burrowing mammal, has its place in the world and its function in the biosphere.

However, to carry these compelling facts to a point where humanity is seen either as a blight on nature or the "lord of creation" leads to a very sinister result. Both views serve to pit humanity against nature, whether as "blight" or as "lord." Humanity (insofar as this word denotes a species rather than highly divided social beings who live in sharp conflict with each other as oppressed and oppressor) is plucked out of the evolution of life and placed on a shelf like an inanimate object. Isolated from the world of life with either curses or praises, it is then dispatched back into a primal world of the distant past or catapulted up to the stars, regaled with space suits and exotic weapons. Neither of these images touches upon an all-important fact: human beings exist in various *societies,* all of which are profoundly relevant to our ecological problems. As social beings, humans have developed ways of relating to each other through *institutions* that, more than any single factor, determine how they deal with the natural world.

I submit that we must go beyond the superficial layer of ideas created by "biocentricity," "antihumanism," Malthusianism, and "deep ecology" at one extreme, and the belief in growth, competition, human "supremacy," and social power at the other extreme. We must look at the *social* factors that have created both of these extremes in their many different forms and answer key questions about the human condition if we are to harmonize humanity's relationship with nature.

What, after all, *is* human society when we try to view it from an ecological perspective? A "curse?" An unmitigated "blessing?" A "device" for coping with material needs? Or, dare I say, a *product* of natural evolution as well as culture that not only meets a wide variety of human needs, but, potentially at least, can play a major role in fostering the evolution of life on the planet?

What factors have produced ecologically harmful human societies? And what factors could yield ecologically beneficial human societies?

Is a well-developed technology necessarily anti-ecological or can it be used to enhance the biosphere and habitats of life?

What can we learn from history that will answer these questions and advance our thinking beyond the bumper-sticker slogans that we encounter among the misanthropic and liberal environmentalists alike?

Indeed, how should we think out these questions? By means of conventional logic? Intuition? Divine inspiration? Or, perhaps, by developmental ways of thinking that are called "dialectical?"

Lastly, but by no means finally, what kind of social reconstruction do we need to harmonize humanity's relationship with nature — assuming, to be sure, that society should not be dismissed and everyone rush off to claim his or her mountain peak in the High Sierras or Adirondaks? By what political, social, and economic means will such a reconstruction be achieved? And by what ethical principles will it be guided?

These are, at best, preliminary questions. There are many others that we will have to consider before our discussion comes to its end. I hesitate to go further, here, because I have a deep aversion to a mere laundry list of ideas, half-thought-out statements, flow diagrams, and bumper-sticker slogans that are so much in vogue these days. When my young man from California shouted the words "human beings" at me, he did his best *not* to think and he sets an intellectually crude example of mindlessness to others whose minds have been shaped by Hollywood, Disneyland, and television.

Hence, more than ever, we desperately need coherence. I do not mean dogma. Rather, I mean a real *structure* of ideas that places philosophy, anthropology, history, ethics, a new rationality, and utopian visions in the service of freedom — freedom, let me add, for *natural* development as well as human. This is a structure which we shall have to build in the pages that follow, not simply to collect in pell-mell fashion into a mere rubbish heap of ideas. The unfinished thought is as dangerous as the totally finished dogma. Both yield an uncreative vision of reality that can be bent and twisted in every possible direction; hence the extremely contradictory notions that exist in works on "deep ecology."

This book was written to address the questions I have raised in the hope that we can formulate the coherent framework to which I have already alluded and develop a practice of which we are in dire need. It has been initiated by an incident, by an encounter with real life — not by reclusive academic reflections and private vagaries.

If the ecology movement which I helped to pioneer some thirty years ago folds its tents for the mountains or turns to Washington for influence, the loss will be irreparable. Ecological thinking, today, can provide the most important synthesis of ideas we have seen since the Enlightenment, two centuries ago. It can open vistas for a practice that can effectively change the entire social landscape of our time. The stylistic militancy readers encounter in this book stems from a troubled sense of urgency. It is vitally incumbent upon us not to let an ecological way of thinking and the movement it can produce degenerate and go the way of traditional radicalism — into the lost mazes of an irrecoverable history.

SOCIETY AND ECOLOGY

The problems which many people face today in "defining" themselves, in knowing "who they are" — problems that feed a vast psychotherapy industry — are by no means personal ones. These problems exist not only for private individuals; they exist for modern society as a whole. Socially, we live in desperate uncertainty about how people relate to each other. We suffer not only as individuals from alienation and confusion over our identities and goals; our entire society, conceived as a single entity, seems unclear about its own nature and sense of direction. If earlier societies tried to foster a belief in the virtues of cooperation and care, thereby giving an ethical meaning to social life, modern society fosters a belief in the virtues of competition and egotism, thereby divesting human association of all meaning — except, perhaps, as an instrument for gain and mindless consumption.

We tend to believe that men and women of earlier times were guided by firm beliefs and hopes — values that defined them as human beings and gave purpose to their social lives. We speak of the Middle Ages as an "Age of Faith" or the Enlightenment as an "Age of Reason." Even the pre–World War II era and the years that followed it seem like an alluring time of innocence and hope, despite the Great Depression and the terrible conflicts that stained it. As an elderly character in a recent, rather sophisticated, espionage movie put it: what he missed about his younger years during World War II were their "clarity" — a sense of purpose and idealism that guided his behaviour.

That "clarity," today, is gone. It has been replaced by ambiguity. The certainty that technology and science would improve the human condition is mocked by the proliferation of nuclear weapons, by massive hunger in the Third World, and by poverty in the First World. The fervent belief that liberty would triumph over tyranny is belied by the growing centralization of states everywhere and by the disempowerment of people by bureaucracies, police forces, and sophisticated surveillance techniques — in our "democracies" no less than in visibly authoritarian countries. The hope that we would form "one world," a vast community of disparate ethnic groups that would share their resources to improve life everywhere, has been shattered by a rising tide of nationalism, racism, and an unfeeling parochialism that fosters indifference to the plight of millions.

We believe that our values are worse than those held by people of only two or three generations ago. The present generation seems more self-centred, privatized, and mean-spirited by comparison with earlier ones. It lacks the support systems provided by the extended family, community, and a commitment to mutual aid. The encounter of the individual with society seems to occur through cold bureaucratic agencies rather than warm, caring people.

This lack of social identity and meaning is all the more stark in the face of the mounting problems that confront us. War is a chronic condition of our time; economic uncertainty, an all- pervasive presence; human solidarity, a vaporous myth. Not least of the problems we encounter are nightmares of an ecological apocalypse — a catastrophic breakdown of the systems that maintain the stability of the planet. We live under the constant threat that the world of life will be irrevocably undermined by a society gone mad in its need to grow — replacing the organic by the inorganic, soil by concrete, forest by barren earth, and the diversity of life-forms by simplified ecosystems; in short, a turning back of the evolutionary clock to an earlier, more inorganic, mineralized world that was incapable of supporting complex life-forms of any kind, including the human species.

Ambiguity about our fate, meaning, and purpose thus raises a rather startling question: is society itself a curse, a blight on life generally? Are we any better for this new phenomenon called "civilization" that seems to be on the point of destroying the natural world produced over millions of years of organic evolution?

An entire literature has emerged which has gained the attention of millions of readers: a literature that fosters a new pessimism toward civilization as such. This literature pits technology against a presumably "virginal" organic nature; cities against countryside; countryside against "wilderness"; science against a "reverence" for life; reason against the "innocence" of intuition; and, indeed, humanity against the entire biosphere.

We show signs of losing faith in all our uniquely human abilities — our ability to live in peace with each other, our ability to care for our fellow beings and other life-forms. This pessimism is fed daily by sociobiologists who locate our failings in our genes, by antihumanists who deplore our "antinatural" sensibilities, and by "biocentrists" who downgrade our rational qualities with notions that we are no different in our "intrinsic worth" than ants. In short, we are witnessing a widespread assault against the ability of reason, science, and technology to improve the world for ourselves and life generally.

The historic theme that civilization must inevitably be pitted against nature, indeed, that it is corruptive of human nature, has re-surfaced in our midst from the days that reach back to Rousseau — this, precisely at a time when our need for a truly human and ecological civilization has never been greater if we are to rescue our planet and ourselves. Civilization, with its hallmarks of reason and technics, is viewed increasingly as a new blight. Even more basically, society as a phenomenon in its own right is being questioned so much so that its role as integral to the formation of humanity is seen as something harmfully "unnatural" and inherently destructive.

Humanity, in effect, is being defamed by human beings themselves, ironically, as an accursed form of life that all but destroys the world of life and threatens its integrity. To the confusion that we have about our own muddled time and our personal identities, we now have the added confusion that the human condition is seen as a form of chaos produced by our proclivity for wanton destruction and our ability to exercise this proclivity all the more effectively because we possess reason, science, and technology.

Admittedly, few antihumanists, "biocentrists," and misanthropes, who theorize about the human condition, are prepared to follow the logic of their premises to such an absurd point. What is vitally important about this medley of moods and unfinished ideas is that the various forms, institutions, and relationships that make up what we should call "society" are largely ignored. Instead, just as we use vague words like "humanity" or zoological terms like *homo sapiens* that conceal vast differences, often bitter antagonisms, that exist between privileged whites and people of colour, men and women, rich and poor, oppressor and oppressed; so do we, by the same token, use vague words like "society" or "civilization" that conceal vast differences between free, nonhierarchical, class, and stateless societies on the one hand, and others that are, in varying degrees, hierarchical, class-ridden, statist, and authoritarian. Zoology, in effect, replaces socially oriented ecology. Sweeping "natural laws" based on population swings among animals replace conflicting economic and social interests among people.

Simply to pit "society" against "nature," "humanity" against the "biosphere," and "reason," "technology," and "science" against less developed, often primitive forms of human interaction with the natural world, prevents us from examining the highly complex differences and divisions within society so necessary to define our problems and their solutions.

Ancient Egypt, for example, had a significantly different attitude toward nature than ancient Babylonia. Egypt assumed a reverential attitude toward a host of essentially animistic nature deities, many of which were physically part human and part animal, while Babylonians created a pantheon of very human political deities. But Egypt was no less hierarchical than Babylonia in its treatment of people and was equally, if not more, oppressive in its view of human individuality. Certain hunting peoples may have been as destructive of wildlife, despite their strong animistic beliefs, as urban cultures which staked out an over-arching claim to reason. When these many differences are simply swallowed up together with a vast variety of social forms by a word called "society," we do severe violence to thought and even simple intelligence. Society *per se* becomes something "unnatural." "Reason," "technology," and "science" become things that are "destructive" without any regard to the social factors that condition their use. Human attempts to alter the environment are seen as threats — as though our "species" can do little or nothing to improve the planet for life generally.

Of course, we are not any less animals than other mammals, but we are more than herds that browse on the African plains. The way in which we are more — namely, the *kinds* of societies that we form and how we are divided against each other into hierarchies and classes — profoundly affects our behaviour and our effects on the natural world.

Finally, by so radically separating humanity and society from nature or naïvely reducing them to mere zoological entities, we can no longer see how human nature is *derived* from nonhuman nature and social evolution from natural evolution. Humanity becomes estranged or alienated not only from itself in our "age of alienation," but from the natural world in which it has always been rooted as a complex and thinking life-form.

Accordingly, we are fed a steady diet of reproaches by liberal and misanthropic environmentalists alike about how "we" as a species are responsible for the breakdown of the environment. One does not have to go to enclaves of mystics and gurus in San Francisco to find this species-centred, asocial view of ecological problems and their sources. New York City will do just as well. I shall not easily forget an "environmental" presentation staged by the New York Museum of Natural History in the seventies in which the public was exposed to a long series of exhibits, each depicting examples of pollution and ecological disruption. The exhibit which closed the presentation carried a startling sign, "The Most Dangerous Animal on Earth," and it consisted simply of a huge mirror which reflected back the human viewer who stood before it. I clearly recall a black child standing before the mirror while a white school teacher tried to explain the message which this arrogant exhibit tried to convey. There were no exhibits of corporate boards or directors planning to deforest a mountainside or government officials acting in collusion with them. The exhibit primarily conveyed one, basically misanthropic, message: people *as such*, not a rapacious society and its wealthy beneficiaries, are responsible for environmental dislocations — the poor no less than the personally wealthy, people of colour no less than privileged whites, women no less than men, the oppressed no less than the oppressor. A mythical human "species" had replaced classes; individuals had replaced hierarchies; personal tastes (many of which are shaped by a predatory media) had replaced social relationships; and the disempowered who live meagre, isolated lives had replaced giant corporations, self-serving bureaucracies, and the violent paraphernalia of the State.

THE RELATIONSHIP OF SOCIETY TO NATURE

Leaving aside such outrageous "environmental" exhibitions that mirror privileged and underprivileged people in the same frame, it seems appropriate at this point to raise a highly relevant need: the need to bring society back into the ecological picture. More than ever, strong emphases must be placed on the fact that nearly *all ecological problems are social problems*, not simply or primarily the result of religious, spiritual, or political ideologies. That these ideologies may foster an anti-ecological outlook in people of all strata hardly requires emphasis. But rather than simply take ideologies at their face value, it is crucial for us to ask from whence these ideologies develop.

Quite frequently, economic needs may compel people to act against their best impulses, even strongly felt natural values. Lumberjacks who are employed to clear-cut a magnificent forest normally have no "hatred" of trees. They have little or no choice but to cut trees just as stockyard workers have little or no choice but to slaughter domestic animals. Every community or occupation has its fair share of destructive and sadistic individuals, to be sure, including misanthropic environmentalists who would like to see humanity exterminated. But among the vast majority of people, this kind of work, including such onerous tasks as mining, are not freely chosen occupations. They stem from need and, above all, they are the product of social arrangements over which ordinary people have no control.

To understand present-day problems — ecological as well as economic and political — we must examine their social causes and remedy them through social methods. "Deep," "spiritual," antihumanist, and misanthropic ecologies gravely mislead us when they refocus our attention on social symptoms rather than social causes. If our obligation is to look at changes in social relationships in order to understand our most significant ecological changes, these ecologies steer us away from society to "spiritual," "cultural," or vaguely defined "traditional" sources. The Bible did not create European antinaturalism; it served to justify an antinaturalism that already existed on the continent from pagan times, despite the animistic traits of pre–Christian religions. Christianity's antinaturalistic influence became especially marked with the emergence of capitalism. Society must not only be brought into the ecological picture to understand why people tend to choose competing sensibilities — some, strongly naturalistic; others, strongly antinaturalistic — but we must probe more deeply into society itself. We must search out the *relationship of society to nature*, the *reasons* why it can destroy the natural world, and, alternatively, the reasons why it has and still can *enhance, foster*, and *richly contribute* to natural evolution.

Insofar as we can speak of "society" in any abstract and general sense — and let us remember that every society is highly unique and different from others in the long perspective of history — we are obliged to examine what we can best call "socialization," not merely "society." Society is a given arrangement of relationships which we often take for granted and view in a very fixed way. To many people today, it would seem that a market society based on trade and competition has existed "forever," although we may be vaguely mindful that there were pre-market societies based on gifts and cooperation. Socialization, on the other hand, is a *process,* just as individual living is a process. Historically, the *process* of socializing people can be viewed as a sort of social infancy that involves a painful rearing of humanity to social maturity.

When we begin to consider socialization from an in-depth viewpoint, what strikes us is that society itself in its most primal form stems very much *from* nature. Every social evolution, in fact, is virtually an extension of natural evolution into a distinctly human realm. As the Roman orator and philosopher, Cicero, declared some two thousand years ago: "...by the use of our hands, we bring into being within the realm of Nature, a second nature for ourselves." Cicero's observation, to be sure, is very incomplete: the primeval, presumably untouched "realm of Nature" or "first nature," as it has been called, is reworked in whole or part into "second nature" not only by the "use of our hands." Thought, language, and complex, very important biological changes also play a crucial and, at times, a decisive role in developing a "second nature" within "first nature."

I use the term "reworking" advisedly to focus on the fact that "second nature" is not simply a phenomenon that develops outside of "first nature" — hence the special value that should be attached to Cicero's use of the expression *"within* the realm of Nature..." To emphasize that "second nature" or, more precisely, society (to use this word in its broadest possible sense) emerges from *within* primeval "first nature" is to re-establish the fact that social life always has a naturalistic dimension, however much society is pitted against nature in our thinking. *Social* ecology clearly expresses the fact that society is not a sudden "eruption" in the world. Social life does not necessarily face nature as a combatant in an unrelenting war. The emergence of society is a *natural* fact that has its origins in the biology of human socialization.

The human socialization process from which society emerges — be it in the form of families, bands, tribes, or more complex types of human intercourse — has its source in parental relationships, particularly mother and child bonding. The biological mother, to be sure, can be replaced in this process by many surrogates, including fathers, relatives, or, for that matter, all members of a community. It is when *social* parents and *social* siblings — that is, the human community that surrounds the young — begin to participate in a system of care, that is ordinarily undertaken by biological parents, that society begins to truly come into its own.

Society thereupon advances beyond a mere reproductive group toward institutionalized human relationships, and from a relatively formless animal community into a clearly structured social *order*. But at the very inception of society, it seems more than likely that human beings were socialized into "second nature" by means of deeply ingrained blood ties, specifically maternal ties. We shall see that in time the structures or institutions that mark the advance of humanity from a mere animal community into an authentic society began to undergo far-reaching changes and these changes become issues of paramount importance in social ecology. For better or worse, societies develop around status groups, hierarchies, classes, and state formations. But reproduction and family care remain the abiding biological bases for every form of social life as well as the originating factor in the socialization of the young and the formation of a society. As Robert Briffault observed in the early half of this century, the "one known factor which establishes a profound distinction between the constitution of the most rudimentary human group and all other animal groups [is the] association of mothers and offspring which is the sole form of true social solidarity among animals. Throughout the class of mammals, there is a continuous increase in the duration of that association, which is the consequence of the prolongation of the period of infantile dependence,"[4] a prolongation which Briffault correlates with increases in the period of fetal gestation and advances in intelligence.

The biological dimension that Briffault adds to what we call society and socialization cannot be stressed too strongly. It is a decisive presence, not only in the origins of society over ages of animal evolution, but in the daily recreation of society in our everyday lives. The appearance of a newly born infant and the highly extended care it receives for many years reminds us that it is not only a human being that is being reproduced, but society itself. By comparison with the young of other species, children develop slowly and over a long period of time. Living in close association with parents, siblings, kin groups, and an ever-widening community of people, they retain a plasticity of mind that makes for creative individuals and ever-formative social groups. Although nonhuman animals may approximate human forms of association in many ways, they do not create a "second nature" that embodies a cultural tradition, nor do they possess a complex language, elaborate conceptual powers, or an impressive capacity to restructure their environment purposefully according to their own needs.

A chimpanzee, for example, remains an infant for only three years and a juvenile for seven. By the age of ten, it is a full-grown adult. Children, by contrast, are regarded as infants for approximately six years and juveniles for fourteen. A chimpanzee, in short, grows mentally and physically in about half the time required by a human being, and its capacity to learn or, at least to think, is already fixed by comparison with a human being, whose mental abilities may expand for decades. By the same token, chimpanzee associations are often idiosyncratic and fairly limited. Human associations, on the other hand, are basically stable, highly institutionalized, and they are marked by a degree of solidarity, indeed, by a degree of creativity, that has no equal in nonhuman species as far as we know.

This prolonged degree of human mental plasticity, dependency, and social creativity yields two results that are of decisive importance. First, early human association must have fostered a strong predisposition for *interdependence* among members of a group — not the "rugged individualism" we associate with independence. The overwhelming mass of anthropological evidence suggests that participation, mutual aid, solidarity, and empathy were the social virtues early human groups emphasized within their communities. The idea that people are dependent upon each each other for the good life, indeed, for survival, followed from the prolonged dependence of the young upon adults. Independence, not to mention competition, would have seemed utterly alien, if not bizarre, to a creature reared over many years in a largely dependent condition. Care for others would have been seen as the perfectly natural outcome of a highly acculturated being that was, in turn, clearly in need of extended care. Our modern version of individualism, more precisely, of egotism, would have cut across the grain of early solidarity and mutual aid — traits, I may add, without which such a physically fragile animal like a human being could hardly have survived as an adult, much less as a child.

Second, human interdependence must have assumed a highly structured form. There is no evidence that human beings normally relate to each other through the fairly loose systems of bonding we find among our closest primate cousins. That human social bonds can be dissolved or de-institutionalized in periods of radical change or cultural breakdown is too obvious to argue here. But during relatively stable conditions, human society was never the "horde" that anthropologists of the last century presupposed as a basis for rudimentary social life. On the contrary, the evidence we have at hand points to the fact that all humans, perhaps even our distant hominid ancestors, lived in some kind of structured family groups, and, later, in bands, tribes, villages, and other forms. In short, they bonded together (as they still do), not only emotionally and morally, but also structurally in contrived, clearly definable, and fairly permanent institutions.

Nonhuman animals may form loose communities and even take collective protective postures to defend their young from predators. But such communities can hardly be called structured, except in a broad, often ephemeral, sense. Humans, by contrast, create highly formal communities that tend to become increasingly structured over the course of time. In effect, they form not only communities, but a new phenomenon called *societies*.

If we fail to distinguish animal communities from human societies, we risk the danger of ignoring the unique features that distinguish human social life from animal communities — notably, the ability of society to *change* for better or worse and the factors that produce these changes. By reducing a complex society to a mere community, we can easily ignore how societies differed from each other over the course of history. We can also fail to understand how they elaborated simple differences in status into firmly established hierarchies, or hierarchies into economic classes. Indeed, we risk the possibility of totally misunderstanding the very meaning of terms like "hierarchy" as highly organized systems of command and obedience — these, as distinguished from personal, individual, and often short-lived differences in status that may, in all too many cases, involve no acts of compulsion. We tend, in effect, to confuse the strictly institutional creations of human will, purpose, conflicting interests, and traditions, with community life in its most fixed forms, as though we were dealing with inherent, seemingly unalterable, features of society rather than fabricated structures that can be modified, improved, worsened — or simply abandoned. The trick of every ruling elite from the beginnings of history to modern times has been to identify its own socially created hierarchical systems of domination with community life *as such*, with the result being that human-made institutions acquire divine or biological sanction.

A given society and its institutions thus tend to become reified into permanent and unchangeable entities that acquire a mysterious life of their own apart from nature — namely, the products of a seemingly fixed "human nature" that is the result of genetic programming at the very inception of social life. Alternatively, a given society and its institutions may be dissolved into nature as merely another form of animal community with its "alpha males," "guardians," "leaders," and "horde"-like forms of existence. When annoying issues like war and social conflict are raised, they are ascribed to the activity of "genes" that presumably give rise to war and even "greed."

In either case, be it the notion of an abstract society that exists apart from nature or an equally abstract natural community that is indistinguishable from nature, a dualism appears that sharply separates society *from* nature, or a crude reductionism appears that dissolves society *into* nature. These apparently contrasting, but closely related, notions are all the more seductive because they are so simplistic. Although they are often presented by their more sophisticated supporters in a fairly nuanced form, such notions are easily reduced to bumper-sticker slogans that are frozen into hard, popular dogmas.

SOCIAL ECOLOGY

The approach to society and nature advanced by social ecology may seem more intellectually demanding, but it avoids the simplicities of dualism and the crudities of reductionism. Social ecology tries to show how nature slowly *phases* into society without ignoring the differences between society and nature on the one hand, as well as the extent to which they merge with each other on the other. The everyday socialization of the young by the family is no less rooted in biology than the everyday care of the old by the medical establishment is rooted in the hard facts of society. By the same token, we never cease to be mammals who still have primal natural urges, but we institutionalize these urges and their satisfaction in a wide variety of social forms. Hence, the social and the natural continually permeate each other in the most ordinary activities of daily life without losing their identity in a shared process of interaction, indeed, of interactivity.

Obvious as this may seem at first in such day-to-day problems as caretaking, social ecology raises questions that have far-reaching importance for the different ways society and nature have interacted over time and the problems these interactions have produced. How did a divisive, indeed, seemingly combative, relationship between humanity and nature emerge? What were the institutional forms and ideologies that rendered this conflict possible? Given the growth of human needs and technology, was such a conflict really unavoidable? And can it be overcome in a future, ecologically oriented society?

How does a rational, ecologically oriented society fit into the processes of natural evolution? Even more broadly, is there any reason to believe that the human mind — itself a product of natural evolution as well as culture — represents a decisive highpoint in natural development, notably, in the long development of subjectivity from the sensitivity and self-maintenance of the simplest life-forms to the remarkable intellectuality and self-consciousness of the most complex?

In asking these highly provocative questions, I am not trying to justify a strutting arrogance toward nonhuman life-forms. Clearly, we must bring humanity's uniqueness as a species, marked by rich conceptual, social, imaginative, and constructive attributes, into synchronicity with nature's fecundity, diversity, and creativity. I have argued that this synchronicity will not be achieved by opposing nature to society, nonhuman to human life-forms, natural fecundity to technology, or a natural subjectivity to the human mind. Indeed, an important result that emerges from a discussion of the interrelationship of nature to society is the fact that human intellectuality, although distinct, also has a far-reaching natural basis. Our brains and nervous systems did not suddenly spring into existence without a long antecedent natural history. That which we most prize as integral to our humanity — our extraordinary capacity to think on complex conceptual levels — can be traced back to the nerve network of primitive invertebrates, the ganglia of a mollusk, the spinal cord of a fish, the brain of an amphibian, and the cerebral cortex of a primate.

Here, too, in the most intimate of our human attributes, we are no less products of natural evolution than we are of social evolution. As human beings we incorporate within ourselves aeons of organic differentiation and elaboration. Like all complex life-forms, we are not only part of natural evolution; we are also its heirs and the products of natural fecundity.

In trying to show how society slowly grows out of nature, however, social ecology is also obliged to show how society, too, undergoes differentiation and elaboration. In doing so, social ecology must examine those junctures in social evolution where splits occurred which slowly brought society into opposition to the natural world, and explain how this opposition emerged from its inception in prehistoric times to our own era. Indeed, if the human species is a life-form that can consciously and richly enhance the natural world, rather than simply damage it, it is important for social ecology to reveal the factors that have rendered many human beings into parasites on the world of life rather than active partners in organic evolution. This project must be undertaken not in a haphazard way, but with a serious attempt to render natural and social development coherent in terms of each other, and relevant to our times and the construction of an ecological society.

Perhaps one of social ecology's most important contributions to the current ecological discussion is the view that the basic problems which pit society against nature emerge form *within* social development itself — not *between* society and nature. That is to say, the divisions between society and nature have their deepest roots in divisions within the social realm, namely, deep- seated conflicts between human and human that are often obscured by our broad use of the word "humanity."

This crucial view cuts across the grain of nearly all current ecological thinking and even social theorizing. One of the most fixed notions that present-day ecological thinking shares with liberalism, Marxism, and conservatism is the historic belief that the "domination of nature" requires the domination of human by human. This is most obvious in social theory. Nearly all of our contemporary social ideologies have placed the notion of human domination at the centre of their theorizing. It remains one of the most widely accepted notions, from classical times to the present, that human freedom from the "domination of man by nature" entails the domination of human by human as the earliest means of production and the use of human beings as instruments for harness-ing the natural world. Hence, in order to harness the natural world, it has been argued for ages, it is necessary to harness human beings as well, in the form of slaves, serfs, and workers.

That this instrumental notion pervades the ideology of nearly all ruling elites and has provided both liberal and conservative movements with a justification for their accommodation to the status quo, requires little, if any, elaboration. The myth of a "stingy" nature has always been used to justify the "stinginess" of exploiters in their harsh treatment of the exploited — and it has provided the excuse for the political opportunism of liberal, as well as conservative, causes. To "work within the system" has always implied an acceptance of domination as a way of "organizing" social life and, in the best of cases, a way of freeing humans from their presumed domination by nature.

What is perhaps less known, however, is that Marx, too, justified the emergence of class society and the State as stepping stones toward the domination of nature and, presumably, the liberation of humanity. It was on the strength of this historical vision that Marx formulated his materialist conception of history and his belief in the need for class society as a stepping stone in the historic road to communism.

Ironically, much that now passes for antihumanistic, mystical ecology involves exactly the same kind of thinking — but in an inverted form. Like their instrumental opponents, these ecologists, too, assume that humanity is dominated by nature, be it in the form of "natural laws" or an ineffable "earth wisdom" that must guide human behaviour. But while their instrumental opponents argue the need to achieve nature's "surrender" to a "conquering" active-aggressive humanity, anti-humanist and mystical ecologists argue the case for achieving humanity's passive-receptive "surrender" to an "all-conquering" nature. However much the two views may differ in their verbiage and pieties, *domination* remains the underlying notion of both: a natural world conceived as a taskmaster — either to be controlled or obeyed.

Social ecology springs this trap dramatically by re-examining the entire concept of domination, be it in nature and society or in the form of "natural law" and "social law." What we normally call domination in nature is a human projection of highly organized systems of *social* command and obedience onto highly idiosyncratic, individual, and asymmetrical forms of often mildly coercive behaviour in animal communities. Put simply, animals do not "dominate" each other in the same way that a human elite dominates, and often exploits, an oppressed social group. Nor do they "rule" through institutional forms of systematic violence as social elites do. Among apes, for example, there is little or no coercion, but only erratic forms of dominant behaviour. Gibbons and orangutans are notable for their peaceable behaviour toward members of their own kind. Gorillas are often equally pacific, although one can single out "high status," mature, and physically strong males among "lower status," younger and physically weaker ones. The "alpha males" celebrated among chimpanzees do not occupy very fixed "status" positions within what are fairly fluid groups. Any "status" that they do achieve may be due to very diverse causes.

One can merrily skip from one animal species to another, to be sure, falling back on very different, asymmetrical reasons for searching out "high" versus "low status" individuals. The procedure becomes rather silly, however, when words like "status" are used so flexibly that they are allowed to include mere differences in group behaviour and functions, rather than coercive actions.

The same is true for the word "hierarchy." Both in its origins and its strict meaning, this term is highly social, not zoological. A Greek term, initially used to denote different levels of deities and, later, of clergy (characteristically, Hierapolis was an ancient Phrygian city in Asia Minor that was a centre for mother goddess worship), the word has been mindlessly expanded to encompass everything from beehive relationships to the erosive effects of running water in which a stream is seen to wear down and "dominate" its bedrock. Caring female elephants are called "matriarchs" and attentive male apes who exhibit a great deal of courage in defense of their community, while acquiring very few "privileges," are often designated as "patriarchs." The absence of an organized system of rule — so common in hierarchical human communities and subject to radical institutional changes, including popular revolutions — is largely ignored.

Again, the different functions that the presumed animal hierarchies are said to perform, that is, the asymmetrical causes that place one individual in an "alpha status" and others in a lesser one, is understated where it is noted at all. One might, with much the same aplomb, place all tall sequoias in a "superior" status over smaller ones, or, more annoyingly, regard them as an "elite" in a mixed forest "hierarchy" over "submissive" oaks, which, to complicate matters, are more advanced on the evolutionary scale. The tendency to mechanically project social categories onto the natural world is as preposterous as an attempt to project biological concepts onto geology. Minerals do not "reproduce" the way life-forms do. Stalagmites and stalactites in caves certainly do increase in size over time. But in no sense do they grow in a manner that even remotely corresponds to growth in living beings. To take superficial resemblances, often achieved in alien ways, and group them into shared identities, is like speaking of the "metabolism" of rocks and the "morality" of genes.

This raises the issue of repeated attempts to read ethical, as well as social, traits into a natural world that is only *potentially* ethical insofar as it forms a basis for an objective social ethics. Yes, coercion does exist in nature; so does pain and suffering. However, *cruelty* does not. Animal intention and will are too limited to produce an ethics of good and evil or kindness and cruelty. Evidence of inferential and conceptual thought is very limited among animals, except for primates, cetaceans, elephants, and possibly a few other mammals. Even among the most intelligent animals, the limits to thought are immense in comparison with the extraordinary capacities of socialized human beings. Admittedly, we are substantially less than human today in view of our still unknown potential to be creative, caring, and rational. Our prevailing society serves to inhibit, rather than realize, our human potential. We still lack the imagination to know how much our finest human traits could expand with an ethical, ecological, and rational dispensation of human affairs.

By contrast, the known nonhuman world seems to have reached visibly fixed limits in its capacity to survive environmental changes. If mere *adaptation* to environmental changes is seen as the criterion for evolutionary success (as many biologists believe), then insects would have to be placed on a higher plane of development than any mammalian life-form. However, they would be no more capable of making so lofty an intellectual evaluation of themselves than a "queen bee" would be even remotely aware of her "regal" status — a status, I may add, that only humans (who have suffered the social domination of stupid, inept, and cruel kings and queens) would be able to impute to a largely mindless insect.

None of these remarks are meant to metaphysically oppose nature to society or society to nature. On the contrary, they are meant to argue that what unites society with nature in a graded evolutionary continuum is the remarkable extent to which human beings, living in a rational, ecologically oriented society, could *embody* the *creativity* of nature — this, as distinguished from a purely *adaptive* criterion of evolutionary success. The great achievements of human thought, art, science, and technology serve not only to monumentalize culture, *they serve also to monumentalize natural evolution itself.* They provide heroic evidence that the human species is a warm-blooded, excitingly versatile, and keenly intelligent life-form — not a cold-blooded, genetically programmed, and mindless insect — that expresses *nature's* greatest powers of creativity.

Life-forms that create and consciously alter their environment, hopefully in ways that make it more rational and ecological, represent a vast and indefinite extension of nature into fascinating, perhaps unbounded, lines of evolution which no branch of insects could ever achieve — notably, the evolution of a fully *self-conscious* nature. If this be humanism — more precisely, ecological humanism — the current crop of antihumanists and misanthropes are welcome to make the most of it.

Nature, in turn, is not a scenic view we admire through a picture window — a view that is frozen into a landscape or a static panorama. Such "landscape" images of nature may be spiritually elevating but they are ecologically deceptive. Fixed in time and place, this imagery makes it easy for us to forget that nature is not a static vision of the natural world but the long, indeed cumulative, *history* of natural development. This history involves the evolution of the inorganic, as well as the organic, realms of phenomena. Wherever we stand in an open field, forest, or on a mountain top, our feet rest on ages of development, be they geological strata, fossils of long-extinct life-forms, the decaying remains of the newly dead, or the quiet stirring of newly emerging life. Nature is not a "person," a "caring Mother," or, in the crude materialist language of the last century, "matter and motion." Nor is it a mere "process" that involves repetitive cycles like seasonal changes and the building-up and breaking-down process of metabolic activity — some "process philosophies" to the contrary notwithstanding. Rather, natural history is a *cumulative* evolution toward ever more varied, differentiated, and complex forms and relationships.

This *evolutionary* development of increasingly variegated entities, most notably, of life-forms, is also an evolutionary development which contains exciting, latent possibilities. With variety, differentiation, and complexity, nature, in the course of its own unfolding, opens new directions for still further development along alternative lines of natural evolution. To the degree that animals become complex, self-aware, and increasingly intelligent, they begin to make those elementary choices that influence their own evolution. They are less and less the passive objects of "natural selection" and more and more the active subjects of their own development.

A brown hare that mutates into a white one and sees a snow- covered terrain in which to camouflage itself is *acting* on behalf of its own survival, not simply "adapting" in order to survive. It is not merely being "selected" by its environment; it is selecting its own environment and making a *choice* that expresses a small measure of subjectivity and judgement.

The greater the variety of habitats that emerge in the evolutionary process, the more a given life-form, particularly a neurologically complex one, is likely to play an active and judgemental role in preserving itself. To the extent that natural evolution follows this path of neurological development, it gives rise to life-forms that exercise an ever-wider latitude of choice and a nascent form of freedom in developing themselves.

Given this conception of nature as the cumulative history of more differentiated levels of material organization (especially of life-forms) and of increasing subjectivity, social ecology establishes a basis for a meaningful understanding of humanity and society's place in natural evolution. Natural history is not a "catch-as-catch-can" phenomenon. It is marked by tendency, by direction, and, as far as human beings are concerned, by conscious purpose. Human beings and the social worlds they create can open a remarkably expansive horizon for development of the natural world — a horizon marked by consciousness, reflection, and an unprecedented freedom of choice and capacity for conscious creativity. The factors that reduce many life-forms to largely adaptive roles in changing environments are replaced by a capacity for consciously adapting environments *to* existing and new life-forms.

Adaptation, in effect, increasingly gives way to creativity and the seemingly ruthless action of "natural law" to greater freedom. What earlier generations called "blind nature" to denote nature's lack of any moral direction, turns into "free nature," a nature that slowly finds a voice and the means to relieve the needless tribulations of life for all species in a highly conscious humanity and an ecological society. The

"Noah Principle" of preserving every existing life-form simply for its own sake — a principle advanced by the antihumanist, David Ehrenfeld — has little meaning without the presupposition, at the very least, of the existence of a "Noah" — that is, a conscious life-form called humanity that might well rescue life- forms that nature itself would extinguish in ice ages, land desiccation, or cosmic collisions with asteroids.[5] Grizzly bears, wolves, pumas, and the like, are not safer from extinction because they are exclusively in the "caring" hands of a putative "Mother Nature." If there is any truth to the theory that the great Mesozoic reptiles were extinguished by climatic changes that presumably followed the collision of an asteroid with the earth, the survival of existing mammals might well be just as precarious in the face of an equally meaningless natural catastrophe unless there is a conscious, ecologically oriented life-form that has the technological means to rescue them.

The issue, then, is not whether social evolution stands opposed to natural evolution. The issue is *how* social evolution can be situated *in* natural evolution and *why* it has been thrown — needlessly, as I will argue — against natural evolution to the detriment of life as a whole. The capacity to be rational and free does not assure us that this capacity will be realized. If social evolution is seen as the potentiality for expanding the horizon of natural evolution along unprecedented creative lines, and human beings are seen as the potentiality for nature to become self-conscious and free, the issue we face is *why* these potentialities have been warped and *how* they can be realized.

It is part of social ecology's commitment to natural evolution that these potentialities are indeed real and that they can be fulfilled. This commitment stands flatly at odds with a "scenic" image of nature as a static view to awe mountain men or a romantic view for conjuring up mystical images of a personified deity that is so much in vogue today. The splits between natural and social evolution, nonhuman and human life, an intractable "stingy" nature and a grasping, devouring humanity, have all been specious and misleading when they are seen as inevitabilities. No less specious and misleading have been reductionist attempts to absorb social into natural evolution, to collapse culture into nature in an orgy of irrationalism, theism, and mysticism, to equate the human with mere animality, or to impose a contrived "natural law" on an obedient human society.

Whatever has turned human beings into "aliens" in nature are social changes that have made many human beings "aliens" in their own social world: the domination of the young by the old, of women by men, and of men by men. Today, as for many centuries in the past, there are still oppressive human beings who literally own society and others who are owned by it. Until society can be reclaimed by an undivided humanity that will use its collective wisdom, cultural achievements, technological innovations, scientific knowledge, and innate creativity for its own benefit and for that of the natural world, all ecological problems will have their roots in social problems.

HIERARCHIES, CLASSES, AND STATES

Up to now, I have tried to show that humanity and the human capacity to think are products of natural evolution, not "aliens" in the natural world. Indeed, every intuition tells us that human beings and their consciousness are results of an evolutionary tendency toward increasing differentiation, complexity, and subjectivity. Like most sound intuitions, this one has its basis in fact: the palaeontological evidence for this tendency. The simplest unicellular fossils of the distant past and the most complex mammalian remains of recent times all testify to the reality of a remarkable biological drama. This drama is the story of a nature rendered more and more aware of itself, a nature that slowly acquires new powers of subjectivity, and one that gives rise to a remarkable primate life-form, called human beings, that have the power to choose, alter, and reconstruct their environment — and raise the moral issue of what *ought* to be, not merely live unquestioningly with what *is*.

Nature, as I have argued, is not a frozen scene that we observe from a picture window or a mountain top. Defined more broadly and richly than a slogan on a bumper-sticker, nature *is* the very history of its evolutionary differentiation. If we think of nature as a development, we discern the presence of this tendency toward self-consciousness and, ultimately, toward freedom. Discussions about whether the presence of this tendency is evidence of a predetermined "goal," a "guiding hand," or a "God" are simply irrelevant for the purposes of this discussion. The fact is that such a tendency can be shown to exist in the fossil record, in the elaboration of existing life-forms from previous ones, and in the existence of humanity itself.

Moreover, to ask what humanity's "place" in nature may be is to implicitly acknowledge that the human species has evolved as a life-form that is organized to *make* a place for itself in the natural world, not simply to *adapt* to nature. The human species and its enormous powers to alter the environment were not invented by a group of ideologues called "humanists" who decided that nature was "made" to serve humanity and its needs. Humanity's powers have emerged out of aeons of evolutionary development and out of centuries of cultural development. The question of this species' "place" in nature is no longer a zoological problem, a problem of locating humanity in the overall evolution of life, as it was in Darwin's time. The problem of the "descent of man," to use the title of Darwin's great work, is as accepted by thinking people today as are the enormous powers our species possesses.

To ask what humanity's "place" in nature may be has now become a moral and social question — and one that no other animal can ask of itself, as much as many antihumanists would like to dissolve humanity into a mere species in a "biospheric democracy." And for humans to ask what their "place" in nature may be is to ask whether humanity's powers will be brought to the *service* of future evolutionary development or whether they will be used to *destroy* the biosphere. The extent to which humanity's powers will be brought to or against the service for future evolutionary development has very much to do with the kind of society or "second nature" human beings will establish: whether society will be a domineering, hierarchical, and exploitative one, or whether it will be a free, egalitarian, and ecologically oriented one. To sidestep the social basis of our ecological problems, to obscure it with primitivistic cobwebs spun by self-indulgent mystics and anti-rationalists, is to literally turn back the clock of ecological thinking to an atavistic level of trite sentiment that can by used for utterly reactionary purposes.

But if society is so basic to an understanding of our ecological problems, it, too, cannot be viewed as a frozen scenic view that we observe from the rarefied heights of an academic tower, the balcony of a governmental building, or the windows of a room for a corporate board of directors. Society, too, has emerged out of nature, as I have tried to show in my account of human socialization and the everyday reproduction of that socializing process up to the present day. To regard society as "alien" to nature reinforces the dualism between the social and the natural so prevalent in modern thinking. Indeed, such an antihumanistic view serves to clear the field for exactly all the anti-ecological forces that pit society against nature and reduce the natural world to mere natural resources.

By the same token, to dissolve society into nature by rooting social problems in genetic, instinctive, irrational, and mystical factors is to clear the field for exactly all those primitivistic forces that promote racist, misanthropic, and sexist tendencies, be they among women or among men.

Far from being a frozen scene, one that makes it easy for reactionary elements to identify the existing society with society *as such*, — just as the oppressed and their oppressors are grouped into a single species called *homo sapiens* and are held equally responsible for our present ecological crisis — society *is* the history of social development with its many different social forms and possibilities. Culturally, we are all the repositories of social history, just as our bodies are the repositories of natural history. We carry with us, often unconsciously, a vast body of beliefs, habits, attitudes, and sentiments that foster highly regressive views toward nature as well as toward each other.

We have fixed images, often inexplicable to ourselves, of a static "human nature," as well as a nonhuman nature, that subtly shape a multitude of our attitudes toward members of the two sexes, the young, the elderly, family bonds, kinship loyalties, and political authority, not to mention different ethnic, vocational, and social groups. Archaic images of hierarchy still shape our views of the most elementary differences between people and between all living beings. Our mental arrangement of the most simple differences among phenomena into hierarchical orders, say, of "one-to-ten," have been formed by socially ancestral distinctions that go back to a time that is too remote for us to remember.

These hierarchical distinctions have been developed over the course of history, often from harmless differences in mere status, into full-blown hierarchies of harsh command and abject obedience. To know our present and to shape our future calls for a meaningful and coherent understanding of the past — a past which always shapes us in varying degrees, and which profoundly influences our views of humanity and nature.

THE NOTION OF DOMINATION

To gain a clear understanding of how the past bears upon the present, I must briefly examine a basic view in social ecology, one that has now percolated into current environmental thinking. I refer to social ecology's insight that all our notions of dominating nature stem from the very real domination of human by human. This statement, with its use of the word "stem," must be examined in terms of its intent. Not only is it a historical statement of the human condition, but it is also a challenge to our contemporary condition which has far-reaching implications for social change. As a historical statement it declares, in no uncertain terms, that the domination of human by human *preceded* the notion of dominating nature. Indeed, human domination of human gave rise to the very *idea* of dominating nature.

In emphasizing that human domination precedes the notion of dominating nature, I have carefully avoided the use of a slippery verb that is very much in use today: namely, that the domination of nature "involves" the domination of human by human. I find the use of this verb particularly repellent because it confuses the order in which domination emerged in the world and, hence, the extent to which it must be eliminated if we are to achieve a free society. Men did not think of dominating nature until they had already begun to dominate the young, women, and, eventually, each other. And it is not until we eliminate domination in all its forms, as we shall see, that we will really create a rational, ecological society.

However much the writings of liberals and Marx convey the belief that attempts to dominate nature "led" to the domination of human by human, no such "project" ever existed in the annals of what we call "history." At no time in the history of humanity did the oppressed of any period joyfully accede to their oppression in a starry-eyed belief that their misery would ultimately confer a state of blissful freedom from the "domination of nature" to their descendants in some future era.

To take issue, as social ecology does, with words like "involve" or "led" is not a form of medieval casuistry. On the contrary, the way these words are used raises issues of radical differences in the interpretation of history and the problems that lie before us.

Domination of human by human did not arise because people created a socially oppressive "mechanism" — be it Marx's class structures or Lewis Mumford's human-constructed "mega-machine" — in order to "free" themselves from the "domination by nature." It is exactly this very queasy idea that gave rise to the myth that the domination of nature "requires," "presupposes," or "involves" the domination of human by human.

Implied in this basically reactionary myth is the notion that forms of domination, like classes and the State, have their sources in economic conditions and needs; indeed, that freedom can only be attained after the "domination of nature" has been achieved, with the resulting establishment of a classless society. Hierarchy somehow seems to disappear here in a shuffle of vague ideas or it is subsumed under the goal of abolishing classes, as though a classless society were necessarily one that is free of hierarchy. If we are to accept Engel's view, and to some degree Marx's, in fact, hierarchy in some form is "unavoidable" in an industrial society and even under communism. There is a surprising agreement between liberals, conservatives, and many socialists, as I have already noted, that hierarchy is unavoidable for the very existence of social life, and is an infrastructure for its organization and stability.

In contending that the notion of dominating nature *stems* from the domination of human by human, social ecology radically reverses the equation of human oppression and broadens its scope enormously. It tries to search into institutionalized systems of coercion, command, and obedience that preceded the emergence of economic classes, and that are not necessarily economically motivated at all. The "social question" of inequality and oppression that has plagued us for centuries is thereby extended by social ecology well beyond economic forms of exploitation into cultural forms of domination that exist in the family, between generations and sexes, among ethnic groups, in institutions of political, economic, and social management, and very significantly, in the way we experience reality as a whole, including nature and nonhuman life-forms.

In short, social ecology raises the issue of command and obedience in personal, social, historical, and reconstructive terms on a scale that encompasses, but goes far beyond, the more restricted economic interpretations of the "social question" that are prevalent today. Social ecology extends, as we shall see, the "social question" beyond the limited realm of justice into the unbounded realm of freedom; beyond a domineering rationality, science, and technology into libertarian ones; and beyond visions of social reform into those of radical social reconstruction.

EARLY HUMAN COMMUNITIES

We, of this era, are still victims of our own recent history. Modern capitalism, the most unique, as well as the most pernicious, social order to emerge in the course of human history, identifies human progress with bitter competition and rivalry; social status with the rapacious and limitless accumulation of wealth; the most personal values with greed and selfishness; the production of commodities, of goods explicitly made for sale and profit, as the motive force of nearly every economic and artistic endeavour; and profit and enrichment as the reason for the existence of social life.

No society known to history has made these factors so central to its existence or, worse, identified them with "human nature" as such. Every vice that, in earlier times, was seen as the apotheosis of evil has been turned into a "virtue" by capitalist society.

So deeply ingrained are these bourgeois attributes of our everyday lives and ways of thinking that we find it difficult to understand how much precapitalist societies held to the very opposite images of human values, however much they may have been honoured in the breach. It is hard for the modern mind to appreciate that precapitalist societies identified social excellence with cooperation rather than competition; disaccumulation rather than accumulation; public service rather than private interest; the giving of gifts rather than the sale of commodities; and care and mutual aid rather than profit and rivalry.

These values were identified with an uncorrupted human nature. In many respects, they are still a part of a caring socialization process in our own lives that tends to foster interdependence, not an aggressive, self-serving "independence" we call "rugged individualism." To understand from whence we came socially and how we came to be where we are, it is necessary to peel away our present system of values and examine, however summarily, a body of ideas that provide a clearer picture of a more organic, indeed, an ecological society that emerged from the natural world.

This organic, basically preliterate or "tribal," society was strikingly nondomineering — not only in its institutionalized structure but in its very language. If the linguistic analyses of anthropologists like the late Dorothy Lee are sound, Indian communities like the Wintu of the Pacific Coast lacked transitive verbs like "to have," "to take," and "to own" which denote power over individuals and objects. Rather, a mother "went" with her child into the shade, a chief "stood" with his people, and, more commonly, people "lived with" objects rather than "possessed" them.

However much these communities may have differed from each other in many social respects, we hear in their language, and detect in their behavioural traits, attitudes that go back to a shared body of beliefs, values, and basic lifeways. As Paul Radin, one of Americas most gifted anthropologists, observed, there was a basic sense of respect between individuals and a concern over their material needs that Radin called the principle of the "irreducible minimum." Everyone was entitled to the means of life, irrespective of his or her productive contribution. The right to live went unquestioned so that concepts like "equality" had no meaning if only because the "inequalities" that afflict us all — from the burdens of age to the incapacities of ill-health — had to be compensated for by the community.

Early notions of formal "equality," in which we are all "equally" free to starve or die of neglect, had yet to replace the *substantive* equality in which those less able to be fully productive were neverthe-less reasonably well provided for. Equality thus existed, as Dorothy Lee tells us, "in the very nature of things, as a by-product of the democratic structure of the culture itself, not as a principle to be supplied."[6] There was no need in these organic societies to "achieve" equality, for what existed was an absolute respect for man, for all individuals apart from any personal traits.

This broad appraisal by Lee was to be echoed by Radin, who for decades had lived among the Winnebago Indians and enjoyed their full confidence:

> If I were asked to state briefly and succinctly what are the outstanding features of aboriginal civilization, I, for one, would have no hesitation in answering that there are three: the respect for the individual, irrespective of age or sex; the amazing degree of social and political integration achieved by them; and the existence of a personal security which transcends all governmental forms and all tribal and group interests and conflicts.[7]

The respect for the individual, which Radin lists first as an aboriginal attribute, deserves to be emphasized, today, in an era that rejects the collective as destructive of individuality on the one hand, and, yet, in an orgy of pure egotism, has actually destroyed all the ego boundaries of free-floating, isolated, and atomized individuals on the other hand. A strong collectivity may be even more supportive of the individual, as close studies of certain aboriginal societies reveal, than a "free market" society with emphasis on an egoistic, but impoverished, self.

No less striking than the substantive equality achieved by many organic societies was the extent to which their sense of communal harmony was also projected onto the natural world as a whole. In the absence of any hierarchical social structures, the aboriginal vision of nature was also strikingly nonhierarchical. Accounts of many aboriginal ceremonies among hunting and horticultural communities leave us with the strong impression that the participant saw themselves as part of a larger world of life. Dances seemed to resemble simulations of nature, particularly animals, rather than human attempts to coerce nature, be it game or forces like rainfall.

Magic, which the last century called the "primitive man's science," apparently had a twofold aspect to it. One of these aspects seems to have been recognizably "coercive" in the sense that a given ritual was expected to necessarily produce a given effect. This kind of magic, presumably, had its own form of hard "causality," not unlike what we would expect to find in chemistry.

However, as I have suggested elsewhere, there were rituals — especially group rituals — that may have preceded in time the more familiar, cause-effect magical activities; rituals that were not coercive, but rather *persuasive*. Wildlife was seen in a complementary relationship of "give-and-take" in which game gave of itself to the hunter as a participant in the broad orbit of life — an orbit based on propitiation, respect, and mutual need. Humanity was no less a part than animals in this complementary orbit in which human and nonhuman were seen to give of themselves to each other according to mutual need rather than "trade-offs."[8]

This high sense of complementarity in rituals apparently reflected an active sense of social equality that viewed personal differences as parts of a larger natural whole rather than a pyramid-structured hierarchy of being. The attempt of organic society to place human beings in the same community on a par with each other, to see in each an interactive partner with others, yielded a highly egalitarian notion of difference as such.

Which is not to say that aboriginal people regarded themselves as "equal" to nonhuman creatures. In fact, they were acutely aware of the inequalities that existed in nature and society, inequalities created by differences in physical prowess, age, intelligence, genetic attributes, infirmities, and the like. Tribal peoples tried to compensate for these inequalities within their own groups, hence the emergence of an "irreducible minimum," as Radin called it, that gave every member of the community access to the means of life, irrespective of his or her abilities or contribution to the common fund. Often, special "privileges" were allowed to individuals who were burdened by infirmities to equalize their situations with respect to more endowed members of the community.

But in no sense did aboriginal people equate themselves with animals. They did not act or think "biocentrically," "eco-centrically" (to use words that have recently come into vogue), or, for that matter, "anthropocentrically" in dealing with nonhuman life-forms. It would be more accurate to say that they had no sense of "centricity" as such, except toward their own communities. The belief held by a tribe that it was "The People," as distinguished from outsiders or other communities, was a parochial weakness of tribal societies as a whole and generally made for fear of strangers, wars, and a self-enclosed mentality that the emergence of cities began to overcome. Indeed, until territorial ways of living that appear with cities began to replace loyalties based on blood ties, the notion of a common humanity was vague indeed, and tribalism remained very restrictive in its view of outsiders and strangers.

In this inner world of substantive equality, land and those "resources" our present society denotes as "property," were available to everyone in the community for use, at least to the extent that they were needed. But in principle, such "resources" could not be "possessed" in any personal sense, much less "owned" as property. Thus, in addition to the principles of the "irreducible minimum," substantive equality, the arts of persuasion, and a conception of differentiation as complementarity, organic preliterate societies seem to have been guided by a commitment to *usufruct*. Things were available to individuals and families of a community because they were needed, not because they were owned or created by the labour of a possessor.

The substantive equality of organic preliterate communities was not only the product of institutional structures and ancestral custom. It entered into the very sensibility of the individual: the way he or she perceived differences, other human beings, nonhuman life, material objects, land and forests, indeed, the natural world as a whole. Nature and society, which are so sharply divided against each other in our society and or sensibilities, were thereby slowly graded into each other as a shared continuum of interaction and everyday experience.

Needless to say, neither humanity "mastered" nature nor did nature "master" humanity. Quite to the contrary: nature was seen as a fecund source of life, well-being, indeed, a providential parent of humanity, not a "stingy" or "withholding" taskmaster that had to be coerced into yielding the means of life and its hidden "secrets" to a Faustian man. An image of nature as "stingy" would have produced "stingy" communities and self-seeking human participants.

This nature was anything but the relatively lifeless phenomenon it has become in our era — the object of laboratory research and the "matter" of technical manipulation. It consisted of wildlife that, in the aboriginal mind, was structured along kinship lines like human clans; forests, that were seen as a caring haven; and cosmic forces, like winds, torrential rainfall, a blazing sun, and a benign moon. Nature literally permeated the community not only as a providential environment, but as the blood flow of the kinship tie that united human to human and generation to generation.

The loyalty of kin to each other in the form of the blood oath — an oath that combined an expression of duty to one's relatives with vengeance for their offenders — became the organic source of communal continuity. Fictitious as this source would eventually become, especially in more recent times when the word "kin" has become a tenuous surrogate for authentic kinship ties, there is little reason to doubt its viability as a means for establishing one's place in early human communities. It was one's affiliations by blood, be it because of a shared ancestry or shared offspring, that determined whether an individual was an accepted part of a group, who he or she could marry, the responsibility he or she had to others, as well as the responsibility he or she had to him or her — indeed, the whole array of rights and duties that a community's members had in relation to each other.

It was on the basis of this biological fact of blood ties that nature penetrated the most basic institutions of preliterate society. The continuity of the blood tie was literally a means of *defining* social association and even self-identity. Whether one belonged to a given group or not, and who one was, in relation to others, was determined, at least juridically, by one's blood affiliations.

But still another biological fact defined one as a member of a community: whether one was a male or female. Unlike the kinship tie, which was to be slowly thinned out as distinctly nonbiological institutions like the State were gradually to encroach on the claims of genealogy and paternity, the sexual structuring of society has remained with us to this day, however much it has been modified by social development.

Lastly, a third biological fact defined one as a member of a group, namely, one's age. As we shall see, the earliest, truly social examples of status based on biological differences were essentially the age-groups to which one belonged and the ceremonies that legitimated one's age-status. Kinship established the basic fact that one shared a common ancestry with members of a given community. It defined one's rights and responsibilities to others of the same bloodline — rights and responsibilities that might involve who one could marry of a particular genealogical group, who was to be aided and supported in the normal demands of life, and who one could turn to for aid in difficulties of any kind. The bloodline literally gave definition to an individual and a group, much as skin forms the boundary that distinguishes one person from another.

Sexual differences, also biological in origin, defined the kind of work one did in the community and the role of a parent in rearing the young. Women essentially gathered and prepared food; men hunted animals and assumed a protective role for the community as a whole. These basically different tasks also gave rise to sororal and fraternal cultures in which women developed associations, whether informal or structured, and engaged in ceremonies and revered deities that were dissimilar from those of men, who had a culture very much of their own.

But none of these gender differences — not to mention genealogical ones — initially conferred a commanding position on one member of a sexual group or an obedient one on another. Women exercised full control over the domestic world: the home, family hearth, and the preparation of the most immediate means of life such as skins and food. Often, a woman built her own shelter and tended to her own garden as society advanced toward a horticultural economy.

Men, in turn, dealt with what we might call "civil" affairs — the administration of the nascent, barely developed "political" affairs of the community such as relations between bands, clans, tribes, and intercommunal hostilities. Later, as we shall see, these "civil" affairs became highly elaborate as population movements brought communities into conflict with each other. Warrior fraternities began to emerge within early societies that ultimately specialized in hunting men as well as animals.

What is reasonably clear is that in early phases of social development, woman's and man's cultures complemented each other and co-jointly fostered social stability as well as provided the means of life for the community as a whole. The two cultures were not in conflict with each other. Indeed, it is doubtful that an early human community could have survived if gender-oriented cultures initially tried to exercise any commanding position, much less an antagonistic one, over the other. The stability of the community required a respectful balance between potentially hostile elements if the community was to survive in a fairly precarious environment.

Today, it is largely because "civil" or, if you like, "political" affairs are so important in our own society that we read back into the preliterate world a "commanding" role among men in their monopoly of "civil" affairs. We easily forget that early human communities were really domestic societies, structured mainly around the work of women, and were often strongly oriented in reality, as well as mythology, toward woman's world.

Age groups, however, have more ambiguous social implications. Physically, the old people of a community were the most infirm, dependent, and often the most vulnerable members of the group in periods of difficulty. It was they who were expected to give up their lives in times of want that threatened the existence of a community. Hence, they were its most insecure members — psychologically as well as physically.

At the same time, the old people of a community were the living repositories of its lore, traditions, knowledge, and collective experience. In a world that had no written language, they were the custodians of its identity and history. In the tension between extreme personal vulnerability on the one hand and the embodiment of the community's traditions on the other hand, they may have been more disposed to enhance their status, to surround it with a quasi-religious aura and a social power, as it were, that rendered them more secure with the loss of their physical power.

THE EMERGENCE OF HIERARCHIES AND CLASSES

The logical beginnings of hierarchy, as well as a good deal of anthropological data at our disposal, suggest that hierarchy stems from the ascendancy of the elders, who seem to have initiated the earliest institutionalized systems of command and obedience. This system of rule by the elders, benign as it may have been initially, has been designated as a "gerontocracy" and it often included old women as well as old men. We detect evidence of its basic, probably primary, role in virtually all existing societies up to recent times — be it as councils of elders that were adapted to clan, tribal, urban and state forms, or, for that matter, in such striking cultural features as ancestor-worship and an etiquette of deference to older people in many different kinds of societies.

The rise of growing male power in society did not necessarily remove old women from high-status positions in this earliest of all hierarchies. Biblical figures like Sara had a distinctly authoritative and commanding voice in public as well as domestic affairs, even in the patriarchal and polygamous family of Hebrew bedouins. In reality, Sara is not an atypical figure in explicitly patriarchal families; indeed, in many traditional societies, once a woman aged beyond the child-bearing years of her life, she often acquired the status of what has been called a "matriarch" who enjoyed enormous influence within the community at large, at times even exceeding that of older males.

But even an early gerontocracy has a somewhat egalitarian dimension. If one lives long enough, one may eventually become an "elder" in an honorific sense, or, for that matter, a domineering "patriarch" and even a "matriarch." Hierarchy in this early form seems to be less structurally rigid because of a kind of biological "upward mobility." Its existence is still consistent with the egalitarian spirit of early communal societies.

The situation changes, however, when the biological facts that initially underpin early communal life become increasingly social — that is to say, when society comes increasingly into its own and transforms the form and content of relationships within and between social groups. It is important to emphasize that the biological facts that enter into the blood relationship, gender differences, and age-groups do not simply disappear once society begins to acquire its own self-generative forces of development. Nature is deeply interwoven with many of these social changes. But the natural dimension of society is modified, complicated, and altered by the socialization of the biological facts that exist in social life at all times.

Consider one of the major shifts in early societies that was to profoundly influence social evolution: the growing authority of men over women. By no means is it clear that the hierarchical supremacy of males was the first or necessarily the most inflexible system of hierarchy to corrode the egalitarian structures of early human society. Gerontocracy probably preceded "patricentricity," the orientation of society toward male values, or (in its most exaggerated form) "patriarchal" hierarchies. Indeed, what often passes for Biblical types of patriarchy are patricentric modifications of gerontocracy in which *all* younger members of the family — male as well as female — are under the complete rule of the oldest male and often his oldest female consort, the so-called matriarch.

That males are born into a special status in relationship to females becomes an obvious social fact. But it also rests on biological facts that are reworked for distinct social ends. Males are physically larger, more muscular, and normally possessed of greater hemoglobin, within the same ethnic group, than females. I am obliged to add that they produce significantly greater quantities of testosterone than females — an androgen that not only stimulates the synthesis of protein and produces a greater musculature, but also fosters behavioural traits that we associate with a high degree of physical dynamism. To deny these evolutionary adaptations, which provide males with greater athleticism in the hunting of game and, later, of people, by invoking individual exceptions to these male traits is to simply overlook important biological facts.

None of these factors and traits need yield the subordination of females to males. Nor is it likely that they did so. Certainly, male domination served no function when woman's role was so central to the stability of the early human community. Attempts to institutionalize the subordination of women, given their own rich cultural domain and their decisive role in maintaining the community, would have been utterly destructive to intragroup harmony. Indeed, the very idea of domination, not to mention hierarchy, had yet to emerge in early human communities that were socialized into the values of the irreducible minimum, complementarity, substantive equality, and usufruct. These values were not simply a moral credo; they were part of an all-encompassing sensibility that embraced the nonhuman as well as the human world.

Yet we know that men began to dominate women and began to give primacy to their "civil" over woman's "domestic" culture. That this occurred in a very shadowy and uncertain fashion is a problem that has not received the careful attention it deserves. The two cultures — male and female — retained a considerable distance from each other well into history, even as the male seemed to move to the social forefront in nearly every field of endeavour. There is a sense in which male "civil" affairs simply upstaged female "domestic" affairs without fully supplanting them. We have many ceremonies in tribal societies in which women seem to bestow powers on men that the men do not really have, such as ceremonial re-enactments of the ability to give birth.

But as "civil" society became more problematic because of invaders, intercommunal strife, and finally, systematic warfare, the male world became more assertive and agonistic — traits that are likely to make male anthropologists give the "civil" sphere greater prominence in their literature, especially if they have no meaningful contact with the women of a preliterate community. That women often mocked male bellicosity and lived full lives of their own in very close personal relationships, seems to wane to the footnote level in most accounts by male anthropologists. The "men's hut" stood actively opposed to the woman's home, where the everyday domain of child-rearing, food preparation, and an intensely familial social life remained almost unnoticed by male anthropologists, although it was psychologically pivotal to the sullen men of a community. Indeed, sororal life retained an amazing vitality and exuberance long after the emergence of urban societies. Women's talk, however, was deprecated as "gossip" and their work was called "menial" even in Euro-American societies.

Ironically, the degradation of women, itself always variable and often inconsistent, appears when males form hierarchies among themselves, as Janet Biehl has so ably shown in her splendid work on hierarchy.[9] With increasing intercommunal conflicts, systematic warfare, and institutionalized violence, "civil" problems became chronic. They demanded greater resources, the mobilization of men, and they placed demands on woman's domain for material resources.

Out of the skin of the most able hunter emerged a new kind of creature: the "big man," who was also a "great warrior." Slowly, every domain of preliterate society was reoriented toward maintaining his heightened "civil" functions. The blood oath, based on kinship loyalties, was gradually replaced by oaths of fealty by his soldierly "companions" who were drawn from clans other than his own, indeed, from solitary strangers, thereby cutting across traditional bloodlines and their sanctity. "Lesser men" appeared who were obliged to craft his weapons, provide for his sustenance, build and adorn his dwellings, and finally, erect his fortifications and monumentalize his achievements with impressive palaces and burial sites.

Even woman's world, with its secretive underpinnings, was reshaped, to a lesser or greater degree, in order to support him with young soldiers or able serfs, clothing to adorn him, concubines to indulge his pleasures, and, with the growth of female aristocracies, heroes and heirs to bear his name into the future. All the servile plaudits to his great stature, that are commonly seen as signs of feminine weakness, emerged, throwing into sharp contrast and prominence a cultural ensemble based on masculine strength.

Servility to male chiefs, warriors, and kings was not simply a condition imposed by warriors on women. Side by side with the servile woman is the unchanging image of the servile man, whose back provides a footrest for arrogant monarchs and demeaning capitalists. The humiliation of man by man began early on in the "men's hut," when cowering boys lived on a diet of mockery for their inexperience at the hands of adult males; and "small men" lived on a diet of disdain for their limited accomplishments by comparison with those of "big men."

Hierarchy, which first rears its head tentatively with gerontocracies, did not suddenly explode into prehistory. It expanded its place slowly, cautiously, and often unnoticeably, by an almost metabolic form of growth when "big men" began to dominate "small men," when warriors and their "companions" began to gradually dominate their followers, when chiefs began to dominate the community, and finally, when nobles began to dominate peasants and serfs.

By the same token, the "civil" sphere of the male began to slowly encroach upon the "domestic" sphere of the female. By degrees, it placed the female world increasingly in the service of the male, without destroying it. The sororal world, far from disappearing, took on a hidden form, indeed, a confidential form, that women shared with each other behind the backs of men, as they confronted new "civil" relationships created by males.

Hence, in gender relationships as well as in intramale relationships, there was no sudden leap from the sexual egalitarianism of early preliterate societies to male "priority." Indeed, it would be quite impossible, as Biehl has pointed out, to divorce the domination of woman by man from the domination of man by man. The two always interacted dialectically to reinforce each other with attitudes of command and obedience that gradually permeated society as a whole, even producing hierarchies of a more unstable nature among women. At the bottom of every social ladder always stood the resident outsider—male or female — and the assortment of war captives who, with economic changes, became a very sizeable population of slaves.

The transition from a largely "domestic" to a largely "civil" society was also conditioned by many less noticeable, but very important, factors. Long before domination became rigorously institutionalized, gerontocracy had already created a state of mind that was structured around the power of elders to command and the obligation of the young to obey. This state of mind went far beyond the indispensable care and attention required for the instruction of children and youths in the arts of survival. In many preliterate communities, elders acquired major decision-making powers that dealt with marriage, group ceremonies, decisions about war, and intracommunal squabbles between persons and clans. This state of mind, or, if you like, conditioning, was a troubling presence that presaged even greater troubles as hierarchy generally extended itself over society.

But hierarchy even in early societies was still further reinforced by shamans and, later, by shamanistic guilds that gained prestige and privileges by virtue of their very uncertain monopoly over magical practices. Be they "primitive man's science" or not, the arts of the shaman were naïve at best and fraudulent at worst — and more often the latter than the former, present-day cults, covens, and pop-literature on the subject to the contrary notwithstanding. Repeated failures by shamans in their use of magical techniques could be fatal, not only to a troubled community or a sick person. Their failure could be dangerous to the shaman as well, who might just as well be speared as exiled in disgrace.

Hence, as Paul Radin notes in his excellent discussion of West African shamans, shamanistic guilds always sought influential allies who could buffer them from popular anger and incredulity. Such allies were often elders who felt insecure as a result of their own failing powers or rising chiefs who were in need of ideological legitimation from the spirit world.[10]

Still another refinement of hierarchy was the transition from the "big man's" status — whose prestige depended as much on his distribution of gifts as it did upon his prowess as a hunter — to the status of a hereditary chief. Here, we witness the remarkable transmutation of a "big man," who must actively earn public admiration with impressive actions of all kinds, into a wise chiefly advisor, who commands respect without any prerogative of power, and finally, into a quasi- monarchical figure who evokes fear, be it because of his considerable entourage of armed "companions," his status as a demi-god with supernatural powers of his own, or both.

This graded development of a "big man" into an outright autocrat was leavened by basic alterations in the kinship bond and its importance. The kinship bond is surprisingly egalitarian when it is not twisted out of shape. It evokes a simple sense of loyalty, responsibility, mutual respect, and mutual aid. It rests on the *moral* strength of a shared sense of ancestry, on the belief that we are all "brothers" and "sisters," however fictitious these ancestral ties may become in reality — not on the basis of material interest, power, fear, or coercion.

The "big man," chief, and finally, the autocrat undermines this essentially egalitarian bond. He may do so by asserting the supremacy of his own kin group over other ones, in which case an entire clan may acquire a royal or dynastic status in relations to other clans in the community. Or he may bypass his own kinspeople entirely and adopt "companions," be they warriors, retainers, and the like, who are drawn into his fold exclusively on the basis of their own prowess and fealty without any regard to blood affiliations.

This is a highly corrosive process. A new kind of "person" is created again: a person who is neither a member of the "big man's" kin group or, for that matter, a member of the community. Like the mercenaries of the Renaissance or even classical antiquity, he is a "companion," with other companions like himself, who collects into a military "company" that has no social loyalties or traditions.

Such "companies" can easily be set against the community or reared above it into a coercive monarchy and aristocracy. Gilgamesh in the famous Sumerian epic adopted Enkidu, a total stranger, as his "companion," thereby challenging the integrity of the entire kinship system as a form of social cement and undermining its complex network of commitments that were so essential to the egalitarian values of preliterate society.

What I would like to emphasize is how much hierarchical differentiation simply reworked existing relationships in early society into a system of status long before the strictly economic relationship we call "classes" emerged. Age status merged with changes in gender status; "domestic" society was placed in the service of "civil" society; shamanistic guilds networked with gerontocracies and warrior groups; and warrior groups reworked kinship ties, ultimately reducing tribal blood communities to territorial communities based on residence rather than blood ties and composed of peasants, serfs, and slaves.

Our present era is the heir to this vast reworking of differentiation of humanity — not only along class lines but, much earlier in time, into hierarchies in which class systems were incubated. These hierarchies still form the fertile ground in our own time for the existence of hidden oppressions by age groups, of women by men, and of men by men — indeed, a vast landscape of domination that also gives rise in great part to largely exploitative economic systems based on classes.

Only later was this immense system of social domination extended into the notion of dominating nature by "humanity." No ecological society, however communal or benign in its ideals, can ever remove the "goal" of dominating the natural world until it has radically eliminated the domination of human by human, or, in essence, the entire hierarchical structure within society in which the very notion of domination rests. Such an ecological society must reach into the overlaid muck of hierarchy — a muck that oozes out from fissures in family relationships that exist between generations and genders, churches and schools, friendships and lovers, exploiters and exploited, and hierarchical sensibilities toward the entire world of life.

To recover and go beyond the nonhierarchical world that once formed human society and its values of the irreducible minimum, complementarity, and usufruct, is an agenda that belongs to the closing portions of this book. It suffices, here, to bear in mind that social ecology has made the understanding of hierarchy — its rise, scope, and impact — the centrepiece of its message of a liberating, rational, and ecological society. Any agenda that contains less than these imperatives is obscure at best and grossly misleading at worst.

At the risk of repetition, let me emphasize that the word hierarchy should be viewed strictly as a *social* term. To extend this term to cover all forms of coercion is to permanently root consciously organized and institutionalized systems of command and obedience in nature and give it an aura of eternality that is comparable only to the genetic programming of a "social" insect. We have more to learn from the fate of our own royal figures in human history that from the behaviour of "queen bees" in beehives.

Figures like Louis XVI of France and Nicholas II of Russia, for example, did not become autocrats because they had genetically programmed strong personalities and physiques, much less keen minds. They were inept, awkward, psychologically weak, and conspicuously stupid men (even according to royalist accounts of their reigns) who lived in times of revolutionary social upheaval. Yet their power was virtually absolute until it was curtailed by revolution.

What gave them the enormous power they enjoyed? Their power can only be explained by the rise of humanly contrived and supportive institutions like bureaucracies, armies, police, legal codes and judiciaries that consciously favoured absolutism, and a far- flung, and largely servile, Church that itself was structured along highly hierarchical lines — in short, a vast, deeply entrenched institutional apparatus that had been in the making for centuries and was overthrown in revolutionary upheavals in a matter of weeks. Apart from genetically programmed insects, we have absolutely no equivalent of such hierarchies in the nonhuman world. Remove the word "hierarchy" from its social context in human life and we create the utmost confusion in trying to understand its origins in our midst and the means for removing it — a social capacity, I may add, that we alone, as human beings, possess.

By the same token, the word "domination" should be viewed strictly as a *social* term if we are not to lose sight of its various institutionalized forms — forms that are unique to human beings. Animals certainly do coerce each other, usually as individuals, occasionally even as small "gangs" that presumably demand access to seeming "privileges," (a word which can also be stretched beyond all recognition if we examine "privilege" comparatively, as it exists from one species to another.)

But not only is this "domineering" behaviour associated with one or a few individual animals; it is highly tentative, often episodic, informal, and among apes in particular, highly diffuse. The "privileges" our closest animal relatives claim are very different from one species to another, even one group to another. Lasting institutions like armies, police, and even criminal groups, do not exist in the animal world. Where they seem to exist, as among "soldiers" in insects like ants, they are examples of genetically programmed behaviour, not socially con- trived institutions open to radical change by rebellion.

It is tempting to ask *why* such coercive social institutions, indeed, status systems and hierarchies, arose among human beings in the first place, not only *how* they arose. In other words, what were the *causes* that gave rise to institutionalized dominance and submission apart from descriptions of their emergence and development?

Status, as I have already pointed out, appeared between age- groups, albeit in an initially benign form. Hence, a psycho-social setting of deference to the elderly was already present in early society even before older generations began to claim very real privileges from younger ones. I've cited the infirmities and insecurities aging produces in the elderly and their capacity to bring their greater experience and knowledge to the service of their increasing status.

Their gerontocracies present no real mystery as a source of status- *consciousness*. That age-hierarchies would appear is often merely a matter of time: the socialization process with its need for careful instruction, growing knowledge, and an increasing reservoir of ex- perience virtually guarantees that elders would earn a justifiable degree of respect and, in precarious situations, seek a certain amount of power.

The most challenging form of social status, however, is probably the power that "big men" gained and concentrated, initially in their own persons, later in their increasingly institutionalized "companies." Here, we encounter a very subtle and complex dialectic. "Big men" were notable, as we have seen, for their generosity, not only for their prowess. Their ceremonial distribution of gifts to people — a system for the redistribution of wealth that acquired highly neurotic traits in the potlatch ceremonies of the Northwest Indians, where bitter contests between "big men" led to an orgiastic "disaccumulation" of everything they owned in order to "accumulate" prestige within the community — may have had very benign origins. To be generous and giving was a social etiquette that promoted the unity, and contributed to the very survival, of the early human community.

Given time and the likely susceptibility of men to seek communal approval, a susceptibility that was rooted in their sense of "manliness" and the community's respect for their physical prowess, it is likely that "bigness" meant little more than generosity and a high regard for skill and courage. These would have been attributes that *any* preliterate community would have prized in a male, just as women had many different skills that were deeply valued. This kind of "bigness," as potlatch ceremonies suggest, could have easily become reified as an end in itself. Or, as in certain communities like the Hopi, by contrast, it could be seen as socially disruptive because of its strident in- dividuality, and thus, it was sharply curtailed. Accordingly, when Euro-American "educators" of the Hopi tried to teach Hopi children to play competitive sports, they had immense difficulties in getting the children to keep scores. Hopi custom discouraged rivalry and self- assertiveness as harmful to community solidarity.

Everywhere along the way, in effect, conflicting alternatives con- fronted each community as potential hierarchies began to appear: first, as gerontocracies, later, as individual "big men" and warrior groups. Such potential hierarchies could have been developed very much on their own momentum, initially with very little divisive effects on the community, or they could have been sharply curtailed even after they began to appear. There is evidence to show that such opposing tenden- cies appeared in many different preliterate communities, either advancing into full-blown hierarchies or being arrested at various levels of development, when they were not simply pushed back to a more egalitarian condition.

In fact, custom, socialization, and basic precepts like the irreducible minimum, complementarity, and usufruct, might very well have tended to favour the *curtailment* of hierarchy rather than its cultivation. This is evident in the large number of human communities that existed well into Euro-American history with little or no hierarchical institutions. Only a surprisingly small part of humanity developed societies that were structured overwhelmingly around hierarchies, classes, and the State. Perhaps a majority avoided in varying degrees this dark path of social development or, at least, entered onto it to a limited extent.

But one fact should be clearly noted: a community that does develop along hierarchical, class, and statist lines has a profound impact upon all the communities around it that continue to follow an egalitarian direction. A warrior community led by an aggressive chiefdom compels highly pacific neighbouring communities to create their own military formations and chiefs if they are to survive. An entire region may thus be drastically changed —culturally, morally, and institutionally — merely as a result of aggressive hierarchies in a single community.

We can trace this clearly by studying one community's grave sites in the Andes which was initially free of weapons and distinctive status-oriented ornaments, only to find that these sites began to exhibit warrior and prestige artifacts at a later level of development. Actually, this change could be attributed to the emergence of a neighbouring community that had embarked upon an aggressive, warrior-oriented social development earlier in time, thereby profoundly affecting the internal life of more peaceful communities which surrounded it. So it may have been in many parts of the world, each one in isolation from the others.

No less striking is the evidence we find of changes in American Indian societies from highly centralized, war-like, and quasi-statist "empires" to decentralized, fairly pacific, and relatively nonhierarchical communities. In their centralistic and militaristic phases, these "empires" apparently became so top-heavy, exploitative, and exhausting to the communities they controlled that they either collapsed under their own weight or were simply overthrown by local rebellions. The

Indian mound-builders of the American midwest or the Mayans of Mexico may very well have embarked on a vigorous militaristic expansion, only to disappear when they could no longer sustain themselves or retain the obedience of subject populations. This historic see-saw of communal institutions between centralization and decentralization, warrior and peaceful communities, expansive and contractive societies, all appeared in the West as well until the rise of the nation-state in Europe during the fifteenth and sixteenth centuries.

In so far as women were reduced to the spectators of the intracommunity changes that gave rise to hierarchy, they were not significant participants in its development. Victimized as they were, they shared with the lower strata of male hierarchies an oppression and degradation that all ruling elites inflicted on their underlings. Men not only degraded, oppressed, and often used women as objects; they also oppressed and killed other men in an orgy of slaughtering and cruelty. The early kingdoms of the Near East were reluctant to keep male prisoners of war because they were regarded as potentially too rebellious, so they were normally put to death rather than enslaved. When male slaves began to appear in large numbers, they were often exploited ruthlessly and were treated, especially in mines and large-scale agriculture, with appalling ruthlessness. Male physical strength became a liability, not an asset, when it was used for exploitative purposes.

The causes of hierarchy, then, are not a mystery. They are quite comprehensible when we dig into their roots in the more mundane aspects of daily life such as the family, the rearing of young people, the segmentation of society in to age-groups, the expectations that are placed on the individual as a male or female in the everyday domestic or "civil" worlds, and in the most personal aspects of acculturation as well as community ceremonies. And hierarchy will not disappear until we change these roots of daily life radically, not only economically, with the removal of class society.

Not only did hierarchies precede classes, but, as Biehl has shown, male domination over other males generally preceded the domination of women. Women became the degraded bystanders of a male-oriented civilization that reared itself up beside woman's own culture, corroded it, and established systematic ways of manipulating it. When men tried to absorb woman's culture, they warped it and subordinated it — but they succeeded in only a limited degree. Sororal relationships, affections, and lifeways continued behind the backs of men and often outside the range of their vision in the secret alcoves of history, as it were.

Men, in turn, were often the objects of ridicule to women, even in cultures that were overbearingly patriarchal. Nor did women always aspire to participate in a "civil" society that was even more brutal to men than to domestic animals. Let us not forget that it was not oxen that dragged huge blocks of stone up the ramparts of the great pyramids of ancient Egypt, but usually male serfs and slaves, who were regarded as more expendable than cattle.

THE EMERGENCE OF THE STATE

The institutionalized apex of male civilization was the State. Here, again, we find a tricky dialectic which, if we ignore its subtleties, can lead us into very simplistic discussions of state formation in which state institutions suddenly erupt into history, fully grown and overtly coercive. Indeed, such eruptions of states, from seemingly "democratic" to highly "authoritarian" institutions, are more of a modern than a premodern phenomenon, notably the sudden substitution of republican by totalitarian states. Except in periods of invasions, when alien aristocracies were rapidly imposed on relatively egalitarian communities, rapid changes in state institutions were a comparative rarity. Unless we consider how the State began to emerge, how far it developed, and how stable it was, we encounter many difficulties even in defining the State, much less in exploring the forms it took in different societies.

Minimally, the State is a professional system of social coercion — not merely a system of social administration as it is still naïvely regarded by the public and by many political theorists. The word "professional" should be emphasized as much as the word "coercion." Coercion exists in nature, in personal relationships, in stateless, nonhierarchical communities. If coercion alone were used to define a State, we would despairingly have to reduce it to a natural phenomenon — which it surely is not. It is only when coercion is *institutionalized* into a professional, systematic, and organized form of social control — that is, when people are plucked out of their everyday lives in a community and expected not only to "administer" it but to do so with the backing of a monopoly of violence — that we can properly speak of a State.

There may be varying approximations of a State, notably incipient, quasi, or partial states. Indeed, to ignore these gradations of coercion, professionalization, and institutionalization toward fully developed states is to overlook the fact that statehood, as we know it today, is the product of a long and complex development. Quasi, semi, and even fully developed States have often been very unstable and have often haemorrhaged power over years that resulted in what essentially became stateless societies. Hence, we have the swings, historically, from highly centralized empires to feudal manorial societies and even fairly democratic "city-states," often with swings back again to empires and nation-states, be they autocratic or republican in form. The simplistic notions that states merely come into existence like a new-born baby, omit the all-important gestation process of state development and have resulted in a great deal of political confusion to this very day. We still live with confused notions of statecraft, politics, and society, each of which is deeply in need of careful distinction from the other.

Each State is not necessarily an institutionalized system of violence in the interests of a specific ruling class, as Marxism would have us believe. There are many examples of States that *were* the "ruling class" and whose own interests existed quite apart from — even in antagonism to — privileged, presumably "ruling" classes in a given society. The ancient world bears witness to distinctly capitalistic classes, often highly privileged and exploitative, that were bilked by the State, circumscribed by it, and ultimately devoured by it — which is in part why a capitalist society never emerged out of the ancient world. Nor did the State "represent" other class interests, such as landed nobles, merchants, craftsmen, and the like. The Ptolemaic State in Hellenistic Egypt was an interest in its own right and "represented" no other interest than its own. The same is true of the Aztec and the Inca States until they were replaced by Spanish invaders. Under the Emperor Domitian, the Roman State became the principal "interest" in the empire, superseding the interests of even the landed aristocracy which held such primacy in Mediterranean society.

I shall have a good deal to say about the State when I distinguish statecraft from politics and the authentically political from the social. For the present, we must glance at state-*like* formations that eventually produced different kinds of States.

A chieftainship, surrounded by a "company" of supportive warriors such as the Aztec State, is still an incipient type of state formation. The seemingly absolute monarch was selected from a royal clan by a council of clan elders, was carefully tested for his qualifications, and could be removed if he proved to be inadequate to meet his responsibilities. Like the highly militaristic Spartan State, chieftains or kings were still circumscribed by tribal traditions that had been reworked to produce the centralization of power.

Near-Eastern States, like the Egyptian, Babylonian, and Persian, were virtually extended households of individual monarchs. They formed a remarkable amalgam of a "domestic" society with a territorial one: an "empire" was seen primarily as the land attached to the king's palace, not a strictly territorial administrative unit. Pharaohs, kings, and emperors nominally held the land (often co-jointly with the priesthood) in the trust of the deities, who were either embodied in the monarch or were represented by him. The empires of Asian and North African kings were "households" and the population was seen as "servants of the palace," not as citizens in any Western sense of the term.

These "states," in effect, were not simply engines of exploitation or control in the interests of a privileged "class." They were resplendent households with vast bureaucracies and aristocratic entourages that were self-serving and self-perpetuating states. Administration was seen as the task of maintaining a very costly household with monuments to its power that taxed and virtually undermined the entire economy. In Egypt's Old Kingdom, possibly as much effort went into building pyramids, temples, palaces, and manors as was devoted to the maintenance of the Nile valley's all-important irrigation system. The Egyptian State was very real but it "represented" nothing other than itself. Conceived as a "household" and a sacred terrain in which the Pharaoh embodied a deity, the State was almost congruent with society itself. It was, in effect, a huge *social* State in which the differentiation of politics out of society was really minimal. The State did not exist above society or apart from it; the two were essentially one — an extended social household, not an assortment of independent coercive institutions.

The Greek *polis* of the classical era does not offer us any more a complete picture of the State than we encounter in the Near East. Athens may be regarded as the apogee of class *politics* as distinguished from the private world of the household based on family life, work, friendships, and material needs which we can properly call *social*, or the administration of armies, bureaucrats, judicial systems, police, and the like, which we can properly call *statecraft*. Placed within the context of this threefold distinction — social, political, and statist — the Athenian *polis* is very difficult to define. The State, more properly the *quasi-* state created by the Athenians in the Periklean Age, possessed highly tribalistic attributes that directly involved the participation of a sizeable male citizenry in seemingly statist activities. These Athenians had invented *politics* — the direct administration of public affairs by a community as a whole.

Admittedly, this political community or "public domain," as it has been called, existed within a wider domain of disenfranchised alien residents, women of all classes, and slaves. These large disenfranchised populations provided the material means for many Athenian male citizens to convene in popular assemblies, function as mass juries in trials, and collectively administer the affairs of the community. Politics here, had begun to differentiate itself from the social domain of the family and work.

But was this *polis* really a State? That the Athenians of the classical era used coercion against slaves, women, aliens, and rival *poleis* is clearly evident. Within the eastern Mediterranean, Athenian influence became increasingly imperial as the city forced other *poleis* to join the Athenian-controlled Delian League and taxed them, using these funds to maintain the Athenian citizenry and aggrandize the *polis*. Women, of upper and well-to-do strata, were often confined to their homes and obliged to maintain a domestic establishment for their husbands' public life.

It does not absolve the limitations of the Athenian democracy to say that women were degraded throughout much of the Mediterranean world, perhaps even more so in Athens than other regions. Nor does it absolve it to say that Athenians were generally less severe in their treatment of slaves than Romans. But, by the same token, we cannot ignore the fact that classical Athens was historically unique, indeed unprecedented, in much of human history, because of the democratic forms it created, the extent to which they worked, and its faith in the competence of its citizens to manage public affairs. These institutions were forms of a direct democracy, as we shall see, and reflected a public aversion to bureaucracy that made them structurally the most democratic in the career of human political life. The Athenian State, in effect, was not a fully developed phenomenon.

Indeed, I cannot stress too strongly that Athens, like so many "city-states," would have normally developed toward an oligarchy if we explore the way in which so many autonomous cities eventually became increasingly authoritarian and internally stratified. This was the case with Rome, the late medieval Italian city-states, the German city federations, and New England townships of America. One can go on endlessly and cite decentralized, seemingly free and independent cities that eventually turned from fairly democratic communities into aristocracies.

What is remarkable about Athens is that the apparently "normal" trend toward oligarchy was consciously reversed by the radical changes introduced by Solon, Kleisthenes, and Perikles in the *polis's* entire institutional structure. Aristocratic institutions were steadily weakened and consciously abolished or reduced to mere ceremonial bodies, while democratic ones were granted increasing power and eventually embraced the entire male citizenry, irrespective of property ownership and wealth. The army was turned into a militia of foot-soldiers whose power began to exceed, by far, that of the aristocratic cavalry. Thus all the negative features of the Athenian democracy, so common to the Mediterranean and the era as a whole, must be seen in the context of a revolutionary reversal of the normal trend toward oligarchy in most city-states.

It is easy to deprecate this democracy because it rested on a large slave population and degraded the status of women. But to do this with lofty arrogance from a distance of more than two thousand years, with a hindsight that is enriched by endless social debate, is to lift oneself up by one's bootstraps from the rich wealth of historical facts. Indeed, it is to ignore those rare moments of democratic creativity that appeared in the West and have nourished rich utopian and libertarian traditions.

Indeed, we do not encounter the State as a fully professional and distinctive apparatus rooted in class interest until we see the emergence of modern nations in Europe. The nation-state, as we know it today, finally divests politics of all its seemingly traditional features: direct democracy, citizen participation in the affairs of governmental life, and a sensitive responsiveness to the communal welfare. The word "democracy" itself undergoes degradation. It becomes "representative" rather than face-to-face; highly centralized rather than freely confederal between relatively independent communities, and divested of its grassroots institutions.

Educated, knowledgeable citizens become reduced to mere taxpayers who exchange money for "services," and education surrenders its civic orientation to a curriculum designed to train the young for financially rewarding skills. We have yet to see how far this appalling trend will go in a world that is being taken over by mechanical robots, computers that can so easily be used for surveillance, and genetic engineers who have very limited moral scruples.

Hence, it is of enormous importance that we know how we arrived at a condition where our preening "control" of nature has actually rendered us more servile to domineering society than at any time in the past. By the same token, it is immensely important to know precisely those human achievements in history, however faulty, that reveal how freedom can be institutionalized — and, hopefully, expanded beyond any horizon we can find in the past.

There is no way that we can return to the naïve egalitarianism of the preliterate world or to the democratic *polis* of classical antiquity. Nor should we want to do so. Atavism, primitivism, and attempts to recapture a distant world with drums, rattles, contrived rituals, and chants whose repetition and fantasies bring a supernatural presence into our midst — however much this may be denied or affirmed as innocent or "immanent" — deflect us from the need for rational discussion, a searching investigation of community, and a searing critique of the present social system. Ecology is based on the wondrous qualities, fecundity, and creativity of natural evolution, all of which warrant our deepest emotional, aesthetic, and, yes, intellectual appreciation — not on anthropomorphically projected deities, be they "immanent" or "transcendental." Nothing is gained by going beyond a naturalistic, truly ecological, framework and indulging mystical fantasies that are regressive psychologically and atavistic historically.

Nor will ecological creativity be served by dropping on all fours and baying at the moon like coyotes or wolves. Human beings, no less a product of natural evolution than other mammals, have definitively entered the social world. By their very own biologically rooted mental power, they are literally *constituted* by evolution to intervene into the biosphere. Tainted as the biosphere may be by present social conditions, their presence in the world of life marks a crucial change in evolution's direction from one that is largely adaptive to one that is, at least, potentially creative and moral. In great part, their human nature is formed socially — by prolonged dependence, social interdependence, increasing rationality, and the use of technical devices and their willful application. All of these human attributes are mutually biological and social, the latter forming one of natural evolution's greatest achievements.

Hierarchies, classes, and states warp the creative powers of humanity. They decide whether humanity's ecological creativity will be placed in the service of life or in the service of power and privilege. Whether humanity will be irrevocably separated from the world of life by hierarchical society, or brought together with life by an ecological society depends on our understanding of the origins, development, and, above all, the scope of hierarchy — the extent to which it penetrates our daily lives, divides us into age group against age group, gender against gender, man against man, and yields the absorption of the social and political into the all-pervasive State. The conflicts within a divided humanity, structured around domination, inevitably lead to conflicts with nature. The ecological crisis with its embattled division between humanity and nature stems, above all, from divisions between human and human.

Our times exploit these divisions in a very cunning way: they *mystify* them. Divisions are seen not as social but personal. Real conflicts between people are mollified, even concealed, by appeals to a social "harmony" that has no reality in society. Like the atavistic ritual with its barely concealed appeal to the spirit world and its theistic "spiritualism," the encounter group has become a privatized arena for learning how to "conciliate" — this, while storms of conflict rage around us and threaten to annihilate us. That this use of "encounter" groups and theistic "spirituality" to mollify and despiritualize has come so much into vogue from its breeding ground in the American sunbelt is no accident. It occurs when a veritable campaign, under the name of "post-modernism," is going on to discard the past, to dilute our knowledge of history, to mystify the origins of our problems, to foster dememorization and the loss of our most enlightened ideals.

Hence, never before has it been more necessary to recover the past, to deepen our knowledge of history, to demystify the origins of our problems, to regain our memory of forms of freedom and advances that were made in liberating humanity of its superstitions, irrationalities, and, above all, a loss of faith in humanity's potentialities. If we are to re-enter the continuum of natural evolution and play a creative role in it, we must re-enter the continuum of social evolution and play a creative role there as well.

There will be no "re-enchantment" of nature or of the world until we achieve a "re-enchantment" of humanity and the potentialities of human reason.

TURNING POINTS IN HISTORY

I have tried to show how far we must go and how deeply we must enter into the most everyday aspects of our lives in order to root out the notion of dominating nature.

In so doing, I have tried to emphasize the extent to which the domination of human by human precedes the notion of dominating nature, indeed, even precedes the emergence of classes and the State. I have asked — and tried to answer — how hierarchies emerged, why they emerged, and the way they became increasingly differentiated into initially temporary and, later, firmly based status groups, and, finally, classes and the State.

My purpose has been to let these trends unfold from their own inner logic and examine all their nuanced forms along the way. The reader has been persistently reminded that humanity and its social origins are no less a product of natural evolution than other mammals and their communities; indeed, that human beings can express a conscious creativity in nature's evolutionary development and can enlarge it — not arrest or reverse it.

Whether humanity will play such a role, I have contended, depends upon the kind of society that emerges and the sensibility society fosters.

It is now important to examine those turning points in history which could have led people to either achieve a rational, ecological society, or an irrational, anti-ecological one.

THE RISE OF THE WARRIORS

Perhaps the earliest change in social development that veered society in a direction that became seriously harmful, both to humanity and the natural world, was the hierarchical growth of male's civil domain — namely, the rise of male gerontocracies, warrior groups, aristocratic elites, and the State. To reduce these highly complex developments to "patriarchy," as many writers are prone to do, is as naïve as it is simplistic. "Men" — a generic word that is as vague as the word "humanity" and ignores the oppression of men by men as well as of women by men — did not simply "take over" society. Nor did the male's civil society simply subvert woman's domestic world through invasions by patriarchal Indo-European and Semitic pastoralists, important as these invasions may have been in the subjugation of many early horticultural societies. The emphasis of certain eco-feminists, mystics, and Christian or pagan acolytes on this "take-over" and "invasions" theory simply creates another unresolved mystery: how did dramatic changes, like the emergence of patriarchy, occur in the pastoral societies that did the invading? We have evidence that the rise of the male civil domain with its concern for intertribal affairs and warfare gained ascendancy slowly and that some pastoral communities were oriented toward women in such strategic areas as descent and the inheritance of property, however much these communities were led by bellicose warriors.

In many cases, the male's civil domain developed slowly and probably gained importance with increases in neighbouring populations. Men were, in fact, needed to protect the community as a whole — including its women — from other marauding men. Warfare may have even emerged or developed among seemingly "pacific" and matricentric horticultural communities which tried to expel more pristine hunting and gathering peoples from woodlands that later were turned into farm lands. Let us be quite frank about this: matricentric or pacific as early farming communities may have been, they probably were very warlike in the eyes of the hunters they managed to displace

— that is, those hunting peoples and cultures that were by no means predisposed to abandon their free-ranging ways and take up food cultivation. The statements of the great Indian orators, the words of Wovoka, the Paiute Indian messiah of the late nineteenth-century Ghost Dance, on plow agriculture, are still evocative of this mentality: "Shall I plunge a blade into the breast of my mother, the Earth?"

But there can be little doubt that the slow shift from rule by the elderly, later the oldest male or patriarch, the change from the influence of animistic shamans to deity worshipping priesthoods, and the rise of warrior groups that finally culminated in supreme monarchs — all formed a major turning point in history toward domination, classes, and the emergence of the State. There is the possibility that matricentric communities of villagers might have shaped a pathway of an entirely different character for humanity as a whole. Based on gardening, simple tools, usufruct, the irreducible minimum, complementarity, and so-called feminine values of care and nurture (which, in any case, have been with us in the socialization of their children up to recent times), society might have taken a relatively benign turn in history. The concern that mothers normally share with their young might have been generalized into a concern that people could have shared with each other. Technical development based on limited wants could have continued very slowly into increasingly more sophisticated social forms and cultural life could have been elaborated with considerable sensitivity.

Whether unavoidable or not, the fact remains that this fork in the road of early history was to be marked by a turn to patriarchal, priestly, monarchical, and statist lines, not along matricentric and nonhierarchical lines. Warrior values of combat, class domination, and state rule were to form the basic infrastructure of all "civilized" development — no less in Asia than in Europe and no less in large areas of the New World, like Mexico and the Andes, than in the Old World.

The wistful attempts by many people in the ecology and feminist movements to return, in one way or another, to a presumably untroubled Neolithic village world are understandable in the face of "civilization's" more nightmarish results. But their imagery of this distant world and their growing hatred of "civilization" *as such*, leaves room for considerable doubt.

Certainly, it is not likely that pristine hunting and gathering communities had more love for equally pristine gardening societies than a Wovoka, whether or not they shared a belief in the same Mother Goddess. Nor is it likely that, with growing population, gardening societies could have retained the tender sentiments celebrated by the more atavistic feminists of our day. Patricentric pastoralists and sea invaders may have telescoped a development that might have been more benign, to be sure, but it would have been one that was difficult to avoid. If "civilization" was conceived in "original sin," it was probably a "sin" or evil that pitted food cultivators against hunters (both of whom may have been matricentric and animistic) and, much later, pastoralists against food cultivators.

In any case, there was a great deal in tribal and village society — be it composed of hunters or food cultivators — that needed remedying. First of all, tribal and village societies are notoriously parochial. A shared descent, be it fictional or real, leads to an exclusion of the stranger — except, perhaps, when canons of hospitality are invoked. Although the rules of exogamy and the imperatives of trade tend to foster alliances between the "insider" and "outsider" of a tribal and village community, an "outsider" can be killed summarily by an "insider." Rules of retribution for theft, assault, and murder apply exclusively to the "insider" and his or her relatives, not to any authority that exists apart from the common descent group.

Tribal and village societies, in effect, are very closed societies — closed to outsiders unless they are needed for their skills, to repopulate the community after costly wars and lethal epidemics, or as a result of marriage. And they are closed societies not only to outsiders, but often to cultural and technological innovations. While many cultural traits may spread slowly from one tribal and village community to another, such communities tend to be highly conservative in their view of basic innovations. For better or worse, traditional lifeways tend to become deeply entrenched with the passing of time. Unless they are developed locally, new technologies tend to be resisted — for understandable reasons, to be sure, if one bears in mind the socially disruptive effects they may have on time-honoured customs and institutions. But the harsh fact is that this conservatism makes a tribal and village community highly vulnerable to control, indeed, to eradication by other communities that have more effective technological devices.

A second troubling feature of tribal and village societies is their cultural limitations. These are not societies that are likely to develop complex systems of writing, hence the terms "nonliterate" and "preliterate" that are used by many anthropologists to designate them. Today, when irrationalism, mysticism, and primitivism have become rather fashionable among affluent middle-class people (ironically, through written works), the inability of nonliterate people to maintain a recorded history and culture, or to communicate through pictographs, is regarded as a pristine blessing. That the absence of alphabetic writing, in fact, not only severely limited the scope of the cultural landscape of early times but even fostered hierarchy, is easily overlooked. Knowledge of lore, ancestral ties, rituals, and survival techniques became the special preserve of the elderly who, through experience, rote learning, or both, were strategically positioned to manipulate younger people.

Gerontocracy, in my view the earliest form of hierarchy, became possible because young people had to consult their elders for knowledge. No scrolls or books were available to replace the wisdom inscribed on the brains of older people. Elders used their monopoly of knowledge with telling effect to establish the earliest form of rule in prehistory. Patriarchy itself owes a good deal of power to the knowledge which the eldest male of a clan commanded by virtue of the experience conferred upon him by age. Writing could easily have democratized social experience and culture — a fact shrewdly known to ruling elites and especially to priesthoods, who retained stringent control over literacy and confined a knowledge of writing to "clerks" or clerics.

A large literature has emerged, today, that mystifies primitivism. It is important to remind thinking people that humanity was not born into a Hobbesian world of a war of "all against all"; that the two sexes were once complementary to each other culturally as well as economically; that disaccumulation, gift-giving, the irreducible minimum, and substantive equality formed the basic norms of early organic societies; that humanity lived in a harmonious relationship with nature because it lived in a condition of internal social harmony within the same community. However, we cannot ignore that this innocent world, vulnerable to internal tendencies toward hierarchy as well as invaders who placed them in subjugation to warrior elites, had major flaws that kept humans from the full realization of their potentialities.

The idea of a shared *humanitas*, that could bring people of ethnically, even tribally, diverse backgrounds together in the common project of building a fully cooperative society for all to enjoy, did not exist. Tribal confederations certainly formed over time, often to mitigate bloody intertribal warfare and for expansionist purposes to displace "other" people of their land. The Iroquois Confederacy is perhaps one of the most celebrated examples of intertribal cooperation based on strong democratic traditions. But it was a Confederacy that was entirely focused on its own interests, for all its merits. Indeed, it earned the bitter hatred of the other Indian peoples like the Hurons and the Illinois, whose lands it invaded and whose communities it ravaged.

THE EMERGENCE OF THE CITY

After the shift from a matricentric to a patricentric warrior pathway of development, the next major turning point we encounter historically is the emergence and development of the city. The city was to form an entirely new social arena — a *territorial* arena in which one's place of residence and economic interests steadily replaced one's ancestral affinities based on blood ties.

The radical nature of this shift and its impact on history are difficult to appreciate today. Urbanity is so much a part of modern social life that it is simply taken for granted. Moreover, so much emphasis has been placed on the extent to which the city accelerated cultural development (writing, art, religion, philosophy, and science) and the impetus it gave to economic development (technology, classes, and the division of labour between crafts and agriculture) that we often fail to stress the new kinds of *human* association urbanity produced.

Perhaps for the first time, so far as we can judge, human beings were able to interact with each other with relatively little regard for their ancestral and blood ties. The notion that people were basically alike, irrespective of their tribal and village ancestry, began to gain ascendancy over their ethnic differences. The city increasingly replaced the *biological* fact of lineage, and the accident of birth into a particular kin group, by the *social* fact of residence and economic interests. People were not simply *born* into a distinct social condition; in varying degrees they could begin to *choose* and *change* their social condition. Social institutions and the development of a purely human ecumene came to the foreground of society and gradually edged the folk community into the background of social life. Kinship retreated more and more into the private realm of family affairs, and fading clan-type relations began to shrink into the narrower extended family of immediate relatives rather than a far-flung system of clan "cousins."

What is vastly important about the new social dispensation created by the city was the fact that the stranger or "outsider" could now find a secure place in a large community of human beings. Initially, this new place did not confer equality on the "outsider." Despite its avowed openness to resident aliens, Periklean Athens, for example, rarely gave them citizenship and the right to plead their court cases, except through the voices of Athenian citizens. But early cities did provide strangers with increased protection from abuse by the "insider." In many cases of newly emerging cities, a compromise was struck between tribal values based on blood ties and social values based on the realities of residence in which the "outsider" acquired basic rights that tribal society rarely conferred, while restricting citizenship to the "insider" and giving him a wider latitude of civil rights.

Even more than hospitality, then, the city offered the "outsider" *de facto* or *de jure* justice — but it did so in the form of protection provided by a monarch and, in later years, by written law codes. Minimally, both the "outsider" and the "insider" were now seen as human beings with a shared body of rights, not simply as mutually exclusive in their humanity and needs. With the rise and development of the city, the germinal idea that *all* people were in a certain sense *one* people, came to fruition and achieved a new historic universality.

I do not wish to suggest that this enormous step in developing the idea of a common *humanitas* occurred overnight or that it was not accompanied by some very questionable changes in the human condition, as we shall see shortly. Perhaps the most liberal cities like the Greek *poleis*, particularly democratic Athens, ceased to confer citizenship on resident aliens, as I have noted, in Perikles's time. Solon, a century or so earlier, had indeed freely and openly granted citizenship to all foreigners who brought skills needed by Athens from abroad. Perikles, the most democratic of the Athenian leaders, regrettably abandoned Solon's liberality and made citizenship a privilege for men of proven Athenian ancestry.

Tribalistic beliefs and institutions also permeated early cities. They lingered on in the form of highly archaic religious views: the deification of ancestors, followed by tribal chiefs who eventually become divine monarchs; patriarchal authority in domestic life; and feudal aristocracies that were inherited from village societies of the late Neolithic and Bronze Ages. On the other hand, in Athens and Rome, the tribal and village assembly form of decision-making was not only retained but revitalized and, in Athens at least, given supreme authority during the Periklean era.

The city existed in tension with these beliefs and institutions. It continually tried to rework traditional religions into civic ones that fostered loyalty to the city. The power of the nobility was steadily eroded and that of the patriarch to command the lives of his sons was repeatedly challenged in order to bring young men into the service of civic institutions, such as the bureaucracy and the army.

This tension never completely disappeared. Indeed, it formed an on-going drama of civic politics for nearly three thousand years and surfaced in such violent conflicts as the attempts by medieval towns to subdue overbearing territorial nobles and bishops. Cities sought to bring rationality, a measure of impartial justice, a cosmopolitan culture, and greater individuality to a world that was permeated by mysticism, arbitrary power, parochialism, and the subordination of the individual to the command of aristocratic and religious elites.

Legally, at least, the city did not attain civic maturity until the Emperor Caracalla in the third century C.E. proclaimed all free men in the Roman Empire citizens of Rome. Caracalla's motives may be justly regarded with suspicion: he was patently interested in expanding the empire's tax base to meet rising imperial costs. But even as a legal gesture, this act created a worldly sense that all human beings, even slaves, belonged to the same species — that men and women were one, irrespective of their ethnic background, wealth, occupations, or station in life. The notion of a vast human ecumene had received legitimation on a scale that was unknown in the past, except in philosophy and certain religions — Judaism, no less than Christianity.

Caracalla's edict, to be sure, did not dissolve the parochial barriers that still divided differing ethnic groups, towns, and villages. Inland, near the frontiers of the Empire and beyond, these differences were as strong as they had been for millennia. But the edict, later reinforced by Christianity's vision of a unified world under the rule of a single creator-deity and a commitment to individual free will, set a new standard for human affinity that could only have emerged with the city and its increasingly cosmopolitan, rationalistic, and individualistic values. It is not accidental that Augustine's most famous tract in defense of Christianity was called the *City of God* and that the Christian fathers were to look as longingly toward the city of Jerusalem as did the Jews.

The sweeping social dispensation initiated by the city was not achieved without the loss of many profoundly important attributes of tribal and early village life. The communal ownership of land and of so-called natural resources gave way to private ownership. Classes, those categories based on the ownership and management of these "resources," crystallized out of more traditional status hierarchies into economic ones, so that slaves stood opposed to masters, plebians to patricians, serfs to lords, and, later, proletarians to capitalists.

Nor did earlier and more basic hierarchies structured around status groups like gerontocracies, patriarchies, chiefdoms, and, in time, bureaucracies, disappear. As largely status groups, they formed the hidden bases for more visible and stormy class relationships. Indeed, status groups were simply taken for granted as a "natural" state of affairs so that the young, women, the sons, and the common masses of people began to enter unthinkingly into complicity with their own domination by elites. Hierarchy, in effect, became embedded in the human unconscious while classes, whose legitimacy was more easy to challenge because of the visibility of exploitation, came to the foreground of an embattled and bitterly divided humanity.

Viewed from its negative side, then, the city consolidated the privatization of property in one form or another: class structures, and quasi-statist or fully developed statist institutions. A tension between advances achieved by the emergence of the city and the loss of certain archaic but deeply cherished values, including usufruct, complementarity, and the principle of the irreducible minimum, raised a puzzling issue in human development that could properly be called the "social question." This phrase, once so popular among radical theorists, referred to the fact that "civilization," despite its many far-reaching advances, has never been fully rational and free of exploitation. To use this phrase more expansively, here, and with a more ethical meaning, one might say that all of humanity's extraordinary gains under "civilization" have always been tainted by the "evil" of hierarchy.

Evil was not a word that Marx was wont to use when he tried to turn the critique of capitalism into an "objective" science, freed of all moral connotations. But it is to Michael Bakunin's credit that "evil" was indeed a condition to be reckoned with in his thinking and he quite properly tried to show that many social changes, however "necessary" or unavoidable they seemed in their own time, turned into an "evil" in the overall drama of history. In his *Federalism, Socialism, and Anti-Theologism*, Bakunin observes: "And I do not hesitate to say that the State is an evil but is a historically necessary evil, as necessary in the past as its complete extinction will be necessary sooner or later, just as necessary as primitive bestiality and theological divagations were necessary to the past."

Putting Bakunin's reference to a "primitive bestiality" aside as a prejudice that was understandable more than a century ago, his recognition that humanity developed as much through the medium of "evil" as it did through the medium of "virtue," touches upon the subtle dialectic of "civilization" itself. Biblical precept did not curse humanity in vain; there is an ancient recognition that certain evils could not easily be avoided in humanity's ascent out of animality. Human beings were no more aware that they were creating hierarchy when they invested authority in the elders than they were aware that they were creating hierarchy when they invested authority in priesthoods. The ability to reason out certain premises to their conclusion does not come too easily in what is, after all, a largely unconscious primate whose capacity to be rational is more of a potentiality than an actuality. In this respect, preliterate people were no better equipped to deal with the development of their social reality than those who have been tainted by the worst aspects of "civilization." The "social question" for us, today, exists precisely in the fact that we raised ourselves into the light of freedom with half-open eyes, burdened by dark atavisms, ancient hierarchies, and deeply ingrained prejudices to which we may still regress, if the present counter-Enlightenment of mysticism and antirationalism persists, and that may yet lead us to our ruin. We hold a proverbial knife in our hands that easily could be used to cut both ways — for our emancipation or our ruination.

"Civilization" has sharpened that knife into a razor's edge, but it has not provided us with a better guide to how we will use so dangerous an instrument beyond the power conferred upon us by consciousness itself.

THE NATION-STATE AND CAPITALISM

A third turning point we encounter historically is the emergence of the nation-state and capitalism. The two — the nation-state and capitalism — do not necessarily go together. But capitalism succeeds so rapidly with the rise of the nation-state that they are often seen as co-jointly developing phenomena.

In point of fact, nation-building goes back as far as the twelfth century when Henry II of England and Philip Augustus of France tried to centralize monarchical power and acquire territories that were to eventually form their respective nations. The nation was to slowly eat away at all local power, ultimately pacifying parochial rivalries among baronies and towns. The imperial patrimonies of the ancient world had created immense states, but they were not lasting ones. Patched together from completely different ethnic groups, these empires lived in strange balance with archaic village communities that had hardly changed, culturally and technologically, since Neolithic times.

The main function of this village society was to supply monarchs with tribute and with corvée labour. Otherwise, they were usually left alone. Hence, local life was subterranean, but intense. A great deal of common land existed around these villages which were open to use by all. There is evidence that even "private" land was regularly redistributed to families according to their changing needs. Interference from the top down was often minimal. The greatest dangers to this stable village society came from invading armies and warring nobles. Otherwise they were usually left to themselves, that is, when they were not plundered by aristocrats and tax gatherers.

Justice, in this kind of society, was often arbitrary. The complaints by the Greek farmer, Hesiod, about unfair, self-seeking local barons echoes a long-standing grievance that seldom surfaces in the historical literature we have at our disposal. The great law codes that were handed down by the absolute monarch of Babylonia, Hammurabi, were not the rule in the pre–Roman world. More often than not, avaricious nobles made their own "law" to suit their own needs. The peasant may have sought the protection of nobles for himself and his community from pillaging outsiders, but rarely justice. Empires were too big to manage administratively, much less juridically. The Roman Empire was a major exception to this rule, largely because it was more of a coastal and fairly urbanized entity rather than a vast inland area with very few cities.

European nations, by contrast, were formed out of continents that history sculpted into increasingly manageable territories. Road systems, to be sure, were poor and communication was primitive. But as strong kings emerged like Henry II of England and Philip Augustus of France, royal justice and bureaucrats began to penetrate into once-remote areas and reach deeper into the everyday life of the people. There is no question that the "king's justice" was welcomed by commoners and his officials acted as a buffer between arrogant nobles and the cowed masses. The early development of the nation-state, in effect, was marked by a genuine sense of promise and relief.

But the royal power was usually an interest in its own right, not a moral agency for the redress of popular grievances, and it eventually became as oppressive as the local nobles it displaced. Moreover, it was not a pliant tool for achieving the ascendancy of the emerging bourgeoisie. The Stuart kings of England, who catapulted England into revolution in the 1640s, viewed their nations as personal patrimonies which both the powerful nobles and wealthy bourgeoisie threatened to subvert.

The notion that the nation-state was "formed" by the bourgeoisie is a myth that should be dispatched by now. In the first place, what we call a "bourgeois" in the late Middle Ages was nothing like the "industrialist" or industrial capitalist we know today. Apart from some wealthy banking houses and commercial capitalists engaged in a far-ranging carrying trade, the nascent bourgeois was generally a master craftsman who functioned within a highly restrictive guild system. He seldom exploited a proletarian of the kind we encounter today.

Disparities in wealth, to be sure, eventually gave rise to craftsmen who closed out apprentices and turned their guilds into privileged societies for themselves and their sons. But this was not the rule. In most of Europe, guilds fixed prices, determined the quality and quantity of goods that were produced, and were open to apprentices who, in time, could hope to be masters in their own right. This system, which carefully regulated growth, was hardly capitalistic. Work was done mainly by hand in small shops where master sat side by side with apprentice and attended to the needs of a limited, highly personalized market.

By the late Middle Ages, the manorial economy with its elaborate hierarchy and its land-based serfs was in dissolution, although by no means did it disappear completely. Relatively independent farmers began to appear who worked as owners of their land or as tenants of absentee nobles. Looking over the broad landscape of Europe between the fifteenth and eighteenth centuries, one encounters a highly mixed economy. Together with serfs, tenant farmers, and yeomen, there were craftsmen, some well-to-do and others of modest means, who co-existed with capitalists, most of whom were engaged in commerce rather than industry.

Europe, in effect, was the centre of a highly mixed economy, not a capitalistic one, and its technology, despite major advances throughout the Middle Ages, was still based on handicrafts, not on industry. Even mass production, such as the system organized in the huge arsenal of Venice (which employed three thousand workers), involved artisans, each of whom worked in a very traditional fashion in small alcoves and shops.

It is important to stress these features of the world that directly preceded the Industrial Revolution because they greatly conditioned the social options that were open to Europe. Prior to the era of the Stuart monarchy in England, the Bourbon in France, and the Hapsburg in Spain, European towns enjoyed an extraordinary amount of autonomy. Italian and German cities, in particular, although by no means exclusively, formed strong states in their own right, ranging in political forms from simple democracies in their early years, to oligarchies in later periods. They also formed confederations to struggle against local lords, foreign invaders, and absolute monarchs. Civic life flourished in these centuries — not only economically, but culturally. Citizens generally owed their allegiances primarily to their cities and only secondarily to their territorial lords and emerging nations.

The growth of power of the nation-state from the sixteenth century onward became as much a source of conflict as it was a source of order in controlling unruly nobles. Attempts by monarchs to impose royal sovereignty on the towns and cities of the period produced an era of near-insurrectionary attacks on representatives of the crown. Royal records were destroyed, bureaucrats assaulted, and their offices demolished. Although the person of the monarch was given the customary respect accorded to a head of state, his edicts were often ignored and his officials were all but lynched. The Fronde, a series of conflicts initiated by the French nobility and Parisian burghers against growing royal power during the youth of Louis XIV, virtually demolished absolutism and drove the young king out of Paris until the monarchy reasserted its power.

Behind these upsurges in many parts of Europe we find a mounting resistance to encroachments by the centralized nation-state on the prerogatives of the towns and cities. This municipal upsurge reached its height in the early sixteenth century when the cities of Castile rose up against Charles II of Spain and tried to establish what was essentially a municipal confederation. The struggle, which went on for more than a year, ended in the defeat of the Castilian cities after a series of striking victories on their part — and their defeat marked the economic and cultural decline of Spain for nearly three centuries. To the extent that the Spanish monarchy was in the vanguard of royal absolutism during that century and played a major role in European politics, the uprising of the cities — or *Comuneros*, as their partisans were called — created the prospect of an alternative pathway to the continent's development toward nation-states: namely, a confederation of towns and cities. Europe genuinely vacillated for a time between these two alternatives and it was not until the late seventeenth century that the nation-state gained ascendancy over a confederal pathway.

Nor did the idea of confederation ever die. It surfaced among radicals in the English Revolution who were condemned by the followers of Cromwell as "Switzering anarchists." It reappeared, again, in confederations that radical farmers tried to establish in New England in the aftermath of the American Revolution. And, again, in France in radical sectional movements — the neighbourhood assemblies of Paris and other French cities established during the Great Revolution — and, finally, in the Paris Commune of 1871, which called for a "Commune of communes" and the dissolution of the nation- state.

In the era that immediately preceded the formation of the nation-state, Europe stood poised at a fork in the historic road. Depending upon the fortunes of the *Comuneros* and the *sans culottes* who packed the Parisian sections of 1793, the future of the nation-state hung very much in the balance. Had the continent moved in the direction of urban confederations, its future would have taken a socially more benign course, perhaps even a more revolutionary, democratic, and cooperative form than it was to acquire in the nineteenth and twentieth centuries.

By the same token, it is quite unclear that an industrial capitalist development of the kind that exists today was preordained by history. That capitalism greatly accelerated technological development at a rate that has no precedent in history hardly requires any detailed discussion. And I shall have much to say about what this technological development *did* to humanity and nature — and what it *could* do in a truly ecological society. But capitalism, like the nation-state, was neither an unavoidable "necessity," nor was it a "precondition" for the establishment of a cooperative or socialist democracy.

Indeed, important forces tended to inhibit its development and ascendancy. As a bitterly competitive market system based on production for exchange and the accumulation of wealth, capitalism and a capitalistic mentality, with its emphasis on individual egoism, stood very much at odds with deeply ingrained traditions, customs, and even the lived realities of precapitalist societies. All precapitalist societies had placed a high premium on cooperation rather than competition, however much this emphasis was commonly disregarded or, indeed, used to mobilize collective labour forces in the service of elites and monarchs. Nevertheless, competition as a way of life — as "healthy competition," to use modern bourgeois parlance — was simply inconceivable. Agonistic male behaviour in ancient and medieval times, to be sure, was not uncommon, but it was generally focused on public service in one form or another — not on material self-aggrandizement.

The market system was essentially marginal to a precapitalist world, particularly one that emphasized self-sufficiency. Where the market achieved prominence, say, in medieval times, it was carefully regulated by guilds and Christian precepts against the taking of interest and excessive profiteering. Capitalism, to be sure, always existed — as Marx observed, "in the interstices of an ancient world" and, one can add, medieval world — but it largely failed to achieve a socially dominant status. The early bourgeoisie, in fact, did not have overly capitalistic aspirations; its ultimate goals were shaped by the aristocracy so that the capitalists of ancient and medieval times invested their profits in land and tried to live like gentry after retiring from business affairs.

Growth, too, was frowned upon as a serious violation of religious and social taboos. The ideal of "limit," the classical Greek belief in the "golden mean," never entirely lost its impact on the precapitalist world. Indeed, from tribal times well into historical times, virtue was defined as a strong commitment by the individual to the community's welfare and prestige was earned by disposing of wealth in the form of gifts, not by accumulating it.

Not surprisingly, the capitalist market and the capitalist spirit that emphasized endless growth, accumulation, competition, and still more growth and accumulation for competitive advantages in the market — all encountered endless obstacles in precapitalist societies. The nascent capitalists of the ancient world rarely rose to a status of more than functionaries of imperial monarchs who needed merchants to acquire rare and exotic commodities from faraway places. Their profits were fixed and their social ambitions were curtailed.

The Roman emperors gave a greater leeway to the early bourgeoisie, to be sure, but plundered it freely by means of taxation and episodic expropriations. The medieval world in Europe gave the bourgeoisie a substantially more freer hand, particularly in England, Flanders, and northern Italy. But even in the more individualistic Christian world, capitalists came up against entrenched guild systems that sharply circumscribed the market and were usually mesmerized by aristocratic values of high living that worked against the bourgeois virtues of parsimony and material accumulation.

Indeed, in most of Europe, the bourgeoisie was seen as a contemptible underclass — demonic in its passion for wealth, parvenu in its ambitions to belong to the nobility, culturally unsettling in its proclivity for growth, and threatening in its fascination for technological innovation. Its supremacy in Renaissance Italy and Flanders was highly unstable. Free-spending *condotierri* like the Medici, who gained control of major northern Italian cities, devoured the gains of trade in lavish expenditures for palaces, civic monuments, and warfare. Changes in trade routes, such as the shift of commerce from the Mediterranean to the Atlantic in the years following the Turkish capture of Constantinople (1453), ultimately doomed the Italian city-states to occupy a secondary place in Europe. It was the historic breakthrough of capitalism in England that gave this economy national, and finally global, supremacy.

This breakthrough, too, was not an unavoidable fact of history, nor was the form it took predetermined in any way by suprahuman social forces. The English economy and state were perhaps the most loosely constructed of any in Europe. The monarchy never achieved the absolutism attained by Louis XIV of France, nor was England a clearly definable nation. It never came to terms with its Celtic neighbours in Scotland, Wales, and most certainly, in Ireland, despite endless attempts to incorporate them into Anglo-Saxon society. Nor was feudalism deeply entrenched in the realm, despite the current English preoccupation with status. In so porous a society with so unstable a history, the merchant and, later, the industrially oriented capitalist found a greater degree of freedom for development there than elsewhere.

The English nobility, in turn, was largely a *nouveau élite* that had been installed by the Tudor monarchs after the traditional Norman nobility all but destroyed itself in the bloody Wars of the Roses in the fifteenth century. The nobles, often of humble birth, were not averse to turning a penny in trade. To raise substantial fortunes by selling wool in the Flanders textile industry, they wantonly enclosed the common lands of the peasantry and turned them into sheep runs.

The spread of the capitalist "putting out" system, moreover, in which so-called factors brought wool to family cottages, passing on unfinished yarn to weavers and then to dyers, eventually led to the concentration of all the cottagers in "factories," where they were obliged to work under harsh, exploitative, and highly disciplined conditions. In this way, the new industrial bourgeoisie circumvented the traditional guild restrictions in the towns and brought a growing class of dispossessed proletarians into its service. Each worker could now be competitively played against others in a presumably "free" labour market, driving down the wages and providing immense profits in the new factory system that developed near England's major urban centres.

In the so-called Glorious Revolution of 1688 — not to be confused with the stormy English Revolution of the 1640s — the avaricious English nobles and their bourgeois counterparts came to a political compromise. The aristocracy was permitted to run the state, the monarchy was reduced to a mere symbol of interclass unity, and the bourgeoisie was granted a free hand in running the economy. Allowing for quarrels between various ruling elites, the English capitalist class enjoyed the virtually unrestrained right to plunder England and to move its operations abroad to claim India, large parts of Africa, and commercially strategic strongholds in Asia.

Market economies had existed before capitalism. Indeed, they coexisted with fairly communal economies. There are periods in the Middle Ages that bear witness to a fascinating balance between town and country, crafts and agriculture, burghers and food cultivators, and technological innovations and cultural constraints. This world was to be idealized by romantic writers in the nineteenth century and by Peter Kropotkin, the Russian anarchist, who exhibited an acute sensitivity to the various alternatives to capitalism offered by a cooperative society and mentality at various periods in history.

The upsurge of English capitalism in the eighteenth century, and its global outreach in the nineteenth century, altered such prospects radically. For the first time, competition was seen to be "healthy"; trade, as "free"; accumulation, as evidence of "parsimony"; and egoism, as evidence of a self-interest that worked like a "hidden hand" in the service of the public good. Concepts of "health," "freedom," "parsimony," and the "public good" were to subserve unlimited expansion and wanton plunder — not only of nature, but of human beings. No class of proletarians in England suffered less during the Industrial Revolution than the huge bison herds that were exterminated on the American plains. No human values and communities were warped any less than the ecosystems of plants and animals that were despoiled in the original forests of Africa and South America. To speak of "humanity's" depredation of nature makes a mockery of the unbridled depredation of human by human as depicted in the tormented novels of Charles Dickens and Emile Zola. Capitalism divided the human species against itself as sharply and brutally as it divided society against nature.

Competition began to permeate every level of society, not only to throw capitalist against capitalist for control of the marketplace. It pitted buyer against seller, need against greed, and individual against individual on the most elementary levels of human encounters. In the marketplace, one individual faced another with a snarl, even as working people, each seeking, as a matter of sheer survival, to get the better of the other. No amount of moralizing and pietizing can alter the fact that rivalry at the most molecular base of society is a bourgeois law of life, in the literal sense of the word "life." Accumulation to undermine, buy out, or otherwise absorb or outwit a competitor *is a condition for existence in a capitalist economic order*.

That nature, too, is a victim of this competitive, accumulative, and ever-expanding social fury, should be obvious if it were not for the fact that there is a strong tendency to date this social trend's origins back to technology and industry as such. That modern technology *magnifies* more fundamental economic factors, notably, growth as a law of life in a competitive economy and the commodification of humanity and nature, is an apparent fact. But technology and industry in themselves do not turn every ecosystem, species, tract of soil, waterway, or, for that matter, the oceans and the air, into mere natural resources. They do not monetize and give a price-tag to everything that could be exploited in the competitive struggle for survival and growth.[11] To speak of "limits to growth" under a capitalistic market economy is as meaningless as to speak of limits to warfare under a warrior society. The moral pieties, that are voiced today by many well-meaning environmentalists, are as naïve as the moral pieties of multinationals are manipulative. Capitalism can no more be "persuaded" to limit growth than a human being can be "persuaded" to stop breathing. Attempts to "green" capitalism, to make it "ecological," are doomed by the very nature of the system *as* a system of endless growth.

Indeed, the most basic precepts of ecology, such as the concern for balance, a harmonious development toward greater differentiation, and ultimately, the evolution of greater subjectivity and consciousness, stand *radically* at odds with an economy that homogenizes society, nature, and the individual, and that divides human against human and society against nature with a ferocity that must ultimately tear down the planet.

For generations, radical theorists opined about the "inner limits" of the capitalist system, the "internal" mechanisms within its operations as an economy, that would yield its self-destruction. Marx gained the plaudits of endless writers for advancing the possibility that capitalism would be destroyed and replaced by socialism because it would enter a chronic crisis of diminishing profits, economic stagnation, and class war with an ever-impoverished proletariat. In the face of vast bio-geochemical dislocations that have opened vast holes in the earth's ozone layer and increased the temperature of the planet by the "green-house effect," these limits are now clearly ecological. Whatever may be the destiny of capitalism as a system that has "internal limits" economically, we can emphatically say that it has *external* limits ecologically.

Indeed, capitalism completely incarnates Bakunin's notion of "evil" without the qualification that it is "socially necessary." Beyond the capitalist system there are no further "turning points in history." Capitalism marks the end of the road for a long social development in which evil permeated the good and irrationality permeated the rational. Capitalism, in effect, constitutes the point of *absolute negativity* for society and the natural world. One cannot improve this social order, reform it, or remake it on its own terms with an ecological prefix such as "eco-capitalism." The only choice one has is to destroy it, for it embodies *every* social disease — from patriarchal values, class exploitation, and statism to avarice, militarism, and now, growth for the sake of growth — that has afflicted "civilization" and tainted all its great advances.

IDEALS OF FREEDOM

I have touched upon popular attempts to resist the immersion of society into "evil," namely, the resistance of the Spanish *Comuneros* and the French *sans culottes* to the nation-state and, less directly, of craftsmen and independent farmers to capitalism.

But the drift of patricentric, urban, and economic institutions in an increasingly antihumanistic and anti-ecological direction was fought by people on a very sweeping scale and with more explosive ideas than I have indicated. Today, when we run the risk of losing all knowledge of history and, particularly, of the revolutionary tradition and utopian alternatives it offered, it is very important that we examine the libertarian movements that emerged at each of history's turning points and the ideas of freedom they advanced. Here, we shall find a remarkable development of ideas that sought to countervail "civilization's" immersion into evil. Indeed, we shall find progress in its truly authentic sense: a widening of social struggles to encompass more and more fundamental issues and a sophistication of the concept of freedom itself.

From the outset, let me draw a very important distinction: namely, between the ideals of freedom and the notions of justice. The two words have been used so interchangeably that they have almost become synonymous. Actually, justice differs profoundly from freedom, and it is important that we clearly disengage one from the other. Historically, they have given rise to very different kinds of struggles and they have voiced radically different demands from systems of authority to this very day. The distinction between mere reforms and fundamental changes in society rests, in great part, on demands for justice and demands for freedom, however much the two have been closely related to each other in highly fluid social situations.

Justice is the demand for equity, for "fair play," and a share in the benefits of life that are commensurable with one's contribution. In Thomas Jefferson's words, it is "equal and exact..." based on a respect for the principle of equivalence. This fair, or equivalent, apportionment of treatment one receives — socially, juridically, and materially — in return for what one gives has traditionally been depicted by the balance or scale Justitia, the Roman goddess, holds in one hand, the sword she holds in the other, and the blindfold that covers her eyes. Taken together, the accoutrements of Justitia testify to the quantification of an equity which can be parcelled out and apportioned on both tables of the scale; the power of violence that stands behind her judgement in the form of her sword (under conditions of "civilization," the sword was to become the equivalent of the State); the "objectivity" of her views as expressed by the blindfold.

Elaborate discussions of theories of justice, from Aristotle's in the ancient world to those of John Rawls in the modern, need not be examined here. They involve explorations into natural law, contract, reciprocity, and egoism — issues that are not of immediate concern to our exploration. But the blindfold around Justitia's eyes and the scale she holds in her hands are symbols of a highly problematic relationship that we cannot afford to ignore. In the presence of Justitia, all human beings are presumably "equal." They stand "naked" before Justitia, to use a common word, bereft of social privilege, special rights, and status. The famous "cry for Justice!" has a long and complex pedigree. From the earliest days of systematic oppression and exploitation, people gave Justitia a voice — blindfold or not — and made her the spokesperson of the downtrodden against unfeeling inequity and violations of the principle of equivalence.

Initially, Justitia was pitted against the tribal canon of blood vengeance, of unreasoning retribution for the harm inflicted on one's kin. The famous *lex talionis* — an eye for an eye, a tooth for a tooth, a life for a life — was applied exclusively for losses inflicted on one's relatives, not to people in general. Rational as the demand for tribal equity may seem in its command for equivalence of treatment, this principle was parochial and restricted. No one stood up for the stranger who was abused or killed — apart from his or her kin in a distant territory. Punishment, in turn, was often very arbitrary. More than one life was commonly claimed for crimes that existed only in the eyes of the beholder, with the harsh result that blood feuds could go on for generations, claiming entire communities and people who were patent-ly innocent of infractions that had long faded from the memory of the combatants.

The highly debated meaning of Aeskylos's *Orestaeia* — a dramatic Greek trilogy in which tribal vengeance for the murder of a mother by her son in retribution for the death she inflicted on his father — has several different themes. Important among them was the higher sense of obligation a son (as well as a daughter) had to a mother under a system of so-called matriarchal law, in which women, rather than men, presumably formed the socially recognized knots of kinship and an-cestry. But no less important as a theme — and possibly more so for classical Athenians, who prized this trilogy — was the need to bring justice out of an archaic world of crude, unreasoning vengeance into a domain of rational and objective equity: to render justice "equal and exact."

Which is not to say that justice had its origins in Greece. In the period following the transition from tribal societies to feudal aristocracies and absolute monarchies, the cry for justice — indeed, for written codes of law that clearly spelled out penalties for crimes — became a major demand of the oppressed. Equivalence in the form of justice "equal and exact" was slowly shorn of its class biases, be it in the Hebrew Deuteronomic Code or the reforms of Solon in Athens. Roman law, the basis for much of modern Western jurisprudence, sophisticated early popular gains enormously, acknowledging in the *jus naturale* and the *jus gentium* that men were really equal by nature, however much they were rendered unequal by society. Even chattel slavery was acknowledged as a "contract" of sorts in which a slave, whose life could have been claimed in warfare, was kept alive if he forfeited his body and labour to the victor.

What is problematic about justice "equal and exact," however, is that all people are *not* equal naturally, despite the *formal* equality that is conferred upon them in a "just" society. Some individuals are born physically strong; others may be born weaker, by comparison. Still others differ markedly from each other by virtue of health, age, infirmities, talent, intelligence, and the material means of life at their disposal. These differences may be either trivial or highly important in terms of the demands that are imposed upon them in everyday life.

Ironically, then, the notion of equality can be used subtly for dealing with people on highly unequal terms: the same burdens are imposed on very disparate individuals who have very different abilities to deal with them. The rights they acquire, "equal and exact" as they may be, become meaningless for those who cannot exercise them because of physical or material liabilities. Justice thus becomes very unequal in *substance* precisely because it is established in mere *form*. An *inequality of equals* may emerge from a society that deals with everyone as juridically equal, that is, without regard for his or her physical and mental condition.

So-called egalitarian tribal societies actually recognized that such major inequalities did exist and tried to find *compensatory* mechanisms to establish substantive equality. The principle of the irreducible minimum, for example, created a bedrock basis for overcoming economic disparities that, in modern society, make many people who are formally equal highly unequal in substance. Everyone, irrespective of his or her status, capacities, or even willingness to contribute materially to the community, was entitled to the basic means of life. These means could not be denied to anyone who was a member of the community. Whenever possible, special treatment was given to the infirm, the elderly, and the weak to "equalize" their material position and to minimize their feelings of dependency. There is evidence that such care goes back to Neanderthal communities some fifty thousand years ago. Skeletal remains have been found of a mature man who was seriously handicapped at birth and whose survival would not have been possible without the special attention he received from his community. Certainly on the level of economic life, the guiding maxim of justice — the inequality of equals — had not yet fully emerged. Preliterate peoples seem to have been guided by another maxim — *the equality of unequals* — a maxim that forms the foundations for the ideal of freedom.

The attempt to equalize unavoidable inequalities, to compensate at nearly every level of life for lacks produced by circumstances over which one has no control — be it a physical impairment of any kind or even a lack of rights because of shortcomings that may arise for a host of inescapable factors — forms the point of departure for a free society. I speak, here, not only of the obvious compensatory mechanisms that come into play when an individual is ill or impaired. I speak of attitudes as well; indeed, of an outlook that manifests itself in a sense of care, responsibility, and a decent concern for human and nonhuman beings whose suffering, plight, and difficulties can be lightened or removed by our intervention. The concept of the equality of unequals may rest on emotional determinants such as a sense of sympathy, community, and a tradition that evokes a sense of solidarity; indeed, even an aesthetic sense that finds beauty in nature and freedom in wilderness. The basically libertarian notion that what often passes for justice "exact and equal" is inadequate — indeed, that it may doom countless people to underprivileged lives or worse, because of factors that can be remedied by rational means — is the cornerstone of freedom conceived as an ethics. To "freely" realize one's potentialities and achieve fulfillment presupposes that these very potentialities *are* realizable because society lives by an ethic of the equality of unequals.

Let me stress the word "ethic," here. Preliterate communities lived by the maxim of the equality of unequals as a matter of *custom* — as a dim form of inherited tradition. Owing to their parochialism, moreover, custom applied exclusively to members of the community, not to "outsiders." Viewed against the broad landscape of early society, preliterate peoples were as vulnerable to onslaughts against their customs as they were to invasions by technically more sophisticated communities. It was not very difficult to shatter customs like the equality of unequals and to replace them with systems of privilege that lacked even the notion of justice. Once customary freedoms had been destroyed, the "cry for justice" came to the forefront — a poor but necessary substitute for the unbridled power of nobles and kings. Moral injunctions, later to be formulated into laws, began to confine their power. Biblical prophets, particularly the anarchic Amos, cast not only rhetorical thunderbolts against the privileged and the kings of Judah; they also extended the boundaries of unthinking custom, based on tradition, into the domain of *morality*.

No longer were the oppressed obliged to find the authority for the redress of injustice in the dim mists of tradition. They could establish moral codes, based on already existing systems of authority, to retain the limited rights they claimed. But no serious attempt was made to formulate these rights in rational terms, that is to say, to turn them into a coherent ethics that lent itself to reason and discourse.

For many centuries, then, justice remained a moral concern which took the form of quasi-religious, often outright supernatural, commandments rather than discursive judgements. "Equal and exact" meant precision, not a reasoned case for right and wrong. Indeed, right and wrong were said to be ordained from the heavens and treated more often as "virtue" and "sin" than as "just" and "unjust." We must turn mainly to the Greeks and Romans — and as much to their philosophers as to their jurists — to find reasoned debates in the secular language of the real world around justice and, eventually, freedom.

It was among these thinkers that justice, conceived as a rational and secular affair, was to take the form of an ethical problem. People began to reason out the differences between just and unjust acts, not simply adopt them as moral injunctions by a deity or inherit them as a time-honoured custom. Freedom, in turn, began to emerge not only as a wistful longing but as an ever-expansive body of ideas, sophisticated by critique and by thoughtful projects to remake society. A new realm of evolution was initiated which was not only natural and social but also ethical and emancipatory. Ideals of freedom began to become part of the evolution of the good society and, in our own time, of an ecological society.

MYTH

I have drawn a fairly sharp distinction between custom, morality, and ethics because the ideals of freedom over the course of history were to take very different forms when they began to advance from a traditional to a prescriptive, and finally, to a rational outlook.

These distinctions are not merely matters of historical interest. Today, justice has become more entangled with freedom than at any time in the recent past, so that mere reforms are often unthinkingly confused with radical social change. Attempts to achieve a just society that involve little more than corrective alterations in a basically irrational society are becoming muddled with attempts to achieve a free society that involve fundamental social reconstruction. Present-day society, in effect, is not being remade; it is being *modified* by means of cosmetic alterations rather than basic changes. Reforms in the name of justice are being advanced, in effect, to *manage* a profound and growing crisis rather than eliminate it.

No less troubling is the fact that reason, with its demands for fundamental critique, analyses, and intellectual coherence, is being subverted by "pop" moralizing, often of a blatantly religious character, while mystical mythmaking is invading even moral interpretations of freedom, evoking primitivistic and potentially reactionary images of liberation. These atavistic tendencies are usually personally oriented rather than socially oriented. Personal therapy is replacing politics under the aegis of "self-liberation"; mythmaking is mingling with religion to produce a luxuriant growth of mystical exotica. All, taken together, are being thrown against rationality in the name of cosmic "Oneness" — a "night," to use Hegel's expression, "in which all cows are black."

The regressive character of this development deserves careful scrutiny. Early ideas of freedom were confined to a mythopoeic imagination. Their realization was doomed to failure largely because they lived in dreamlike fantasies of a return to a "golden age" that was beyond recovery, because of the extent to which even early humanity was separated from a presumed state of pristine animality. It was only in myths, such as Homer's Island of the Lotus-eaters, that we fancifully imagined a condition where nature completely prevails and animality completely permeates the human community so that even memory is effaced. The placidity of the Lotus-eaters, who have no will and no sense of identity, divests them of any past or future in its timeless immediacy and seemingly "natural" eternality. Odysseus's seamen, who are ordered to reconnoitre the island, are received "kindly" and served "the honeyed fruit of the lotus," which deprives them "of any desire to return or send word" to their ship. Not only are they "content to stay" and allow themselves to be sedated; they become "forgetful of home" and of themselves as individuated beings. Like modern-day offspring of the therapeutic and mystical age, they have no "self" to fulfill because they possess no "self" to be evoked.

This mythic fantasy of prehistory and of a lost harmony with nature that is more vegetative than even animalistic, is a libel on human beings as a whole — beings that possess intellect as well as physiological functions and a sense of the "ought-to-be" as well as the "is." That mind and body have been wrongly thrown into sharp opposition to each other by religion as well as philosophy does not remove the fact that they are different from each other in very marked ways.

None of these remarks are meant to deny that humanity did live in harmony with nature in varying degrees in the past. But that harmony was never so *static,* so *timeless,* and so divested of *development* as it corresponds to the world of the Lotus-eaters in all its variations in different myths. Here, the utterly arbitrary character of myth, its lack of any critical correction by reason, delivers us to complete falsehoods. Viewed from a primitivistic viewpoint, "freedom" takes on the treacherous form of an absence of desire, activity, and will — a condition so purposeless that humanity ceases to be capable of reflecting upon itself rationally and thereby preventing emerging ruling elites from completely dominating it. In such a mythic — and mystified — world, there would be no basis for being guarded against hierarchy or for resisting it.

Nor is nature, however pristine and "wild," so fixed in time, so lacking in dynamism, and so eternal that it is little more than the scene one seems to behold from the picture-window of a middle-class summer home. This basically *suburban* image of nature belies its fecundity, its wealth of change, and its richness of development. Nature is turbulently active, even if the Lotus-eaters are not. We shall see, in fact, that ruling class ideology fosters such static and mindless visions of paradise all the more to render freedom remote and desire incompatible with its fulfillment. Indeed, the island of the Lotus-eaters is a regressive myth of a return to infancy and passivity, when the newly born merely responds to caresses, a full breast, and is lulled into a sedated receptivity by an ever-attentive mother. The fact that the earliest word for "freedom" is *amargi*, the Summerian expression for a "return to mother," is ambiguous. It may well be as regressive as it is suggestive of a belief that nature in the past was bountiful and freedom existed only in the cradle of matricentric society.

That there was a freedom to be *won* by activity, will, and consciousness after society had gone beyond mere custom and that hope was needed to achieve a new, rational, and ecological dispensation for humanity and nature had yet to be discovered. Indeed, once the ties between humanity and nature were severed, this became the harsh work of history. To retreat back into myth, today, is to lay the basis for a dangerous quietism that thrusts us beyond the threshold of history into the dim, often imagined, and largely atavistic world of prehistory. Such a retreat obliges us to forget history and the wealth of experience it has to offer. Personality dissolves into a vegetative state that antedates animal development and nature's evolutionary thrust toward greater sensibility and subjectivity. Thus, even "first nature" is libeled, degraded, and denied its own rich dynamic in favour of a frozen and static image of the natural world where the richly coloured evolution of life is painted in washed-out pastels, bereft of form, activity, and self-directiveness.

Such vegetative images of a "golden age" — and they are being revived today, by mystics in American, English, and central European ecology movements — did not simply spring from the oppressed in history. It is true that, as tribal life gave way to "civilization" in the Near East, Egypt, and Asia, a sense of loss and a wistful look backward to a forsaken garden of Eden permeated the utopian dreams of the underclasses. People spoke longingly of an age when the lion and the lamb lay side by side and nature provided a harmonized humanity with all the means of life. The human condition was conceived in terms of a golden era that was followed by a less paradisial silver one, finally descending into an iron age that ushered in conflict, injustice, and warfare — only to be repeated again into eternity like the seasons of the year. There was very little conception of history in a truly developmental sense — merely degeneration, recovery, and continual repetition.

Let there be no mistake, however, that this imagery was advanced only by the oppressed. The belief in a purely passive relationship with nature and nonhuman beings more easily served the interests of ruling elites in history than it did the ruled, however often it was evoked in the day dreams of oppressed peoples. In the first place, these images remained nothing more than day dreams — myths that functioned as safety valves, for the very real discontents of the dominated, and deflected active attempts to change the world into cathartic rituals and sedated longings. Hoarded up by priests and priestesses, they were served out as carefully choreographed dramas to the beat of drums and the noise of flutes, enacting in controlled rituals the anger that might have overflowed into action and basic social change. No society ever returned to its "golden" past; indeed, the imagery of an inevitable cycle, with its specious promise of an "eternal return," reinforced the priestly manipulation of passive congregants.

Even more ironically, the image of a lost "golden age" was used to justify the tyranny of the "iron age." Priest, priestess, and noble combined to explain the loss of a "golden age" as humanity's penalty for a fall from grace. Be it an Eve who induced Adam to eat the fruit of the tree of knowledge or a Pandora who opened the box that contained the ills that were to afflict humanity, paradise or the "golden age" was lost — so it was claimed — because humanity or its surrogates violated its covenant with supernatural power. Misery, in effect, had been brought upon humanity by its own failings, or by hubris — not by the emergence of hierarchy, property, the State, and ruling elites.

Indeed, rule it is various forms was needed to discipline an unruly humanity that lacked the sense of obedience needed to maintain an orderly world. Hence, we encounter a remarkable persistence of retrospective myths of a "golden age" not only in the myths of the oppressed but in the literature of their oppressors. That myth was cannily used to justify the domination of women in the Pandora story and the domination of men in the *Odyssey* (a truly aristocratic epic in which the next island Odysseus encounters after leaving the Lotus-eaters is the island of the harshly patriarchal Cyclopes), reveals that the drama is surprisingly gender-blind in its treatment of subjugation. Men are no less victims of the various demonic beings who rule the islands Odysseus encounters — each of which seems to be a mythic epoch — than are women.

The gropings of Greek rationalism toward a sense of history — of advances forward rather than returns backward — are far more radical than images based on false notions of a cyclic and basically static nature. Thukidides's history of the Greek people in the opening portions of *The Peloponnesian War* is impeccably secular and naturalistic. No myths burden this matter-of-fact account of the emergence of the *polis* and the settlement of the Greek homeland. Centuries later, Diodorus Siculus is distinctly realistic in his history of humanity's evolution from prehistory into history, a drama of changes that break the bonds of myth, cycles, and parochialism. It is not even the Greeks alone who claim Diodorus's attention, but "the race of all human beings and their history in known parts of the inhabited earth."

Christianity, despite its ambivalences and its retreat from the secularism of the Greek chroniclers, brought a sense of history, futurity, and redemption to masses who were captive to cycles of eternal return. That Christian fathers like Augustine invoked the Fall from innocence in the Garden of Eden was only to be expected from a religion that plainly adapted itself to authority and the Roman State. But its own origins as a popular, even a rebellious Judaic movement, mired it in inconsistency that left it open to radical as well as conservative interpretations. The Jewish religion, for all its transcendental and dualistic visions of a creator god who is clearly separated from his creation, removed the deity from social life as well as nature. As H. and H.A Frankfort have observed, social problems could now be fought out in a largely *secular* domain. No longer were they completely entangled with myth and divine claims to authority. In ancient empires, tyranny had been immersed in the authority of divinity and the claims of monarchs to divine sanction. Indeed, a "sacred cosmos" included a "sacred society," so that social oppression acquired the mystical qualities of nature — a line of thought, as Janet Biehl has pointed out, that has been revived in present-day attempts to treat the natural world as "sacred" and restore Goddess worship to eminence in a nonsocial, myth-ridden form of "eco-feminism."

The Church inherited this transcendental tradition, however much it tried to modify it. Ernst Bloch was to observe that: "...for the first time a *political* utopia appears in history [my emphasis]. In fact, it produces history; history comes to be as *saving history in the direction of the kingdom*, as a single unbroken process extending from Adam to Jesus on the basis of the Stoic unity of mankind and the Christian salvation it is destined for."[12] Utopia, in effect, became an earthbound vision oriented toward the future rather than the past. Despite its religious trapping, salvation could be achieved on earth with the return of Jesus and the sorting out of the evil from the virtuous.

Indeed, the Hebrew scriptures are charged by an activism and a bias for the oppressed that was virtually unknown to other religions of the Near East. As the Frankforts point out, Egyptian texts which give an account of the social upheaval that followed the collapse of the Old Kingdom of pyramid builders "viewed the disturbance of the established order...with horror." The power acquired by the oppressed is evidence "of lamentation and distress...'I show thee how the undermost is turned to uppermost,'" bemoans the chronicler. "The poor man will acquire riches." By contrast, the Hebrew scriptures deal with social revolt by the oppressed with exultance. The birth of the prophet Samuel, for example, is celebrated with the words: "The bows of the mighty men are broken, and they that stumbled are girded with strength. They that were full have hired themselves out for bread; and they that were hungry ceased." The poor are raised "out of the dust" and beggars are lifted "from the dunghill, to set them among princes, and to make them inherit the throne of glory..."[13]

Not only are the mentally numbing effects of myth shaken off, like the lethargic after-effects of a powerful sedative; its fixity and conservatism are replaced by a sense of the dynamic and temporal that yields increasingly expansive ideals of freedom. The Joachimites, one of the most subversive tendencies in medieval Christianity, break away radically from the cloudy and calculated vagueness of official scriptural history, and provocatively divide it into distinct *epochs* of human liberation. Even more important than the great chiliastic popular movements, like half-crazed ascetics such as the Flaggelants and the Shepherds or *Pastoreaux*, who were to aimlessly attack the clergy and Jews in their wanderings, were monks like Joachim of Floris who were to lay the bases for more lasting libertarian tendencies. Writing in the twelfth century, Joachim, a Cistercian abbot of Corazzo, a Calabrian town in Italy, reworked the trinity, a largely mystical unity of the deity's triune nature, into a radical chronology. The Old Testament was said to represent the era of the Father; the New, of the Son; and the Holy Ghost was a "Third Kingdom," yet to come, a world without masters in which people would live in harmony, irrespective of their religious beliefs, and a bountiful nature would supply the means of life for all. From the fourteenth century in England to the sixteenth century in Germany — including the Hussite wars in Bohemia, which produced stormy communistic movements like the extreme Taborites — peasants and artisans fought valiantly in chronic insurrections to retain their communal, guild, and localist rights. Conservative as they seem in the light of "modernity," with its harsh urban, technological, and individualistic values, this centuries-long tide of unremitting conflict gave to freedom a *moral meaning* that it has lost in our own era of "scientific socialism" and narrow economistic analyses.

During the centuries that culminated in the Protestant Reformation, religion became increasingly earth-bound and less supernatural than it had been in the past, despite its abiding influence on peasant and artisan movements. By the time of the English Revolution of the 1640s, the democratic Levellers were largely secular in their outlook and derided Cromwell's opportunistic pieties. It was not Christianity as much as it was a naturalistic pantheism (if a theism of any sort it could be called) that influenced the thinking of communistic revolutionaries like Gerrard Winstanley, who led the small Digger movement in the English civil wars of the 1650s.

Freedom, a relatively exotic word by comparison with the cry for justice, had acquired a distinctly realistic content. Men and women began to fight not only for freedom of religion but also for freedom from religion. They began to fight not only against specific forms of domination, but also against domination *as such* and for freedom to the means of life in a communitarian society. Activism began to replace the vegetative placidity of a wistful reverence of the past. Morality began to efface custom; naturalism began to edge out supernaturalism; opposition to ecclesiastical hierarchy began to produce opposition to civil hierarchy. A refreshing sense of development began to replace the fixity of mythopoesis, its repetitive rituals, and the atavistic grip of a dark superstitious past on the present and future.

REASON

If there is a single fact which marks the expansion of the ideals of freedom, it is the extent to which they were nourished by reason. Contrary to popular histories of philosophy, religion, and morality, rationalism had never been abandoned in the closing centuries of the ancient world and in the Middle Ages. Despite the infestation of the late Roman Empire by the Isis cult and ascetic religions from the East, the Hellenic effort to give a rational interpretation of the world was not only retained but it slowly became differentiated into new interpretations of what constituted reason.

Indeed, we today live in a paralysing ignorance of the different kinds of logic and rationalism that thinkers developed well into our own time. The notion that there is only one kind of reason — a fairly static, formal, and basically syllogistic logic of the kind assembled by Aristotle in his *Organum* — is utterly false. Actually, Aristotle himself used a highly developmental and organic kind of reason in his other writings. Formal kinds of reason were modelled on mathematics, particularly geometry. Organic, or shall we say, *dialectical* reason, on the other hand, stressed *growth* rather than fixity; *potentiality* rather than an inferential succession of propositions; the *fluid* eduction of ever-differentiated phenomena from generalized, nascent, indeed seed-like, beginnings into richly developed wholes rather than the schematic deduction of fixed conclusions based on rigidly stated premises. In short, a richly speculative, organic dialectic co-existed with the formal, commonsensical logic we use for matter-of-fact problems in everyday life.

Theology was, if anything, an attempt to rationally understand the ways of the creator-deity in his interaction with his creation, particularly with humankind. In the "Age of Faith" or medieval world, both systems of thought were used to explicate a good deal more than faith to which, ironically, mysticism turned more readily, in its wistful longing for a long-gone innocence, than clerical scholasticism. Francis of Assisi felt deeply for the suffering of the poor and, more problematically, saw in nonhuman life-forms a tribute primarily to the glory of a creator-god. But the Franciscan order was very easily co-opted by the Papacy and, in inquisitorial times, turned from persecuted into persecutor, including the persecution of its own Joachimite acolytes.

Innocence, intuition, and atavistic longings — our modern mystics to the contrary — are not strong barriers to manipulation. It was often keen thinkers like Galileo who were silenced by house arrest and speculative rationalists like Bruno who were burned at the stake by the Inquisition rather than mystics like Francis or Meister Eckhart.

My point, however, is that reason is not cut from a single cloth. In its dialectical form, reason imparts a sense of history, development, and process to thinking, not "linear," propositional, and syllogistic means and analyses. Similarly, the early glimmerings of an organismic approach to the world, not a mechanistic one, also began to revive with explorations into biology as well as physics. Evolution was already in the air as early as the fifteenth century, if we are to judge from Leonardo da Vinci's writings on the marine fossils that were found in inland mountains, and his remarks that, in an ever-changing world, the Po river will eventually "lay dry land in the Adriatic in the same way it has already deposited a great part of Lombardy." By the eighteenth century, evolution was an accepted fact among the French *philosophes*, thanks to the work of Maupertuis, Diderot, and Buffon.

The recovery of the body, the claims of the sensuous, the right to physical pleasure — not merely a restful happiness — began to raise a major challenge to asceticism, not simply of the kind advanced by official Christianity, but also by its radical spiritualists. The belief, so widely held by the poor, that the privileged should share with them in a presumably god-given fund of misery and self-denial, was steadily undermined by ordinary people themselves. The joys of the body and the full satisfaction of material needs were increasingly seen in Renaissance times as a heavenly dispensation. Lusty utopias like the land of Cockaygne, in which toil was unknown and roasted partridges dropped into one's lap, began to abound among the masses, often in marked contrast to the monastic lifeways of denial preached by their mystical leaders.

Unlike radical millenarians, or even Joachimites, the masses did not place these utopias in some distant future or in the heavens above. They existed geographically in the West, off the known maps of the Renaissance; and they were worlds to be discovered by *active* exploration, not by the lazy play of one's imagination. Indeed, it was not always the rationalistic Christian scholastics who posed the most serious obstacles to this naturalistic trend, but rather medieval mystics like Fra Savonarola, the monkish voice of the oppressed, who burned the artworks of Florence and preached a fiery gospel of self-denial.

By comparison with the rich differentiation of liberatory ideas and visions that appeared as the "Age of Reason" approached, the movements of the oppressed by the likes of Pastoreaux, Flaggelants, and even the Joachimites seem faltering and wayward. Unscrambling the more secular threads of Greek rationalism that had been entangled by Christian and Islamic theology, the Renaissance provided a voice for richly speculative and critical ideas.

What is important is that the best of these ideas, whether they are presented in systematic tracts, dialogues, or imaginary utopias, are amazingly all-sided. They are not only rational (even dialectically so) but sensuous; they advance a message of a new society in which everything human is basically good and should be afforded full expression.

From a social viewpoint, they are *ecological* in the sense that they are fully participatory: all aspects of experience play a complementary role in making a richly differentiated whole. The human body is given citizenship in these new eco-communities no less than the mind; the organic, no less than the inorganic; passion, no less than reason; nature, no less than society; women, no less than men. However time-bound they may sometimes seem from the perspective of our own ideas of modernity, no part of the human and natural landscape seems to escape critical investigation and efforts at reconstruction. They penetrate not only into social organization, culture, morality, technology, and political institutions, but into family relations, education, the status of women, and the most mundane features of everyday life. Like the Renaissance and the Enlightenment themselves, everything is brought up before the bar of reason and is rejected or justified in terms of its value to an emerging secularity and naturalism.

That thinkers can hardly hope to go much beyond their time should not surprise us. We need a true generosity of spirit to appreciate the expansiveness of their ideas — given the periods in which they lived. It is one of the great truths of dialectical wisdom that all great ideas, limited as they may seem to their own time and inadequate as they may appear in ours, lose their relativity when they are viewed as part of an ever-differentiating whole — just as a block of marble ceases to be a piece of mere mineral matter when it is sculpted into a magnificent structure. Seen within the larger whole of which it is a part, it can no longer be viewed as a mere mineral, anymore than the atoms that make up a living organism can be viewed as mere particles. With life emerges metabolism, a phenomenon that never existed on the inorganic level, and one that can never be imputed to an atom, much less to its electromagnetic properties.

So the thinkers of the liberatory, indeed revolutionary, tradition must be appreciated as much for what they add to our time as they did to their own if the abiding character of their work is to be grasped.

Thus, we can distinguish several great tendencies in the expanding ideals of freedom: first, a commitment to the *existing* world, to *secular* reality, not to one that exists in the heavens or lies off the map of the known world. I am not saying, by this, that the radical theorists, utopists, and ideologists of the Renaissance, Enlightenment, and the early part of the last century conformed "realistically" to the world in which they lived. On the contrary, they tried in the best of cases to see far beyond it and they tried to rest their ideals on the best features of the times in which they lived.

Which brings us to the second tendency they expressed: the need for a *carefully structured* society that was free of the explosions produced by unruly nobles in England and on the European continent. The Renaissance, particularly the aristocracy of the age, had thrown society into a condition of chronic warfare. Amidst the ruins left by the Wars of the Roses in England and the religious wars in central Europe, no humane society could be conceived of by radical social theorists and utopists other than one that was totally stable and almost machine-like in the cooperative symmetry of its operations. Long before Descartes had made mechanism into a philosophical world view, explosive social dislocations made it into a radical desideratum. That many utopists had taken the well-regulated monastery as their model is radical in itself; they could have easily opted for the centralized nation-states aborning in their midst, as was to happen in the nineteenth century within the socialist movement. If a "planned economy" was needed in their time, partly to countervail the chaotic behaviour of the nobles, partly to control the depredations of an emerging commercial bourgeoisie on the peasantry and urban poor, the traditional and socially responsible rules adopted by the monastery for the conduct of everyday life seemed more ethical and humane than other alternatives. Only later, in the nineteenth century, and to some degree earlier, would an orderly society and a "planned economy" be identified with the centralized nation-state; this, ironically, in the name of a value-free notion of "scientific socialism" and attempts to achieve a "nationalized" economy.

A third tendency that contributed to the expanding ideals of freedom in the radical thought of the Renaissance and, again, in the Enlightenment, was the high esteem that was placed on *work*. Not only did Thomas More, Tommaso Campanella, Valentin Andreae, and Francis Bacon, among others, impart an honoured role to the artisan and food cultivator, but Denis Diderot brought their crafts and their contributions to society into the pages of the French *Encyclopedia*, where they are given almost unprecedented attention and their skills are explored in breath-taking detail. Kropotkin cites a medieval ordinance which declares: "Everyone must be pleased with his work, and no one shall, while doing nothing, appropriate for himself what others have produced by application and work, because laws must be a shield for applications and work."[14] This constellation of traditions and ideas has no precedent in antiquity and was to be honoured in the breach during the Industrial Revolution. Indeed, deeply humane values permeated the mixed economy of peasants, artisans, freeholders, and proletarians in the centuries that immediately preceded the ascendancy of industrial capitalism in England. Even limits to toil were imposed in this dim, often little-understood era. As the late Marie-Louise Berneri was to observe in her searching work, *Journey Through Utopia*:

> The Utopian idea of a short working day which to us, accustomed to think of the past in terms of the nineteenth century, seems a very radical one, does not appear such an innovation, if it is compared with an ordinance of Ferdinand the First relative to the Imperial coal mines, which settled the miner's day at eight hours. And according to Thorold Rogers, in fifteenth century England men worked forty-eight hours a week.[15]

Lastly, among the tendencies that surface in this mixed society, particularly during the Renaissance, is the high premium that is placed on *community*. This was an era that was directly faced with the disintegration of villages and towns by an ever-growing and atomizing market place. The unruly bourgeois-*cum*-burgher had to be controlled. He assailed not only the fragile bonds that held people together in a shared communal interest, but he also threatened its guilds, religious societies that cared for the poor and ill, its extended family ties, and its high values of human solidarity. To the extent that everything came up for grabs, from common land to kinship responsibilities, radical theorists and utopists tightened their muscles — and their vision — against the asocial behaviour of the new bourgeois and the money oriented aristocrat.

We must not think too harshly, then, of Thomas More for trying to retain strong family ties in his *Utopia* and holding fast to Catholic orthodoxy in the face of a rambunctious monarch, Henry VIII, whose "reformation" replaced the hat of the bishop of Rome with the crown of an English king. More, like so many of his Renaissance contemporaries, leaned more toward a humanistic ecumene as expressed by the principle of the papacy than the nationalism as expressed by a parochial monarch. Indeed, More's reservations about a monarchical dispensation for his ideal society are expressed through Hythloday, the narrator of *Utopia* who speaks for its author, in a very pointed comment: "...most princes apply themselves to affairs of war than to the useful arts of peace; and in these I neither have any knowledge, nor do I much desire it; they are generally set on acquiring new kingdoms, right or wrong, than on governing those they possess..."

Even more far-reaching than More's ideal society is Valentin Andreae's "Christianopolis," a severely moral community that places stringent regulations on behaviour, albeit with a deeply humane attitude toward human needs and suffering. "Christianopolis" is indeed a *polis* — a humanly scaled city with clearly defined walls, not a nation-state. But it is highly standardized in its dwellings and its almost mathematical division of functions, zones, and its balance between industry and agriculture. None of these utopias are based on private property — another monastic feature — and they distribute the means of life according to need. Whether they are described as islands as in the case of "Utopia" or communities as in the case of "Christianopolis," they are really cities, and they have ascetic qualities, however well their populations live. These significantly prenational and precapitalistic traits must not be overlooked; the monastic ideal of service, work, sharing, and regimentation in the interests of a visible community good pervade the radical thinking of the day, particularly among the utopists. They appear in Tommaso Campanella's "City of the Sun," in which women enjoy an unusually high status, with its Platonistic eugenics and the emphasis that is given to the natural sciences. The orderly, work-oriented, and literate world they offer is a tight meld between medieval tradition and modern innovation. The social theorists and utopists of the Renaissance were fascinated by the possibilities for human improvement opened by science, as evident in Francis Bacon's sketchy "New Atlantis," which strongly emphasized the role of education in remaking society.

These themes — particularly, enlightenment through learning, the application of reason and order to human affairs, a keen fascination with science and a high regard for work — were to extend into the Enlightenment of the eighteenth century. By now, the nation-state had clearly established itself and the city had ceased to be the basic unit for radical innovation. With Montesquieu, who sets the tone for the century, political institutions began to supplant property concerns, family relationships, and cultural issues. It is interesting to note that the communistic programs advanced by the Abbe Mably and Morelly are completely marginal to the work of the *philosophes;* indeed, to this day, we do not even know Morelly's first name and his influence was very limited until we arrive at the closing years of the French Revolution, when apparently his *Code of Nature* was read by Gracchus Babeuf, the ill-fated leader of the "Conspiracy of Equals."

The Enlightenment was more particularized than the Renaissance, when entire disciplines were created by single individuals with a flourish of a pen, and it was more oriented toward individual rights than the preservation of community. Its engagement with ecclesiastical authority and a hierarchically structured body politic made the monastery an anachronism at best and anathema at worst. Indeed, more psychological than rationalistic, Enlightenment thinkers were often preoccupied with human nature, not only human reason. Both Diderot and Rousseau, perhaps the era's most important figures, were men of "heart" as well as brilliant minds, and spontaneous passion played as much a role in their works as reason.

ANARCHY AND LIBERTARIAN UTOPIAS

From beneath the surface interchange of radical ideas between the sixteenth and eighteenth centuries, several issues came into sharp confrontation with each other. Could material well-being for people in a time of profound economic distress be acquired only at the expense of the individual's subordination to a well-ordered society, based on monastic discipline and, later, on state authority? Could equality in material things be purchased by surrendering freedom to compulsory economic plans? Did a full, sensuous, even playful, way of life endanger the need for all to work, a need that had nourished the asceticism that afflicts so many utopias and radical ideas about society? Was abundance for all possible in a time that had yet to prove it could meet the most elementary needs of life? And to what extent could men, not to mention women, create a lively, participatory political culture while working eight or even less hours at demanding tasks to satisfy their basic material needs? For all the moral admonitions that the ideals of that extraordinary time advance, most of the visions they embody are patently shaped by questions of this kind. It is simply impossible to understand their possibilities and limitations without taking these questions into account.

But amidst the drift from city to nation, from monastery to state, from ethics to politics, from communal property to private property, and from an artisanal world to an industrial world, a fascinating combination of visions emerged that often contained the best — and the worst — of these sweeping social antinomies. I use the word "antinomies" advisedly rather than "changes" because I am speaking of seemingly contradictory *co-existents*, few of which fully supplanted the earlier ones in the minds of nineteenth century radical thinkers. Indeed, as we shall see, they have re-emerged again, today, as highly modified demands in an entirely new synthesis of ideas under the rubric of social ecology. It is true that paired each against the other, certain radical theorists were to choose one over the other in many cases. Marxism, for example, distinctly chose the nation over the city and the

State over the self-disciplined monastic commonwealth advanced particularly by Andreae, whose views often anticipate Robert Owen's "industrial village."

But other forms of radical thought were to emerge and develop a synthesis for their own time — one of rapid industrialization and urbanization — and give rise to a rich legacy of ideas that radicals can no longer ignore. And the time has come to examine that legacy, free from a biased sense of partisanship that stems more from petty factional hatreds than serious reflection.

I refer to the libertarian utopias and the expressly anarchist ideas that appeared in the nineteenth century: traditions that advanced ideals of freedom that were as rational as they were ethical and as self-reflective as they were passionate. One cannot simply ignore the compelling analyses that were advanced by William Godwin's *Enquiry Concerning Social Justice*, the corpus of Pierre-Joseph Proudhon's writings, the incisive critiques of Michael Bakunin, the reconstructive work of Peter Kropotkin, particularly his far-reaching ecological insights, and the utopian visions of Robert Owen and Charles Fourier without forfeiting the rational and moral wealth of ideas that enter into their works from centuries of liberatory struggles and hopes.

Nor can they be dealt with as visionary "precursors" — or worse, ideological protagonists — of Karl Marx and "scientific socialism." One might with equal arrogance dismiss the naturalism of Aristotle for the philosophical idealism of Hegel, or the historical work of Thukidides for that of Charles Beard. At most, all of these thinkers complement each other; at the very least, they illuminate important problems where they do conflict, each spawned by a different social condition in a drama of history that is *still* unfolding.

The course of human development has no more moved in clearly defined and necessarily "progressive" stages than has the history of human ideas. If we were to return to a more decentralized society, an Aristotle and a Thukidides would be more relevant to our concerns because of their stored wisdom of the Greed *poleis* than a Hegel or Beard, who were concerned with nation-states. We have yet to fully assess the meaning of human history, the paths it should have followed, and the ideas that are most appropriate in the remaking of society based on reason and ecological principles.

The radical theorists and utopists following upon the French Revolution exhibited more expansive ideals of freedom than their predecessors in the Enlightenment — and they were to sum up a sweeping body of alternatives to the course followed by history; alternatives that were naïvely ignored by their socialist successors.

Both of these legacies are of immense importance for modern radicalism — the expansiveness of their ideals and the alternatives that confronted humanity. The anarchist thinkers and libertarian utopists were deeply sensitive to *choices* that could have been made in redirecting human society along rational and liberatory lines. They raised the far-reaching questions of whether community and individuality could be brought into harmony with each other; whether the nation was the necessary, indeed the ethical, successor to the community or *commune*; whether the State was the unavoidable successor to city and regional confederations; whether the communal use of resources had to be supplanted by private ownership; whether the artisanal production of goods and small, humanly scaled, agricultural operations were destined by "historical necessity" to be abandoned for giant assembly lines and mechanized systems of agribusiness. Finally, they raised the question of whether ethics had to give way to statecraft and what would be the destiny of politics if it tried to adapt itself to centralized states.

They saw no contradictions between material well being and a well-ordered society, between substantive equality and freedom, or between sensuousness, play, and work. They envisioned a society where abundance would be possible and a gender-blind political culture would emerge as the working week, superfluous production, and excessive consumption diminished. These questions, anticipated nearly two centuries ago and infused by the moral fervour of more than two thousand years of heretical movements like the Joachimites, have surfaced in the late twentieth century with a vengeance. Words like "precursors" have become simply meaningless from the standpoint of a crisis-ridden society like our own which must re-evaluate the *entire* history of ideas and the alternatives opened by social history in the past. What is immediately striking about their work is their acute sense of the alternatives to the abuses of their day and to the abuses of our own.

We cannot ignore the differences that distinguish the anarchist theorists and the libertarian utopists of the last century from those of a more distant past. Anarchic tendencies such as the primitive Christians, the radical Gnostics, the medieval Brotherhood of Free Spirit, the Joachimites, and the Anabaptists viewed freedom more as a result of a supernaturalistic visitation than as the product of human activity. This basically passive-receptive mentality, based on mystical underpinnings, is crucial. That certain premodern tendencies in the anarchic tradition *did* act to change the world does not alter the fact that even their very actions were seen as the expression of a theistic preordination. In their eyes, action stemmed from the transmutation of the deity's will into human will. It was the product of a social alchemy that was possible because of a supernatural decision, not because of human autonomy. The "philosopher's stone" of change in this early approach reposed in heaven, not on earth. Freedom had to "come," as it were, from agents that were suprahuman, be they a "second coming" of Christ or the preachings of a new messiah. Generally, in accord with Gnostic thinking, there were always elites like "psychics" who were free of evil or leaders blessed with moral perfection. History, in effect, was as much of a clock as it was a Joachimite chronicle: it ticked away a form of metaphysical time until the sins of the world became so intolerable that they activated the deity, who no longer forswore his creation as well as the suffering of the poor, deprived, and oppressed.

The Renaissance, Enlightenment, and, above all, the nineteenth century, radically altered this naïve social dispensation. The "Age of Revolutions," if we are to properly characterize the period from the late 1770s to the mid-twentieth century, banished supernatural visitations and a passive-receptive stance by the oppressed from its historical agenda. The oppressed had to *act* if they wished to free themselves. They had to make their own history willfully, an incisive concept which Jean Jacques Rousseau, for all his failings, added to the history of radical ideas and for which he deserves immortality. The oppressed had to *reason*. There was no appeal to powers other than their own minds. The combination of reason and will, of thought and action, of reflection and intervention, changed the whole landscape of radicalism, divesting it of its mythic, mystical, religious, and intuitive qualities — which, regrettably, are beginning to return today in a disempowered and psychologically therapized world.

The radicalism of the "Age of Revolutions," however, went further. The Joachimite treatment of history moves, not unlike the Marxist, to the drumbeat of an inexorable "final days," an end, even a Hegelian absolute, where all that was had to be, in some sense, all that unfolded, followed the guidance of a "hidden hand," be it of God, Spirit and the "cunning of reason" (to use Hegel's language), or economic interest, however concealed that interest may have been from those who were influenced by it. There were no real alternatives to what was, is, or even would be — as absurd debates about the "inevitability of socialism" revealed a generation or two ago.

The emphasis of anarchist and libertarian utopists on *choice* in history was to create a radically new point of departure from the increasingly teleological visions of religious and later "scientific" socialisms. In great part, this emphasis explains the attention the nineteenth century anarchists and libertarian utopists were to place on individual autonomy, the individual's capacity to make choices based on rational and ethical judgements. This view is markedly different from the liberal tradition with which anarchic views of individuality have been associated by their opponents, particularly by Marxists. Liberalism offered the individual a modicum of "freedom," to be sure, but one that was constricted by the "invisible hand" of the competitive marketplace, not by the capacity of free individuals to act according to ethical considerations. The "free entrepreneur" on whom liberalism modelled its image of individual autonomy was, in fact, completely trapped in a market collectivity, however "emancipated" he seemed from the overtly medieval world commune of guilds and religious obligations. He was the plaything of a "higher law" of market interactions based on competing egos, each of whom cancelled out his egoistic interests in the formation of a general social interest.

Anarchism and the libertarian utopists never cast the free individual in this light. The individual had to be free to function as an *ethical* being, according to anarchist theorists — not as a narrow egoist — in making rational, hopefully disinterested, choices between rational and irrational alternatives in history. The Marxist canard that anarchism is a product of liberal or bourgeois "individualism" has its roots in ideologies that are bourgeois to their very core, such as those based on myths of an "invisible hand" (liberalism), Spirit (Hegelianism), and economic determinism (Marxism). The anarchist and libertarian utopist emphasis on individual freedom meant the emancipation of history itself from an ahistorical preordination and stressed the importance of ethics in influencing choice. The individual is, indeed, truly free and attains true individuality when he or she is guided by a rational, humane, and high-minded notion of the social and communal good.

Finally, anarchist visions of a new world, particularly libertarian utopias, imply that society can always be remade. Indeed, utopia is, by definition, the world as it *should* be according to the canons of reason in contrast to the world as it is, according to the blind, unthinking interaction of uncomprehending forces. The nineteenth-century anarchist tradition, less graphic and pictorial than the utopists who painted a canvas of new and detailed images, reasoned out its theories in accordance with human history, not theological, mystical, or metaphysical history. The world had always made itself through the agency of real flesh-and-blood human beings, facing real choices at turning points of history. And it could remake itself along proven alternative lines that confronted people in the past.

Indeed, much of the anarchist tradition is not a "primitivistic" yearning for the past, as Marxist historians like Hobsbawn would have us believe, but a recognition of past possibilities that remain unfulfilled, such as the far-reaching importance of community, confederation, self-management of the economy, and a new balance between humanity and nature. Marx's famous injunction that the dead should bury the dead is meaningless, however well-intended it may be, when the present tries to parody the past. Only the *living* can bury the dead and they can do so only if they understand what is dead and what is still living; indeed, what is intensely vital in the body-strewn battlefields of history.

Herein lies the power of William Godwin's concern for individual autonomy, for the ethical person whose mind is unfettered by the social burdens of suprahuman forces and all forms of domination, including deities as well as statesmen, the authority of custom as well as the authority of the State. Herein, too, lies the power of Pierre-Joseph Proudhon's concern for municipalism and confederalism as principles of associations, indeed, as ways of life whose freedom is unfettered by the nation-state as well as the pernicious role of property. Herein lies

Michael Bakunin's hypostasization of popular spontaneity and the transformative role of the revolutionary act, of the deed as an expression of will that is unfettered by the constraints of compromise and parliamentary cretinism. Herein, finally, lies the power of Peter Kropotkin's ecological visions, his practical concern with human scale, decentralization, and the harmonization of humanity with nature as distinguished from the explosive growth of urbanization and centralization.

I shall have the opportunity to examine and restate the ideas of these remarkable and little appreciated thinkers in the context of the problems we face today and the need for an ecological society. For the present, let me pause to examine the issue of emancipation of another kind — the emancipation of the body in the form of a new sensuousness and of the human spirit in the form of an ecological sensibility. These issues rarely figure in most discussions of social renovation, although they have a prominent place in utopian thinking.

A sense of sheer *joie de vivre*, of joy of living, is closely wedded to the anarchic tradition, despite the arid patches of asceticism that surface in its midst. Emma Goldman's admonition — "If I can't dance in your revolution, I don't want it!" — is typically anarchic in its disposition. A colourful tradition exists that goes back centuries in time to artisan and even certain peasant anarchists who demanded as much for the emancipation of the senses as they did for their communities. The Ophites in the backwash of antiquity reread the Biblical scriptures to make knowledge the key to salvation; the snake and Eve, the agents of freedom; the ecstatic release of the flesh, the medium for the full expression of soul. The Brethren of the Free Spirit, an abiding movement over many different names in medieval Europe, rejected the ecclesiastical reverence for self-denial and celebrated their version of Christianity as a message of sheer libertinism as well as social liberation. In Rabelais's "Abbey of Theleme" narrative, the maxim, "Do As Thou Wilt!" removed all restraint from the members of its playful order, who were free to rise, dine, love, and cultivate all the pleasures of the flesh and the mind as they chose.

The technical limits of past eras, the fact that pleasure could rarely be separated from parasitism in a demanding world of toil, made all of these movements and utopias elitist. What the Brethren of the Free

Spirit stole from the rich, the rich, in turn, took from the poor. What the members of the Abbey of Theleme enjoyed as a matter of right was expropriated from the labour of builders, food cultivators, cooks, and the grooms who served them. Nature was not bountiful, it was assumed, except in a few usually favoured areas of the world. Emancipation of the senses was often assumed by the poor and their revolutionary prophets to be a ruling class privilege, although it was more widespread in villages and towns than we have been led to believe. And even the oppressed had their dreams of utopistic pleasures, of visions where nature was indeed bountiful and rivers flowed with milk and honey. But always this marvelous dispensation was the product of a being other than themselves who bestowed the gift of plenty upon them in the form of a "promised land" — be it deities or irascible demons rather than technology and new, more equitable, arrangements of work and distribution.

The greatest utopians of the nineteenth century represent a radical change in this traditional mix of outlooks and, in this respect they invite our attention. Robert Owen's early "industrial villages," which combined the most advanced technologies of the time with agriculture in humanly scaled communities were structured around the technological opportunities opened by the Industrial Revolution. Whether "first nature" is bountiful or not, it is clearly "second nature" or human society that is economically productive. Humanity makes its own social utopia rather than awaiting its messianic delivery from suprahuman beings.

And it does so through its own technical ingenuity, powers of cooperation, and social imagination. A technological utopianism was to develop a life of its own, to be sure, culminating in the present century with H.G. Wells's technocratically administered world, and guided by Francis Bacon's "New Atlantis" of centuries earlier, a sketchy scientistic utopia of the sixteenth century. William Morris's utopia, on the other hand, was more artisanal and wistfully medieval, albeit libertarian to the core. His "News from Nowhere," overthrows capitalism and recreates the commune of the Middle Ages with its pride in craftsmanship, its human scale, and its cooperative values. Industry, by and large, goes by the board, together with authority, and quality production compensates for any gains provided by the mass manufacture of shoddy goods.

Morris's utopia, in this respect, is a romantic throwback to a world that was gone forever, but not one that was lacking in lessons for his time and ours. The quality of production and artistry of the artisan still haunts us as a standard of excellence and a means of conserving goods for generations in what is not a "throw-away" economy whose products are transient and insult every canon of good taste. Morris's values were clearly ecological. They advance a message of human scale, the integration of agriculture with crafts, the production of lasting, truly artistic works, and a nonhierarchical society.

The utopist who was to meld these seemingly opposing traditions — sensuousness with mind, the production of lasting goods with industry, the belief in a bountiful nature with human activity, play with work — was neither a socialist nor an idle visionary, namely, Charles Fourier, who turned (in his view) imagination into a science and Newtonian models of an orderly world into a cosmological fantasy. It is not important for the purposes of our discussion to explore Fourier's sense of mission and the depth of his social principles. He was not only not a socialist; he was not an egalitarian. His works are riddled with contradictions, hefty prejudices, and are a totally failed endeavour to make his system of "passionate intercourse" into a mathematical system, and to enlist the support of the powerful and wealthy to establish his ideal phalansteries — enormous palaces that could house the minimum 1,620 people of suitable and complementary dispositions who would make for emotionally balanced communities. Needless to say, his phalanstery was to be as self-sufficient as possible with workshops, farming land surrounding it, residences, educational centres, and ballrooms, all linked by covered galleries to protect the inhabitants from inclement weather and give them easy access to each other.

What is significant about Fourier's phalanstery is not its structural principles, but the principles that guided its way of life, many of which were formulated in opposition to the monotony of industrial work, the puritanical values of the time, the burden of poverty that was inflicted on the senses as well as the body. Accordingly, sexual freedom was to wash out traditional familial inhibitions and philistine conventions. God rules the universe by attraction and not by force. This was a novel viewpoint, indeed, a socially rebellious one. Rule consists of self-satisfaction, not of obedience to authority. The answer to industrial discipline is the daily rotation of work, interspersed by personal delights for body and mind, magnificent cuisine to satisfy the palate, a gallery of highly imaginative suggestions for easing life, and the all-important belief that irksome work could be turned into play by adding charm, festivities, and the company of complementary passionate natures in the form of co-workers. Fourier thereby tried to efface the demanding "realm of necessity," which held everyone in yoke to toil, and replace it with the artful "realm of freedom," which made even hard work a pleasurable desideratum.

The "Harmonian World" Fourier envisioned, based on attraction rather than coercion, became a social program — certainly for his acolytes who were to give it a distinctly anarchic character after his death. There was no contradiction in Fourier's mind between human artifice and natural fecundity, any more than there was between body and mind, play and work, freedom and order, unity and diversity. As yet, these were rebellious intuitions that a naturalistic version of dialectic has to work out. Fourier's writings converge in time, if not in place, with Robert Owen's "industrial village," which realistically combined factories and workshops with farms in fully integrated communities, a vision that was to form the prototype for Kropotkin's idea of a libertarian community.

Between the closing years of the French Revolution and the mid-nineteenth century, the ideals of freedom had acquired a solidly naturalistic, technologically viable, and solidly material base. Here, too, was a remarkable turning point in history when humanity, by whatever action, might well have swerved from a path of market-oriented and profit-oriented expansion to one of community-oriented and ecology-oriented harmony — a harmony between human and human that could have been projected by virtue of a new sensibility into a harmony between humanity and nature. More so than the latter half of the nineteenth century, when society became engulfed by a degree of industrial development that was totally remaking the natural world, if not turning it in time into a synthetic one, the first half of the century was filled with the promise of a new integration between society and nature and a cooperative commonwealth that would have satisfied the most generous impulses toward freedom. That this did not occur was due in no small measure to the extent to which the bourgeois spirit began to enfold the Euro-American mixed society of the past century — and, no less significantly, even the revolutionary project of remaking society that had found such rich expression in the utopians, the visionary socialists, and the anarchists who followed in the wake of the French Revolution.

The revolutionary project had acquired a richly ethical heritage, a commitment to reconciling the dualities of mind, body, and society that pitted reason against sensuality, work against play, town against country, and humanity against nature. Utopian and anarchist thought at their best saw these contradictions clearly and tried to overcome them with an ideal of freedom based on complementarity, the irreducible minimum, and the equality of unequals. The contradictions were seen as evidence of a society mired in "evil," indeed, as a "civilization," to use Fourier's word, that was turned against humanity and culture by the irrational directions it had followed up to the time. Reason, in its power to be employed speculatively beyond the existing state of affairs, was becoming a crude rationalism, which was based on the efficient exploitation of labour and natural resources. Science, in its searching probe of reality and its underlying order, was turning into a cult of scientism, which was little more than the instrumental engineering of control over people and nature. Technology, with its promise of ameliorating labour, was turning into a technocratic ensemble of means for exploiting the human and nonhuman world.

The anarchist theorists and the libertarian utopists, despite their understandable belief that reason, science, and technics could be creative forces for remaking society, voiced a collective protest against the reduction of these forces to purely instrumental ends. They were acutely aware, as we can now see retrospectively from the vantage point of our own historical malaise, of the rapid transitions through which the century was going. Their fiery demands for immediate change along liberatory lines was permeated by a sense of anxiety that society as a whole was faced with "embourgeoisment," to use Bakunin's word for the remarkably anticipatory fears and the fatalism that gripped him in the last years of his life.

Contrary to the philistine judgements of Gerald Brenan and Hobsbawn, the anarchist emphases on "propaganda of the deed" were not primitive acts of violence and mere catharsis in the face of public passivity to the horrors of industrial capitalism. They were, in great part, the product of a desperate insight into the fact that a historic moment in social development was being lost, one whose loss would produce immense obstacles in the future to the realization of the revolutionary project. Imbued with ethical and visionary concepts, they rightly saw their time as one that demanded immediate human emancipation, not as one "stage" among many in the long history of humanity's evolution toward freedom with its endless "preconditions" and technological "substructures."

What the anarchist theorists and libertarian utopists did not see is that ideals of freedom were themselves faced with "embourgeoisment." No one, perhaps not even Marx himself who played so important a role in this infection, could have anticipated that the attempt to make the emancipatory project into a "science" under the rubric of "scientific socialism" would have made it even more of a "dismal science" than economics; indeed, that it would divest it of its ethical heart, its visionary spirit, and its ecological substance. What is no less compelling, is that Marx's "scientific socialism" was to develop in tandem with the bourgeoisie's sinister undoing of the very objective as well as ideological premises of the revolutionary project by justifying the absorption of decentralized units into the centralized state, confederalist visions into chauvinistic nations, and humanly scaled technologies into all-devouring systems of mass production.

DEFINING THE REVOLUTIONARY PROJECT

The ideals of freedom, tainted as they have been, still exist in our midst. But rarely has the revolutionary project been more diluted by the "embourgeoisment" that Bakunin feared toward the end of his life. Nor have its terms been more ambiguous than they are today. Words like "radicalism" and "leftism" have become murky and they are in grave danger of being severely compromised. What passes for revolutionism, radicalism, and leftism, today, would have been dismissed a generation or two ago as reformism and political opportunism. Social thought has moved so deeply into the bowels of the present society that self-styled "leftists" — be they socialists, Marxists, or independent radicals of various kinds — risk the possibility of being digested without even knowing it. There is simply no conscious left of any significance in many Euro-American countries. Indeed, there is not even a critically independent radicalism, apart from small enclaves of revolutionary theorists.

What is perhaps more serious in the long run is that the revolutionary project risks the loss of its very identity, its capacity for self-definition, its sense of direction. Not only do we witness a lack of revolutionary insight today, but there is even an inability to define what is meant by the words "revolutionary change" and the full meaning of terms like "capitalism." Bakunin's troubled remark about the "embourgeois-ment" of the working class can be matched by Marx's fear that a day might come when a future generation of workers would take capitalism so much for granted that it would seem like a "natural" form of human affairs, not a society limited to a specific period of history. To speak of Euro-American society as "capitalist" often invites puzzlement at best or specious contrast with the so-called socialist societies of countries like Russia and China at worst. That the former is a corporate form of capitalism while the latter is a bureaucratic form often seems incomprehensible to conventional wisdom.

It may well be, to be sure, that we still do not understand what capitalism really is. Since the outbreak of the First World War, radicals have described every period of capitalism as its "last stage," even while the system has grown, acquired international dimensions, and innovated technologies that were not foreseeable by science fiction a few generations ago. Capitalism has also exhibited a degree of stability and an ability to co-opt its opposition that would have thoroughly shaken the elders of socialism and anarchism in the last century. Indeed, it may well be that capitalism has not come *completely* into its own as the absolute incarnation of social evil, to use Bakunin's words — that is to say, as a system of unrelenting social rivalry between people at all levels of life and an economy based on competition and accumulation. But this much is clear: it is a system that must *continually* expand until it explodes all the bonds that tie society to nature — as growing holes in the ozone layer and the increase in the greenhouse effect indicate. It is literally the cancer of social life as such.

In this case, nature will take its "revenge." This "revenge," to be sure, may assume the form of an uninhabitable planet for complex life-forms like our own and our mammalian cousins. But given the accelerating rate of technological innovation, including means for plumbing the very secrets of matter and life in the form of nuclear science and bioengineering, it is possible that the breakdown of natural cycles will be dealt with by a completely synthetic substitute in which huge industrial installations will supplant natural processes. It would be utterly blind, today, to overlook such a possibility — and the possibility, too, that future generations will be obliged to accept a nightmarish totalitarian society, structured around a completely technocratic administration of social and natural affairs on a global scale. In that case, the planet, conceived as a self-regulating natural system of checks and balances under the rubric of the "Gaia hypothesis," would be replaced by a partially or totally engineered technological system, perhaps a "Daedalus hypothesis," as it were, without the Greek notion of limit and restraint.

But until such a grim prospect becomes a clear issue on the historical agenda, we desperately need to recover the revolutionary project and the new elements that have been added to it over the past half-century. Nor can we be impeded by taunts that the very idea of a *revolutionary* project is evidence of "sectarianism" or "radical dogmatism." What today calls itself "liberal" or "left-of-centre," to use the prudent political verbiage of our time, is too debilitated intellectually to know what constitutes "sectarianism" as distinguished from a searching analysis of contemporary social and ecological problems.

We, in turn, must resolutely and independently re-examine the past and present periods into which the revolutionary project can be sorted out, such as the era of "proletarian socialism," the "New Left," and the so-called Age of Ecology. We must explore the answers that have been given in the recent past to the problems that have arisen today and the ones that lie ahead. Until we engage in a critical examination of earlier solutions, we will still be groping in the darkness of an unknown history that has much to teach us. We will be burdened by a naïvety and ignorance that can completely mislead us into meaningless, futile, and even frivolous directions.

THE FAILURE OF PROLETARIAN SOCIALISM

To a great extent what sharply confronts us today is the fact that one of the great revolutionary projects of the modern era is no longer viable or meaningful in our present predicament. I refer in part to the Marxist analyses of society — but, as we shall see, to proletarian socialism as a whole, which extended far beyond Marxism into libertarian forms of socialism and even certain utopian ideas. That "being determines consciousness" or, put less philosophically, that material factors determine cultural life, is at once too simplistic to carry the enormous weight it had in the latter half of the last century and the first half of the present one, when *capitalism itself* shaped the mentality of Europe and America along highly economistic lines.

A closer view of history shows that this largely bourgeois image of reality, which Marxism turned into a seemingly "radical" ideology, is limited to specific times in the past, however prevalent it may seem at present. It would have been impossible to understand why capitalism did not become a dominant social order at various times in the ancient world if inherited cultural traditions had not restrained and ultimately undermined the capitalistic drives that were very much at work in the past ages. One could go on with endless examples of the extent to which "consciousness" seemed to determine "being" (if one wants to use such "deterministic" language) by turning our eyes to the histories of Asia, Africa, and Indian America, not to mention many European countries early in modern times. On the broad level of the relationship of consciousness to being — which still carries considerable weight with Marxist academics even as all else in the theory lies in debris — Marxism begs its own questions. Looking back from its entrenched economistic and bourgeois viewpoint, it defines in bourgeois terms a host of problems that have distinctly nonbourgeois and surprisingly noneconomic bases. Even the failure of precapitalist societies to move into capitalism, for example, is explained by a "lack" of technological development, the poverty of science and, as often happens to be the case in many of Marx's less rigorous works like the *Gründrisse*, by the very cultural factors that are supposed to be contingent on economic factors.

Apart from the circular reasoning that characterizes so much of Marxism, what is of more serious concern in trying to define the revolutionary project for our time is the ideal of proletarian socialism and the historical myths that have grown up around it. Revolutionary projects have always been rooted in the special features of their period, however much they have tried to universalize their ideas and speak for humanity at all times. Peasant radicalism dates back almost to the beginnings of settled village life. Dressed in a universal religious morality, it always professed to speak for timeless values and hopes centred on land and village forms. Figures like the Ukrainian anarchist, Nestor Makhno in 1917–1921, and the Mexican populist, Emiliano

Zapata, around the same time period, voiced almost identical goals. By the same token, artisanal radicalism surfaced throughout the Middle Ages and reached its zenith in the *enragés* movement of the French Revolution and the Paris Commune of 1871. Pierre-Joseph Proudhon was perhaps its most conscious spokesperson, although his municipalist and confederalist ideas were more far-reaching in their reconstructive implications than those of any particular class for which he spoke.

Proletarian socialism, which still lingers on today in the ideals of many independent socialists and syndicalists, has a more complex and convoluted pedigree. It stems, in part, from the transformation of many fairly self-sufficient craftsmen, by capitalism, into industrial workers during the explosive years of the Industrial Revolution. Similarly, it was influenced as a movement — all theories aside — by its rural and small town origins, notably, by the proletarianization of peasants, who were obliged to leave their villages and agrarian cultures. That they brought these precapitalist cultures, with their naturalistic rhythms and values, into industrial cities is a matter of crucial importance in explaining the character of their discontent and their militancy. The working classes of traditional industrial capitalism, even as late as the 1920s and 1930s in America and Europe, were not "hereditary" proletarians. American auto workers, for example, were recruited from the Appalachian mountains in the first half of the present century. Many French, and especially Spanish, workers were recruited from villages and small towns, when they were not simply craftspeople in large cities like Paris. The same is true of the working classes that made the 1917 revolution in Russia. Marx, it is worth noting, to his lasting confusion, generally viewed these highly volatile strata as *der alte scheisse* (literally, "the old shit") and in no way counted on them to make the revolutions that his followers were to celebrate after his death.

This agrarian background yielded a highly complex mosaic of attitudes, values, and tensions between pre-industrial and industrial cultures — all of which gave a fiery, almost millenarian, character to men and women who, even though they worked with modern machinery and lived in major, often highly literate, urban areas, were guided by largely artisanal and peasant values. The magnificent anarchist workers who burned the money they found in the looted gunshops of Barcelona during the hectic days of the July, 1936 uprising (as Ronald Fraser reports), were people who acted from deep utopistic and ethical impulses, not simply from the economic interests that capitalism was to imbue in much of the working class as time passed by.[16] The proletariat of the late nineteenth and early twentieth centuries were a very special social breed. They were *délassé* in their thinking, spontaneous in the vital naturalism of their behaviour, angry over the loss of their autonomy, and shaped in their values by a lost world of craftsmanship, a love of land, and community solidarity.

Hence, there was the highly revolutionary spirit that surged up in the workers' movement from the June barricades of Paris in 1848, when a largely artisanal working class raised the red flags of a "social republic," to the May barricades of Barcelona in 1937, where an even more socially conscious working class raised the red and black flags of anarcho-syndicalism.

What has so drastically changed in the decades that followed this century-long movement, and the revolutionary project that was built around it, is the social composition, political culture, heritage, and aims of the present-day proletariat. The agrarian world and the cultural tensions with the industrial world that fostered their revolutionary fervour, have waned from history. So, too, have the people, indeed the very personalities, that embodied this background and these tensions.

The working class has now become completely industrialized, not radicalized as socialists and anarcho-syndicalists so devoutly hoped. It has no sense of contrast, no clash of traditions, and none of the millenarian expectations of its antecedents. Not only has the mass media commandeered it and defined its expectations (a convenient explanation, if one wants to anchor everything in the power of modern media), but the proletariat as a *class* has become the counterpart of the bourgeoisie as a class, not its unyielding antagonist. To use the language that was spawned by proletarian socialism against its own myths, the working class is simply an organ within the body of capitalism, not the developing "embryo" of a future society, a concept that figured so significantly in the revolutionary project of proletarian socialism.

We are simply witnesses not only to its failure as a "historical agent" for revolutionary change, but to its completion as a product spawned by capitalism with the development of capitalism itself. In its "pure" form, the proletariat has never been a threat, as a class, to the capitalist system. It was precisely the "impurities" of the proletariat, like the bits of tin and zinc that turn copper into hardened bronze, that gave the earlier proletariat its militancy and, at certain high points, its millenarian zeal.

We come, here, to a terribly flawed model of social change that Marx introduced into the revolutionary project of the last hundred years — one that was to be implicitly accepted by non–Marxist radicals as well. This is the belief that a new society is born within the womb of the old and eventually grows out of it like a robust child that commandeers or destroys its parents.

Nothing in antiquity supported this "embryo" theory of revolution, if it can be called that. European feudalism replaced ancient society on the northern shores of the Mediterranean — and only there — because feudal relationships were generally the form into which tribal relations decompose almost everywhere when they are not reworked into absolute monarchies of the kind that appeared in the East. The great European hinterland north of the Alps was rapidly losing its tribalistic features when it encountered Roman society. Capitalism was not born within the womb of the new European feudalism and there was no inevitability about its birth, as we are led to believe by Marxist historians of the past or by Ferdinand Braudel and Immanuel Wallerstein in more recent times. I have tried to show elsewhere that Europe, between the fourteenth and eighteenth centuries, was very mixed socially and economically, offering many alternatives to capitalism and the nation-state.[17] The myth of an "embryonic" development of capitalism and the "inevitability" of its predominance was to wreak havoc in the revolutionary project of proletarian socialism.

First, it was to create the myth that the proletariat was the analogue of the bourgeoisie in modern times and presumably, like the medieval bourgeoisie, was developing along revolutionary lines within capitalism itself. That the proletariat never even had the economic predominance assigned by Marx to the early bourgeoisie, indeed, that it would have to seize economic as well as political power — all of this created a can of theoretical worms that should have shown how absurd the "embryo" theory was for the proletariat, even if the medieval bourgeoisie enjoyed the power imputed to it. Precisely how the working class could rise beyond its own narrow interests, in an economy to which it was integrally wedded by its narrow demands for jobs, higher wages, shorter hours, and better working conditions *within* the capitalist system, remained an impenetrable mystery.

Marxian economics, for all its extraordinary insights into the commodity relationship and accumulation process, was a largely contrived ideology to show that capitalism would drive the proletariat to revolt through misery and chronic crises. The proletariat, it was presumed, enjoyed an advantage over all precapitalist oppressed classes in that the industrial system made for cooperation within the factory itself and that time would make it the overwhelming population of the country as capitalism itself expanded. That the factory system would, if anything, utterly *domesticate* the proletariat through the deadening industrial routine of the factory; that it would subdue the proletariat's unruliness by conditioning it to a managerial hierarchy and the rationalized methods of production; that the proletariat would not be driven by sheer desperation to revolution, but would be stratified against itself in the course of which the well-paid and racially "superior" would be resolutely pitted against the poorly paid and racially "inferior"; that hopes of a chronic economic crisis would be dashed by shrewd techniques of crisis-management; that nationalism and even patriotic chauvinism would prevail over international class solidarity; indeed, that technological innovation would reduce the proletariat numerically and bring it into collusion with its own exploitation through Japanese-type management approaches — all of this was not even faintly understood as the logic of the capitalist development.

Second, Marx's myth of an "embryonic" development was to mystify history and remove its essential element of spontaneity. Basically, there could be only one course of development in such a theory, not alternative ones. Choice played a very insignificant role in social evolution. Capitalism, the nation-state, technological innovation, the breakdown of all traditional ties that once fostered a sense of social responsibility — all were seen not only as inevitable but desirable. History, in effect, allowed for minimal human autonomy. "Men make their own history..." wrote Marx — a rather obvious statement that culture-oriented Marxists were to emphasize long after his death and amidst growing contradictions between his theories and objective reality. They often forgot to note, however, that Marx made his statement primarily to emphasize its closing phrase: "...they do not make it under circumstances chosen by themselves, but under circumstances directly encountered, given and transmitted from the past."[18]

The Marxian revolutionary project, but by no means the Marxian alone, became saddled with an array of "stages," "substages," and still further "substages" that rested on technological and political "preconditions." In contrast to the anarchist policy of continually pressing against the society in search of its weak-points and trying to open areas that would make revolutionary change possible, Marxian theory was structured around a strategy of "historical limits" and "stages of development." The Industrial Revolution was welcomed as a technological "precondition" for socialism and Luddite tendencies were denounced as "reactionary"; the nation-state was heralded as a crucial step in the direction of a "proletarian dictatorship" and confederalist demands were denounced as atavistic. Everywhere along the way, centralization of the economy and the State were welcomed as advances in the direction of a "planned economy," that is, of a highly rationalized economy. Indeed, so strongly were Marxists, including Engels personally, committed to these fatal views that the Marxist Social Democrats of Germany were reluctant to pass anti-monopoly legislation in the 1920s (to the lasting chagrin of the German petty bourgeoisie, which soon turned to the Nazis for relief) because the concentration of industry and commerce in fewer corporate hands was seen as "historically progressive" in bringing the country closer to a planned economy.

Third, the proletariat itself, already reduced to a fairly pliant instrument of production by capitalism, was treated as such by its Marxist vanguard. Workers were seen primarily as economic beings and the embodiment of economic interests. Efforts by radicals like Wilhelm Reich to appeal to their sexuality or revolutionary artists like Mayakovsky to appeal to their aesthetic sensibilities invited opprobrium by Marxist parties. Art and culture were treated largely as conduits of propaganda to be placed in the service of workers' organizations.

The Marxian revolutionary project was notable for its lack of interest in urbanism and community. These issues were dismissed as "superstructural" and presumably had no bearing on "basic" economic concerns. Human beings and their wide range of interests as creative people, parents, children, and neighbours were reconstituted artificially into economic beings, so that the Marxian revolutionary project reinforced the very degradation, deculturalization, and depersonalization of the workers produced by the factory system. The worker was at his or her best as a good trade-unionist or a devoted party functionary, not as a culturally sophisticated being with wide human and moral concerns.

Finally, this denaturing of human beings into vacuous class beings led to a denaturing of nature itself. Not only were ecological issues alien to the Marxian revolutionary project, but they were seen as insidiously counterproductive in the literal sense of the word. They inhibited the growth of industry and the mining of the natural world. Nature was treated as "stingy," "blind," a cruel "realm of necessity," and an ensemble of "natural resources" that labour and technology had to subdue, dominate, and rework. The great historical advance produced by capitalism, which Marx welcomed as "necessary," was its ruthless capacity to destroy all restraints and limits on the ravaging of the natural world. Hence we encounter encomiums by Marx to the new industrial dispensation introduced by capital which, in his eyes, was "permanently revolutionary" because of its reduction of nature to "simply an object" for human utility.[19]

Marx's language and his views on the unbridled use of nature for social ends does not reflect the so-called humanism or anthropocentricity that is denigrated these days by so many Anglo-American environmentalists. Marx's "humanism" actually rested on a remarkably insidious reduction of *human beings* to objective forces of "history," their subjugation to a social lawfulness over which they had no control. This is a mentality that is more disconcerting than the most unfeeling form of "anthropocentrism." Nature is turned into mere "natural resources" because human beings are conceived as mere "economic resources." Marx's view of human labour as the means by which "man" discovers himself in conflict with nature has the sinister implication that labour is the "essence" of humankind, a trait that set it aside from all other human traits.

In this respect, Marx cut across the grain of the authentic humanist tradition of the past, which singled out human beings because of their consciousness, morality, aesthetic sensibilities, and empathy for all living things. Even more troubling, if human beings in the Marxist theory are merely "instruments of history," the happiness and welfare of the existing generation can be mortgaged to the emancipation of later generations — an immortality that the Bolsheviks generally, and Stalin in particular, were to use with deadly effect and on a frightful scale to "build the future" on the corpses of the present.

The contribution proletarian socialism made to the revolutionary project was minimal, at best, and largely economic in character. Marx's critique of the bourgeois economy, while largely limited to his own time, was masterful. It revealed the latent power of the commodity to develop into an all-corrosive force in changing history and the subversive power of the market place to erase all traditional forms of social life. It anticipated the accumulative power of capital to a point where monopoly was seen as its outcome and automation as the logic of capitalistic technological innovation. Marx also saw that once capitalism emerged, it produced a profound sense of scarcity that no society before had generated in the human spirit. Alienated humanity lived in awe and fear of the very products of its own labour. Commodities had become fetishes which seemed to govern humanity through the fluctuations of the market place and their mysterious power to decide crucial matters of economic survival. A free society could only hope to come to terms with its own fears, material insecurities, and artificially generated wants when technology had reached a level development where a superfluity of goods would render scarcity meaningless — after which it could be hoped that, in a rational and ecological society, human beings would develop meaningful wants that were not distorted by the mystified economic world created by capitalism. That this mystified world should become personalized, as it has in recent years by various reborn religions — Christian or pagan — and by the hypostasization of myth, shamanism, witchcraft, and other self-indulgent lures of the arcane, is evidence of the extent to which capitalism has infested not only the economy but also private life.

It is important to make the need for a technology that can remove modern fears of scarcity a part of the revolutionary project, that is, a post-scarcity technology. But such a technology must be seen within the context of a social development rather than as a "precondition" for human emancipation under all conditions and in all eras. For all their faults and shortcomings, precapitalist societies were structured around certain powerful moral constraints. I have already cited a medieval ordinance, singled out by Kropotkin, that "Everyone must be pleased with his work..." This was by no means a rarity. The notion that work should be pleasant and that needs and wealth should not expand indefinitely served to greatly condition popular notions of scarcity itself. In fact, wealth was often seen as demonic and an excessive indulgence of needs was regarded as morally debasing. To offer gifts, to divest oneself of needless things, as we have seen, was hypostasized over the accumulation of goods and the expansion of wants. Not that the precapitalist societies consistently lacked an appetite for luxury items and the good things of life — certainly not in imperial Rome. But society quickly reacted against these "vices," as they were seen, with ascetism and paeans to self-denial.

Ironically, it was these very traditions that Marx was to deride in the strongest language, praising capitalism for undermining "the inherited, self-sufficient satisfaction of existing needs confined within well-defined bounds, and the reproduction of the traditional ways of life."[20] Production for its own sake — the typically capitalist disregard for all quality goods and their utility for mere quantity and profit — was to be matched by *consumption* for its own sake. This notion is comparatively recent, to be sure. But it is very deeply entrenched today among broad masses of people in the western world. Given the fetishization of commodities and the identification of material security with affluence, modern notions of consumption can no longer be modified significantly by moral persuasion alone, important as such efforts may be. Present-day consumption patterns must be shown to be irrelevant, indeed ridiculous, by virtue of the fact that technology can provide the good life for all and that the very notion of the good life can now be redefined along rational and ecological lines.

In any case, Marxism began to ebb as a revolutionary project when capitalism restabilized itself after the Second World War without any of the projected "proletarian revolutions" that were expected to end the war and rescue society from the alternative of barbarism. Its decline was still further accelerated by the transparent degeneration of Soviet Russia into another nation-state, riddled by national chauvinism and imperialistic ambitions. That Marxist studies have retreated into the enclaves of academe is testimony to its death as a revolutionary movement. It has become safe and toothless because it is so intrinsically bourgeois in its overall orientation.

Capitalist countries, in turn, have nationalized large areas of their economies. They "plan" production in one way or another and they have buffered economic fluctuation with a large variety of reforms. The working class has become a largely devitalized force for basic social change, not to mention revolution. The red flag of Marxian socialism is now draped over a coffin of myths that celebrate economic and political centralization, industrial rationalization, a simplistic theory of linear progress, and a basically anti-ecological stance, all in the name of radicalism. But red flag or not, it still remains a coffin. The myths it contains were to tragically deflect radical thought and practice from the generous ideals of freedom that had preceded it in the early half of the nineteenth century.

NEW LEFT RADICALISM AND COUNTERCULTURE UTOPIANISM

The revolutionary project did not die with the ebbing of Marxism, to be sure, although vulgar Marxian ideas were to taint it for decades after the thirties. By the late fifties and into the early sixties, an entirely new constellation of ideas began to fall into place. The upsurge of the civil rights movement in the United States created a social momentum around the simple demand for ethnic equality, one that was in many ways redolent of demands for equality that go back to the age of the democratic revolutions in the eighteenth century and their sweeping visions of a new human fraternity.

Martin Luther King's speeches, for example, have a strikingly millenarian quality about them that is almost precapitalist in character. His words are openly utopistic and quasi-religious. They contain references to "dreams," to ascents to the "mountain top" like Moses's; they appeal to an ethical fervour that surpasses a plea for special interests and parochial biases. They are voiced against a background of choral music that advances messages like "Freedom Now!" and "We Shall Overcome!"

The broadening of the idea of emancipation, indeed, its sanctification by a religious terminology and a prayer-like demeanour, replaced the pseudo-science of Marxism. It was a pointedly ethical message of spiritual redemption and a utopian vision of human solidarity that transcended class, property, and economic interests. Ideals of freedom were now being restated in the vernacular of the pre–Marxist revolutionary project — in language, that is, that would have been understandable to the day-dreaming Puritan radicals of the English Revolution and perhaps even the radical yeomen of the American Revolution. By degrees, the movement became more and more secular. Peaceful protests orchestrated primarily by black ministers and pacifists to "bear witness" to the infringement of basic human freedoms, gave way to angry encounters and violent resistance against the rambunctious use of authority. Ordinary assemblies ended in riots until, from 1964 onward, almost every summer in the United States was climaxed by black ghetto uprisings of near-insurrectionary proportions.

The civil rights movement did not monopolize the egalitarian ideals that emerged in the sixties. Preceded to a considerable extent by the "antibomb" movement of the fifties, including the Campaign for Nuclear Disarmament (CND) in England and Women's Strike for Peace in the United States, several trends began to converge to produce the New Left, a movement which sharply distinguished itself from the Old Left in its aims, forms of organization, and strategies for social change. The revolutionary project was being recovered — not in continuity with proletarian socialism, but with *pre*-Marxist libertarian ideals. Percolating into this project were the counterculture strains of the "youth revolt" with its emphasis on new lifestyles, sexual freedom, and a wide-ranging body of communal libertarian values. A richly coloured horizon of social ideas, experiments, and relationships emerged that glowed with extravagant hopes of radical change.

This glow did not come from ideology alone, to be sure. It was fueled by sweeping technological, economic, and social transitions in Euro-American society. Between the end of the Second World War and the early sixties, a good deal more than proletarian socialism had died in the interim that separated the two periods. Other major features of the Old Left were waning, such as the institutionalization of radicalism in the form of hierarchical workers' parties, the economic desperation that marked the Great Depression decade, and an archaic technological heritage based on massive industrial facilities and an oversized, labour-intensive factory system. The industrial plant of the Great Depression years was not very technically innovative. The thirties may have been a decade of earnest but grim hope; the sixties, by contrast, was a decade of exuberant promise, even one that demanded the immediate gratification of its desires.

After World War II, capitalism, far from receding into the chronic depression that preceded the war, had restabilized itself on stronger foundations than it had ever known in history. It created a managed economy based on military production, buoyed by dazzling technological advances in electronics, automation, nucleonics, and agribusiness. Goods in vast quantities and varieties seemed to flow from an endless horn of plenty. This was a wealth so massive, in fact, that sizeable portions of the population could live on its mere leavings. It is difficult from a distance of decades to realize what a buoyant sense of promise infused the era.

This sense of promise was clearly materialistic. The counterculture's rejection of material things did not conflict with its own consumption of stereos, records, television sets, "mind-expanding" pharmaceuticals, exotic clothing, and equally exotic foods. Early liberal treatises like the "Triple Revolution" encouraged the highly justified belief that technologically, in the Western world at least, we had entered an era of greater freedom from toil. That society could be adjusted to take full advantage of these material and social goodies was hardly in doubt, provided, to be sure, that it could create a good life structured around a new ethical viewpoint.

These expectations infused every stratum of society, including those who were most deprived and underprivileged. The civil rights movement did not spring simply from the resentment that black people had suffered during three centuries of oppression and discrimination. In the sixties, it arose even more compellingly from popular expectations of the better life enjoyed by the white middle classes and the belief that there was more than enough to go around for all. The ethical message of King and his lieutenants had deep roots in the tension between black poverty and white affluence, a tension that made black oppression more intolerable than it had been before.

By the same token, the radicalism of the New Left became more encompassing and fundamental to the degree that the economic largess that America enjoyed was so inequitably distributed and so irrationally employed — particularly in military adventures abroad. The buoyancy of the counterculture and its claims became increasingly utopian to the degree that a comfortable life for all became more feasible. Young people, the famous "drop-outs" of the sixties, made an ethical calling of the fact that they could live well from the garbage pails of society and with "a little help from one's friends," to reword the lyrics of a famous song by the Beatles.

I say this not to denigrate the New Left's radicalism and the counterculture's utopianism. Rather, I seek to explain why they took the extravagant forms they did — as well as why they were to fade away when the "crisis management" techniques of the system re-invented the myth of scarcity and pulled in the reins of its welfare programs.

Nor do I claim that ethical ideals of freedom mechanically march in step with material realities of poverty and abundance. The revolt of peasants over five centuries of history and the utopian visions they produced, of artisans over a similar span of time with similar vision, of religious radicals like the Anabaptists and Puritans, finally of rationalistic anarchists and libertarian utopians — most of whom advanced ascetic massages in times that were technologically undeveloped — would be inexplicable in terms of this premise. These revolutionary projects accepted parameters for freedom that were based on poverty, not abundance. What commonly moved them to action were the hard facts of the social transition from village to city, from city to nation-state, from artisanal forms of work to industrial toil, from mixed social forms to capitalism — each a *worse* condition, psychologically as well as materially, than its predecessor.

What moved the New Left to its own revolutionary project and the counterculture to its version of unlicensed utopia were parameters for freedom based on abundance — each period a potentially *better* condition than its predecessor. Indeed, for the first time, it seemed, society could begin to forget about potentialities of technology to produce material well-being for all and concentrate on the ethical well-being of all.

Abundance, at least to the extent that it existed for the middle classes, and a technology of an incalculable productivity fostered a radical ethics of its own: the reasonable certainty that the abolition of oppression in any form — of the senses as well as of the body and mind — could be achieved even on the *bourgeois* grounds of economic instrumentalism. What may very well account for the liberal tone of the New Left's early documents like the "Port Huron Statement" was the assumption that technology was so very productive that it could be used to placate the wealthy and remove traditional fears of dispossession. The wealthy could enjoy their wealth and, leaving questions of power and social control aside, more than enough seemed to be at society's disposal to provide an affluent life for all. Capitalism and the State, in effect, seemed to have lost their *raison d'être*, their reason for being. No longer need the means of life be distributed along hierarchical lines because technology was rendering these means available for the asking.

Hence, toil ceased to be a historically explicable burden on the masses. Sexual repression was no longer necessary to divert one's libidinal energies into arduous labour. Conventions that stood in the way of pleasure were insufferable under these new conditions, and need could be replaced by desire as a truly human impulse. The "realm of necessity," in effect, could finally be replaced by the "realm of freedom" — hence the vogue that Charles Fourier's writings began to enjoy at the time in many parts of the Western world.

In its initial phases, the New Left and the counterculture were profoundly anarchistic and utopistic. Several popular concerns became of focal importance in the projects that began to rise to the surface of their collective consciousness. The first was richly democratic: appeals were voiced for a face-to-face system of decision-making. The words "participatory democracy" came very much into vogue as a description of grassroots control over all aspects of life, not simply political ones. Everyone was expected to be free to enter into the political sphere and to deal with people in everyday life in a "democratic" manner. What this meant, in effect, was that people were expected to be *transparent* in all of their relationships and the ideas they held.

The New Left and, in no small degree, the emerging counterculture that paralleled it, had a strong antiparliamentary ambience that often verged on outright anarchism. Much has been written about the "fire in the streets" that became part of the radical activities of the time. However, there were also strong impulses toward an institutionalization of decision-making processes that went beyond the level of street protests and the demonstrations that were so common during the decade.

The principle American New Left organization, Students for a Democratic Society (SDS) and its German counterpart, the Socialists Students Union (also SDS) were distinguished by the formality of their many conferences and workshops. But few limitations were placed on attendance — which left these organizations open to cynical invasions of parasitic dogmatic radical sects. Many of their conferences and workshops, apart from the fairly large ones, acquired an egalitarian geometry of their own — the circle, in which there was no formal chairperson or leader. Individuals yielded the forum to speakers merely by designating their successors from among the raised hands of those who wanted to voice their views.

This geometry and procedure was not simply an idle form of organizational and democratic symbolism. The entire configuration expressed an earnest belief in the ideal of face-to-face dialogue and a spontaneous form of discussion. Leadership was grossly mistrusted to a point where offices were often rotated and an entrenched officialdom was frowned upon as a step toward authoritarian control. New Left conferences contrasted dramatically with the highly formalized, often carefully orchestrated gatherings that had marked conferences in the workers' movement a generation or two earlier. Indeed, democracy as a radical form of decision-making was seen by proletarian socialism, particularly in its Marxian form, as marginal to economic factors.

In a sense, the New Left, almost knowingly, was reviving traditions that had been spawned by the democratic revolutions of two centuries earlier. Precisely because the means of life seemed to be potentially available to all in abundance, the New Left seemed to sense that democracy and an ethical ideal of freedom was the direct pathway to the very social egalitarianism that proletarian socialism had sought to achieve by largely economic and party-oriented means. This was a remarkable shift in orientation toward the role of ethics in an era when all of humanity's material problems could be solved in principle. The pre–Marxist age of the democratic revolutions, in effect, had melded with pre–Marxist forms of socialism and utopianism under the rubric of a participatory democracy. Economics had now become truly political and the political had begun to shed the patina of statecraft which had surrounded it for a century — a change that had fundamentally anarchic implications.

Secondly such a democratic disposition of social life was meaningless without decentralization. Unless the institutional structure of democratic life could be reduced to comprehensible, indeed a graspable, human scale that all could understand, democracy could hardly acquire a truly participatory form. New units of social intercourse had to be developed and new ways of relating to each other had to be established. In short, the New Left began to grope toward new forms of freedom. But it never developed these new forms beyond conferences that were usually convened on college campuses.

In France, during the 1968 May-June uprising, there is some evidence that neighbourhood assemblies were convened in several Paris *arrondissements*. Neighbourhood projects were started half-heartedly in the United States, notably rent-strike groups and ghetto-oriented service collectives. But the idea of developing new kinds of libertarian municipal forms as counterpower to the prevailing state forms did not take root, except in Spain where the Madrid Citizens' Movement played a major role in marshalling public sentiment against the Franco regime. Thus, demands for decentralization remained an important *inspirational* slogan. But they never took a tangible form off the campus, where radical concerns centred on "student power."

The counterculture offered its own version of decentralized structures in the form of communal lifestyles. The 1960s became the decade *par excellence* for anarchist-type communes, as so many books on the subject have called them. In cities, no less than in the countryside, communal establishments became very widespread. These establishments aimed not so much at the development of new politics than at attempts to develop radically new ways of living that were counter to the conventional ones that surrounded them. They were literally the nuclei of a counter*culture*. These new lifeways involved the communalization of property, the practice of usufruct in dealing with the means of life, a sharing and rotation of work tasks, collective childcare by both sexes, radically new sexual mores, attempts to achieve a certain measure of economic autonomy, and the creation of a new music, poetry, and art that were meant to cut against the grain of received tastes in aesthetics. The human body and its beautification, whatever one may think of the standards that were developed, became part of attempts to beautify the environment. Vehicles, rooms, the exteriors of buildings, even the brick walls of apartment houses were decorated and covered with murals.

The fact that entire neighbourhoods were largely composed of these communes led to informal systems of inter-communal associations and support systems, such as so-called tribal councils. The idea of "tribalism," which the counterculture borrowed rather facilely from American Indian cultures, found its expression more in a vernacular of "love" and the wide use of Indian customs, rituals, and especially jewelry, than in the reality of lasting relationships and mutual aid. Groups did arise which tried to live by these tribalistic, indeed, in some cases, conscious anarchist principles, but they were comparatively rare.

Many young people who made up the counterculture were temporary exiles from middle-class suburbia, to which they were to return after the sixties. But the values of many communal lifestyles were abiding ideals that were to filter into the New Left, which established its own collectives for specific tasks like the printing of literature, the management of "free schools," and even day-care centres. Anarchist terms like "affinity groups," the action and cellular units of the Spanish anarchist movement, came very much into vogue. The Spanish anarchists developed these groups as personal forms of association in opposition to anonymous Socialist Party branches based on residence or places of employment, but the more anarchic elements in the New Left mixed broader counterculture elements, like lifestyle, with action in the affinity groups that they established.

Thirdly, the accumulation of property was viewed with derision. The ability to successfully "liberate" food, clothing, books, and the like, from department stores and shopping centres became a calling, as it were, and a badge of honour. This mentality and practice became so widespread that it even infected conventional middle-class people.

Shop-lifting reached epidemic proportions in the sixties. Property was generally seen as something of a public resource that could be freely used by the public at large or personally "expropriated."

Aesthetic values and utopistic ideals that had been buried away in the artistic as well as political manifestoes of the past underwent an extraordinary revival. Museums were picketed as mausoleums of art, whose works the picketers felt should be located in public places so that they could be part of a living environment. Street theatre for the public was conducted in the most improbable locations, such as the sidewalks of business districts; rock bands conducted their concerts in the streets or in public squares; parks were used as ceremonial areas, or places for discussion, or simply open-air habitats for semi-nude young people, who flagrantly smoked marijuana under the very noses of the police.

Lastly, the imagination of western society became overheated with insurrectionary images. A fatal belief began to develop within the New Left that the entire world was on the verge of violent revolutionary change. The war in Vietnam mobilized crowds in the hundreds of thousands in Washington, New York, and other cities, followed by comparable numbers in European cities as well — mobilizations of people that had not been seen since the days of the Russian Revolution. Black ghetto uprisings became commonplace, followed by bloody encounters between troops as well as police that claimed scores of lives. The assassination of public figures like Martin Luther King and Robert Kennedy were only the most publicized of murders that claimed the lives of civil rights' activists, student protesters, and, in one horrendous crime, black children at a church ceremony. These counter-actions began to place left-wing individual terrorism on the agenda of certain New Left tendencies.

The year 1968 saw the most spectacular upsurges of the student and black movements. In France, during May and June, millions of workers followed the students into a general strike that lasted for weeks. This "near-revolution," as it has recently been called, was echoed throughout the world in various forms, albeit with minimal working class support — indeed, with active hostility by American and German workers, a fact that should have placed a fatal seal on the death of proletarian socialism.

Despite another major upsurge in 1970 by students in the United States, in which a general strike followed the American invasion of Cambodia, the movement was more an imaginative projection of an insurrection than the real thing. In France, workers eventually beat a retreat under the commands of their parties and unions. The middle classes were genuinely in conflict between the material benefits they acquired from the established order and the moral appeal voiced by the New Left, and even by their own children. Books by Theodore Roszak and Charles Reich, which tried to explain the ethical message of the New Left and particularly the counterculture to the older generation, met with a surprisingly favourable reception. Perhaps millions of fairly conventional people might have veered toward an actively sympathetic attitude toward antiwar demonstrators, even toward the New Left itself, if its ideology had been advanced in the populist and libertarian forms that were consistent with America's own revolutionary heritage.

The late sixties, in fact, was a profoundly important period in American history. Had there been a slower, more patient and more graded development by the New Left and the counterculture, large areas of popular consciousness could have been changed. The "American Dream," perhaps like the national "dreams" of other countries, had deep-seated ideological roots, not only material ones. Ideals of liberty, community, mutual aid, even of decentralized confederations, had been carried over to America by its radical Puritan settlers with their congregational form of Protestantism that disallowed any clerical hierarchy. These radicals preached a gospel of a primitive Christian communalism rather than the "rugged individualism" (essentially, a western cowboy ideal of purely personal "anarchism" in which the lonely "campfire" of the armed soloist is substituted for the family hearth of the village yeomanry). Puritans had placed a high premium on face-to-face popular assemblies or town meetings as instruments of self-government rather than centralized government. Perhaps honoured more in the breach than in consistent observance, this gospel still exercised enormous influence on the American imagination, an influence that could have easily wedded the New Left and counterculture ideas with an ethical democracy that many Americans would have accepted.

It is one of the appalling facts of history that the New Left, far from following this historic course, did the very opposite in the late sixties. It separated itself from its anarchic and utopistic origins. What is worse, it uncritically adopted Third World ideologies, inspired by Vietnamese, Chinese, North Korean, and Cuban social models. These were introduced to a sickening extent by the sectarian Marxist debris that lingered on from the thirties, not only in the U.S. but in Europe. The very democracy of the New Left was used against it by Maoist-type authoritarians in an attempt to "capture" SDS in America and Germany. Guilt for a middle-class pedigree was the principle mechanism for imbuing these movements with a subservient attitude to self-styled working class and black groups; indeed, for adopting a rambunctious ultra-revolutionary zealotry that totally marginalized the followers of this trend and eventually demoralized them completely. The failure of many anarchists in American and German SDS, as well as similar movements elsewhere, to develop a well-organized movement within the larger ones (particularly with the "ultra-revolutionary" braggadocio and radical swaggering in the U.S.) played directly into the hands of the more well-organized Maoist tendencies — with disastrous results for the New Left as a whole.

But it was not a lack of ideology and organization alone that brought the New Left and a rather wavering counterculture to an end. The expanding, overheated economy of the sixties was steadily replaced by the cooler, more wavering economy of the seventies. The accelerating rate of economic growth was deliberately arrested and its direction was partly reversed. Under Nixon in America and Thatcher in England, as well as their counterparts in other European countries, a new political and economic climate was created that replaced the ebullient post-scarcity mentality of the sixties with one of economic uncertainty.

The material insecurity of the seventies, and the political reaction that followed the election of conservatives in America and Europe, began to foster a personal retreat from the public sphere. Privatism, careerism and self-interest increasingly gained ascendancy over the desire for a public life, an ethics of care, and a commitment to change. The New Left waned even more rapidly than it rose and the counter-culture became the industry for boutiques and pornographic forms of sexual license. Indeed, the mind-expanding "drug culture" of the sixties gave way to the sedating "drug culture" of the seventies — one which has created national crises in Euro-American society with the discovery of new pharmaceuticals and their exotic combinations in more intense "highs" and "lows."

A perceptive account of the New Left and counterculture, with a full knowledge of the facts that led to their origins, development, and decay, has yet to be written. Much of the material that is now available to us is marked more by sentimentality than serious analyses.

The radicalism of that era, however, has been sensed intuitively. The New Left was never as educated as the Old, which it tried to succeed more by an emphasis on activism than theoretical insight. Despite a spate of high-minded and electrifying propaganda tracts, it produced no perceptive intellectual accounts of the events which it had created or of the real possibilities that it confronted. Unlike the Old Left which, for all its failings, was part of a century-long historical tradition, indeed an epoch, filled with analyses of cumulative experiences and critical evaluations of their outcome, the New Left seems more like an isolated island in history whose very existence is difficult to explain as part of a larger historical era.

Given more to action than to reflection, the New Left seized upon refurbished versions of the most vulgar Marxist dogmas to shore up its guilt-ridden reverence of Third World movements, its own middle-class insecurities, and the hidden elitism of its more opportunistic, media-oriented leaders who were proof that power ultimately does corrupt. The more dedicated of the sixties radical youth went into factories for brief spans of time to "win" a largely indifferent working class, while others turned to "terrorism" — in some cases, a parody of the real thing, in other cases, a costly tragedy that claimed the lives of highly dedicated, if sadly misguided, young people.

Errors that had been repeated generation after generation over the past century were thus being recycled again: a disregard for theory, an emphasis on action that excluded all serious thought, a tendency to fall back on shopworn dogmas when action is reified, and the resulting certainty of defeat and demoralization. And this was precisely what occurred as the sixties began to draw to a close.

But not everything is lost in a development. Proletarian socialism had focused the attention of the revolutionary project on the *economic* aspects of social change — the need to create the material conditions, particularly under capitalism, for a forward-looking vision of human liberation. It revived and fully explored the fact — long emphasized by writers like Aristotle — that people had to be reasonably free from material want to be able to function fully as citizens in the political sphere. Freedom that lacked the material bases for people to act as self-managing and self-governing individuals or collectives was the purely formal freedom of the inequality of equals, the realm of mere justice. Proletarian socialism died partly because of its sobriety and lack of imagination, but it also provided a necessary corrective to a purely ethical emphasis by earlier radicals on political institutions and a largely imaginative vision of the economic arrangements that were so necessary for full popular participation in shaping society.

The New Left restored the anarchic and utopian visions of the pre–Marxian revolutionary project and it greatly expanded them in accordance with the new material possibilities created by technology after the Second World War. To the need for solid economic underpinnings of a free society, the New Left and the counterculture added certain Fourieresque qualities. They advanced the image of a sensuous society, not only one that was well-fed; a society free from toil, not only one that was free from economic exploitation; a substantive democracy, not only a formal one; the release of pleasure, not only the satisfaction of need.

Antihierarchical, decentralist, communalist, and sensuous values were to still persist into the seventies, despite the ideological contortions of the decomposing New Left and its drift into an imaginative world of insurrection, "days of rage," and terrorism.

While it is true that many of the New Left's activists were to find their way into the very university system they despised in the sixties and lead fairly conventional lives, the movement also vastly broadened the definition of freedom and the scope of the revolutionary project, extending them beyond their traditional economic confines into vastly cultural and political domains. No radical movement of any importance in the future could ignore the ethical, aesthetic, and anti-authoritarian legacy created by the New Left and the communalist experiments that emerged in the counterculture, although the two tendencies were by no means identical. But two questions now remained. What specific forms should a future movement assume if it hoped to reach the people generally? And what new possibilities and additional ideas lay before it that would still further expand the ideals of freedom?

FEMINISM AND ECOLOGY

The answers to these questions began to emerge even while the New Left and the counterculture were very much alive and began to centre around two basically new issues: ecology and feminism.

Conservative movements, even environmental movements to correct specific pollution abuses, have a long history in English-speaking countries, particularly in the United States and in central Europe, where nature mysticism reaches back to the late Middle Ages. The emergence of capitalism and the appalling damage it inflicted on the natural world gave these movements a new sense of urgency. The recognition that particular diseases like tuberculosis — the famous "White Plague" of the nineteenth century — have their main origins in poor living and working conditions became a major issue for many socially conscious physicians like Rudolph Virchow, a German liberal, who was deeply concerned with the lack of proper sanitation among Berlin's poor. Similar movements arose in England and spread throughout most of the Western world. A relationship between the environment and health was thus seen as a problem of paramount importance for well over a century.

For the most part, this relationship was seen in very practical terms. The need for cleanliness, good food, airy living quarters, and healthful working conditions were dealt with in rather narrow terms that posed no challenge to the social order. Environmentalism was a *reform* movement. It raised no broad problems beyond the humanitarian treatment of the poor and the working class. In time, and with piecemeal reforms, its supporters could expect that there would be no serious conflict between a strictly environmental orientation and the capitalist system.

Another environmental movement, basically American (albeit fairly widespread in England and Germany), emerged from a mystical passion for wilderness. The various strains that entered into this movement are too complex to unravel, here. American conservationists like John Muir found in wilderness a spiritually reviving form of communion with nonhuman life; one that presumably awakened deep-seated human longings and instincts. This view goes back even further in time to Rousseau's idyllic passion for a solitary way of life amidst natural surroundings. As a sensibility, it has always been marked by a good deal of ambiguity. Wilderness, or what is left of it today, can give one a sense of freedom, a heightened sense of nature's fecundity, a love of nonhuman life-forms, and a richer aesthetic outlook and appreciation of the natural order.

But it also has a less innocent side. It can lead to a rejection of *human* nature, an introverted denial of social intercourse, a needless opposition between wilderness and civilization. Rousseau leaned toward this viewpoint in the eighteenth century for very mixed reasons that need not concern us in this discussion. That Voltaire called Rousseau an "enemy of mankind" is not entirely an overstatement. The wilderness enthusiast who retreats into remote mountain areas and shuns human company has provided a bouquet of innumerable misanthropes over the ages. For tribal peoples, such individual retreats, or "vision quests" are ways of *returning* to their communities with greater wisdom; for the misanthrope it is often a revolt *against* one's own kind; indeed, a disclaiming of natural evolution as it is embodied in human beings.

This pitting of a seemingly wild "first nature" against social "second nature" reflects a blind and tortured inability to distinguish what is irrational and anti-ecological in capitalist society from what *could* be rational and ecological in a free society. Society is simply condemned wholesale. Humanity, irrespective of its own internal conflicts between oppressor and oppressed, is lumped together as a single "species" that constitutes an accursed blight on a presumably pristine, "innocent," and "ethical" natural world.

Such views easily lend themselves to a crude biologism that offers no way of fixing humanity and society in nature, or, more precisely, in natural evolution. The fact that human beings, too, are products of natural evolution and that society grows out of that evolutionary process, incorporating in its own evolution the natural world as transmuted into social life, is generally given a subordinate place to a very static image of nature. This simplistic type of imagery sees nature as a mere piece of scenery of the kind we encounter in picture postcards. There is very little naturalism in this view; rather, this view is largely aesthetic rather than ecological. The wilderness enthusiast is usually a visitor or a vacationer to a world that, uplifting as it may be for a time, is basically alien to his or her authentic social environment. Such wilderness enthusiasts carry their social environment within themselves whether they know it or not, no less than the fact that the knapsacks they shoulder are often products of a highly industrialized society.

The need to go beyond these traditional trends in environmentalism emerged in the early 1960s, when an attempt was made in 1964 by anarchist writers to rework libertarian ideas along broadly ecological lines. Without denying the need to stop the degradation of the environment from pollution, insensate deforestation, the construction of nuclear reactors, and the like, a reformist approach with its focus on single issues was abandoned for a revolutionary one, based on the need to totally reconstruct society along ecological lines.

What is significant about this new approach, rooted in the writings of Kropotkin, was the relationship it established between hierarchy and the notion of dominating nature. Put simply: the very idea of dominating nature, it was argued in this anarchistic interpretation, stemmed from the domination of human by human. As I have pointed out earlier in this book, this interpretation totally reversed the traditional liberal and Marxist view that the domination of human by human stems from a shared historical project to dominate nature by using human labour to overcome a seemingly "stingy," withholding, intractable natural world whose "secrets" had to be unlocked and rendered available to all in order to create a beneficent society.

No ideology, in fact, has done more to justify hierarchy and domination since Aristotle's time than the myth that the domination of nature presupposes the domination of "man by man." Liberalism, Marxism, and earlier ideologies had indissolubly linked the domination of nature with human freedom. Ironically, the domination of human by human, the rise of hierarchy, of classes, and the State, were seen as "preconditions" for their very elimination in the future.

The views advanced by anarchists were deliberately called *social* ecology to emphasize that major ecological problems have their roots in social problems — problems that go back to the very beginnings of patricentric culture itself. The rise of capitalism, with a law of life based on competition, capital accumulation, and limitless growth, brought these problems — ecological and social — to an acute point; indeed, one that was unprecedented in any prior epoch of human development. Capitalist society, by recycling the organic world into an increasingly inanimate, inorganic assemblage of commodities, was destined to simplify the biosphere, thereby cutting across the grain of natural evolution with its ages-long thrust toward differentiation and diversity.

To reverse this trend, capitalism had to be replaced by an ecological society based on nonhierarchical relationships, decentralized communities, eco-technologies like solar power, organic agriculture, and humanly scaled industries — in short, by face-to-face democratic forms of settlement economically and structurally tailored to the ecosystems in which they were located. These views were explored in such pioneering articles like "Ecology and Revolutionary Thought" (1964) and "Toward a Liberatory Technology" (1965), years before "Earth Day" was proclaimed and an obscure word, "ecology," began to enter into everyday discourse.

What should be emphasized is that this literature anchored ecological problems for the first time in hierarchy, not simply in economic classes; that a serious attempt was made to go beyond single-issue environmental problems into deep-seated ecological dislocations of a monumental character; that the relationship of nature to society, formerly seen as an inherently antagonistic one, was explored as part of a long continuum in which society had phased out of nature through a complex and cumulative evolutionary process.

It may have been asking too much of an increasingly Maoist New Left and an increasingly commercialized counterculture, both with a strong predilection for action and a deepening mistrust of theoretical ideas, to absorb social ecology as a whole. The use of words like "hierarchy," a term rarely employed in New Left rhetoric, surfaced widely in the radical discourse of the late sixties and began to assume particular relevance for a new movement — notably, feminism. With the notion that woman, as such, is a victim of a male-oriented "civilization" irrespective of her "class position" and economic status, the term "hierarchy" became particularly relevant to early feminist analyses. Social ecology was increasingly reworked by early radical feminist writers into a critique of hierarchical forms, not simply class forms.

In a broad sense, social ecology and early feminism directly challenged the economistic emphasis Marxism had placed on social analysis and reconstruction. It rendered the New Left's anti-authoritarian outlook more explicit and more clearly definable by singling out hierarchical domination, not simply anti-authoritarian oppression. Woman's degraded status as a gender and status-group was rendered clearly visible against the background of her seeming "equality" in a world guided by justice's inequality of equals. At a time when the New Left was decomposing into Marxist sects and the counterculture was being transformed into a new form of boutique retailing, social ecology and feminism were expanding the ideal of freedom beyond any bounds that had been established in recent memory. Hierarchy *as such* — be it in the form of ways of thinking, basic human relationships, social relations, and society's interaction with nature — could now be disentangled from the traditional nexus of class analyses that concealed it under a carpet of economic interpretations of society. History could now be examined in terms of general interests such as freedom, solidarity, and empathy for one's own kind; indeed, the need to be an active part of the balance of nature.

These interests were no longer specific to a particular class, gender, race, or nationality. They were *universal* interests that were shared by humanity as a whole. Not that economic problems and class conflicts could be ignored, but to confine oneself to them left a vast residue of perverted sensibilities and relationships that had to be confronted and corrected on a broader social horizon.

In terms that were more expansive than any that had been formulated in the sixties or earlier, the revolutionary project could now be clearly defined as the abolition of hierarchy, the reharmonization of humanity with nature through the reharmonization of human with human, the achievement of an ecological society structured on ecologically sound technologies and face-to-face democratic communities. Feminism made it possible to highlight the significance of hierarchy in a very *existential* form. Drawing heavily from the literature and the language of social ecology, it rendered hierarchy concrete, visible, and poignantly real owing to the status of women in all classes, occupations, social institutions, and familial relationships. As long as it revealed the demeaned human condition that all people suffered, particularly women, it demystified subtle forms of rule that existed in the nursery, bedroom, kitchen, playground, and school — not only in the workplace and the public sphere generally. Hence social ecology and feminism logically intertwined with each other and complemented each other in a shared process of demystification. They exposed a demonic incubus that had perverted every advance of "civilization" with the poison of hierarchy and domination. An agenda even larger than that advanced by the early New Left and counterculture had been created by the mid-sixties; one that required elaboration, educational activity, and serious organization to reach people as a whole, not merely a particular sector of the population.

This project could have been reinforced by issues that cut across all traditional class lines and status groups: the subversion of vast natural cycles, the growing pollution of the planet, massive urbanization, and increases in environmentally induced diseases. A growing public began to emerge that felt deeply implicated in environmental problems. Questions of growth, profit, the future of the planet, assumed in their own way an all-encompassing, socially planetary character; they were no longer single issues or class issues but human and ecological issues. That various elites and privileged classes still advanced their own bourgeois interest could have served to highlight the extent to which capitalism was *itself* becoming a special interest whose existence could no longer be justified. It could be made clearly evident that capitalism did not represent a universal historical force, much less a universal human interest.

The close of the sixties and the opening of the seventies formed a period filled with extraordinary alternatives. The revolutionary project had come into its own. Ideals of freedom whose threads had been broken by Marxism were once again picked up and advanced along anarchic and utopian lines to encompass *universal* human interests — the interests of society as a whole, not of the nation-state, the bourgeoisie, or the proletariat as particularistic social phenomena.

Could enough of a New Left and a counterculture be rescued from the process of decomposition that followed 1968 to embrace the expanded revolutionary project opened by social ecology and feminism?

Could a radical sentiment and the energies of radicals generally be mobilized on a scale and with the intellectuality that equaled the broad revolutionary project advanced by these two tendencies?

Vague demands for participatory democracy, social justice, disarmament, and the like, had to be linked together into a coherent outlook and program. They required a sense of direction that could be given only by a deeper theoretical insight, a relevant program, and more definable organizational forms than the New Left of the sixties could generate. Rudi Dutschke's appeal to German SDS for a "Long march through the institutions," which amounted to little more than adapting to the institutions that exist without troubling to create new ones, led to the loss of thousands within the institutions. They went in — and never came out.

FROM HERE TO THERE

The door that can open the way to a New Left of the future, one that embodies the experience of the thirties, sixties, and the decades that have followed them, is still swinging to and fro on its hinges.

It has neither opened fully nor closed. Its swings depend partly upon the hard realities of everyday social life — namely, whether the economy is depressed or rising, the kind of political climate that exists in various parts of the world, events in the Third World as well as the First and Second, the fortunes of radical tendencies at home and abroad, and the sweeping environmental changes that confront humanity in the years that lie ahead.

Ecologically, humanity is faced with major climatic changes, rising levels of pollution, and new, environmentally induced illnesses. Terrible human tragedies in the form of hunger, famine, and malnutrition are claiming millions of lives annually. An incalculable number of animal and plant species face extinction as a result of deforestation from lumbering activities and acid rain. The global changes that are degrading the natural environment, and may eventually render it uninhabitable for complex life-forms, have an almost geological massiveness, and they may be occurring at a pace that verges on the catastrophic for many plant and animal species.

One might have hoped that these planetary changes would have catapulted the ecology movement into the foreground of social thought and added new insights to the ideals of freedom. This has not been the case. The ecology movement has divided into several questionable tendencies that often directly contradict each other. Many people are simply pragmatic environmentalists. Their efforts are focused on single-issue reforms such as the control of toxic wastes, opposition to the construction of nuclear reactors, restrictions on urban growth, and the like. These are necessary struggles, to be sure, that can never be disdained simply because they are limited and piecemeal. They serve to slow down a headlong race to disasters like Chernobyl or Love Canal.

But they cannot supplant the need to get to the roots of environmental dislocations. Indeed, insofar as they are restricted merely to reforms, they often create the dangerous illusion that the present social order is capable of rectifying its own abuses. The denaturing of the environment must always be seen as *inherent* to capitalism, the product of its very law of life, as a system of limitless expansion and capital accumulation. To ignore the anti-ecological core of the present social order — be it in its Western corporate form or its Eastern bureaucratic form — is to allay public concern about the depth of the crisis and lasting means to resolve it.

Environmentalism, conceived as a piecemeal reform movement, easily lends itself to the lure of statecraft, that is, to participation in electoral, parliamentary, and party-oriented activities. It requires no great change in consciousness to turn a lobby into a party or a petitioner into a parliamentarian. Between a person who humbly solicits from power and another who arrogantly exercises it, there exists a sinister and degenerative symbiosis. Both share the same mentality that change can be achieved only through the *exercise* of power, specifically, through the power of a self-corrupting professionalized corps of legislators, bureaucrats, and military forces called the State. The appeal to this power invariably legitimates and strengthens the State, with the result that it actually disempowers the people. Power allows for no vacuum in public life. Whatever power the State gains, it always does so at the expense of popular power. Conversely, whatever power the people gain, they always acquire at the expense of the State. To legitimate State power, in effect, is to delegitimate popular power.

Ecology movements that enter into parliamentary activities not only legitimate State power at the expense of popular power, but they are obliged to function *within* the State, ultimately to become blood of its blood and bone of its bone. They must "play the game," which means that they must shape their priorities according to predetermined rules over which they have no control. This not only involves a given constellation of relationships that emerges with participation in State power; it becomes an ongoing *process* of degeneration, a steady devolution of ideals, practices, and party structures. Each demand for the "effective" exercise of parliamentary power raises the need for a further retreat from presumably cherished standards of belief and conduct.

If the State is a realm of "evil," as Bakunin emphasized, the "art" of statecraft is essentially a realm of lesser or greater evils, not a realm of ethical right and wrong. Ethics itself is radically redefined from the classical time-honoured study of good and evil into the more sinister contemporary study of compromises between lesser and greater evils — in short, what I have elsewhere called an "ethics of evil."[*] This basic redefinition of ethics has had deadly consequences over the course of recent history. Fascism made its way to power in Germany when Social Democracy lived in a diet of choices between liberals and centrists; later, centrists and conservatives; and, finally, between conservatives and Nazis — a steady devolution in which a conservative President, Marshall von Hindenberg, finally appointed the Nazi leader, Adolf Hitler, to the position of Reich Chancellor. That the German working class with its huge parties and its massive trade unions permitted this appointment to occur without any act of resistance is an easily forgotten and dismal event in history. Not only did this moral devolution occur on the level of the State, but also on the level of German popular movements themselves, in a cruel dialectic of political degeneration and moral decomposition.

Environmental movements have not fared better in their relationship to State power. They have bartered away entire forests for token reserves of trees. Vast wilderness areas have been surrendered for national parks. Huge stretches of coastal wetlands have been exchanged for a few acres of pristine beaches. To the extent that environmentalists

---

[*]   See my forthcoming book, *The Ethics of Evil* (Montreal, 1990).

have entered into national parliaments as Greens, they have generally attained little more than public attention for their self-serving parliamentary deputies and achieved very little to arrest environmental decay.

The Hesse coalition of the German Greens with a Social Democratic government in the mid-1980s ended in ignominy. Not only did the "realist wing" of the German Green party taint the movement's finest principles with compromises, it made the party more bureaucratic, manipulative, and "professional" — in short, very much like the rivals it once denounced.

Reformism and parliamentarism, at least, have a tangibility about them that raises real questions of political theory and a sense of social direction. The most recent tendency in the environmental movement, however, is completely ghostly and vaporous. Bluntly put: it consists of attempts to turn ecology into a religion by peopling the natural world with gods, goddesses, woodsprites, and the like — all serviced by a corps of financially astute gurus from India, their home-bred competitors, a variety of witches, and self-styled "wiccan anarchists."

The American roots of this tendency, of course, should be emphasized. The United States is currently the most ill-read, ill-informed, and, culturally, the most illiterate country in the Western world. The sixties counterculture opened a rupture not only with the past, but with all knowledge of the past, including its history, literature, art, and music. The young people who arrogantly refused to "trust anyone over thirty," to use a popular slogan of the day, severed all their ties with the best traditions of the past. In an era of junk food, the opening created by this breach was filled by an appalling mixture of junk ideas. Patently contradictory fantasies were congealed by drugs and rock music into a squalid ooze of atheistic religions, natural supernaturalisms, privatistic politics, and even liberal reactionaries. If this pairing of completely opposing terms seems irrational, the reader should bear in mind that the amalgam was "made in America," where everything is believed to be possible and the absurd is normally the result.

That ecology, an eminently *naturalistic* outlook and discipline, could be infested with supernatural rubbish, would seem explicable if such nonsense were confined strictly to its American borders. What is astonishing, however, is that it has spread like a worldwide pollutant to Europe, especially to England, Germany, and Scandinavia. Given time, it will almost certainly invade the Mediterranean countries as well.

As a form of "cultural feminism," this extension of a quasi-theological ecology to gender relationships already commands a growing, indeed enormous, following in English and German-speaking countries. The hope that ecology would enrich feminism has taken the bizarre form of a theistic "eco-feminism," structured around woman's uniquely "nurturing" role in the biosphere. Leaving aside this crassly anthropomorphic extension of human behaviour to nature as a whole, theistic "eco-feminists" have essentially reversed the eminent role patricentric cultures assign to men by simply inverting the same relationship in woman's favour. Women are privileged in nature just as men are privileged in history, with the result that male chauvinism is simply replaced by female chauvinism.

Accordingly, presumably "pacific" female goddesses are substituted for male warrior gods, as though trading one deity for another is not an extension of religion and superstition into human affairs — whether they are called "immanent," "transcendental," "paganistic," or "Judeo-Christian." Female-oriented myths based on "nurture" are substituted for male-oriented myths based on military conquest, as though myths are not inherently fictitious and arbitrary — whether they are "naturalistic" or "supernaturalistic," "earth-based," or "heaven-based." The world, viewed as a complex biosphere that should invite wonder, admiration, and foster an aesthetic as well as caring sensibility, is re-envisioned as a basically female terrain, occupied by woodsprites, witches, goddesses, and regaled by rituals and mystified by contrived myths — an ensemble that is borne on a lucrative tidal wave of books, artifacts, and bejeweled ornaments.

Political activity and social engagement in this theistic terrain tends to shrivel from activism into quietism and from social organization into privatistic encounter-groups. One has only to cover a personal problem with the patina of gender — be it a failed love affair or a business misfortune — and it is easily designated as "political" or a form of gender victimization. The notion that the "personal is the political," in effect, is stretched to the frivolous point where political issues are cast increasingly in a therapeutic vernacular, so that one's "manner" of presenting ideas is considered more important than their substance. Form is increasingly replacing content and eloquence is increasingly decried as "manipulative," with the result that a deadening mediocrity of form *and* content tends to become the rule in political discourse. The moral outrage that once stirred the human spirit over the ages in the thundering words of the Hebrew prophets is denounced as evidence of "aggressiveness," "dogmatism," "divisiveness," and "male behaviour." What "counts," today, is not what one says but *how* one says it — even if statements are insultingly naïve and vacuous. "Care" can easily regress into naïvety and "concern" into a childishness that makes one's politics more infantile than feminist.

None of this is to deny the feminist claim that woman has been the pariah of a largely male history, a history that has never prevented males from dominating, exploiting, torturing, and murdering each other on a scale that beggars description. But to see woman as the protypical victim of hierarchy and her oppression as the source of all hierarchy, as some feminists claim, is to simplify the development of hierarchy in a very reductive manner. The origins of a phenomenon do not exhaust our understanding of the phenomenon any more than the origins of the cosmos exhaust or understanding of its development from a compact undifferentiated mass into extremely complex forms. Male hierarchies are highly complex affairs. They embody subtle interactions between men as fathers, brothers, sons, workers, and ethnic types, including their cultural status and their individual proclivities. The caring father, who often stands in a warm relationship with his daughter by comparison with a competitive mother, should remind us that hierarchy is intricate enough on the familial level to give us pause when we consider it on the social level.

Nor does anthropology supply conclusive support for the status of woman as the protypical victim of hierarchy. Elderly women, in fact, enjoyed a high status together with elderly men in early hierarchical gerontocracies. Nor were women the sole, or necessarily the most oppressed, victims of patriarchy. Sons of patriarchs were often confronted with unendurable demands and dealt with far more harshly on many occasions by their fathers than were their sisters or mothers.

Indeed, the power of patriarchs was often shared quite openly with their eldest wives, as is evident in the commanding status of Sara in the Hebrew scriptures.

Finally, it is by no means clear that women do not form hierarchies among themselves or that the abolition of male dominance will remove hierarchy as such. Hierarchy embraces vast areas of social life, today, such as bureaucracies, ethnic groups, nationalities, occupational classes, not to mention domestic life in all its aspects. It permeates the human unconscious in ways that often have no direct or even indirect relationship with women. It involves ways of looking at the natural world that in no way relate to the putative assignment of a presumably "instinctive" proclivity of women to be "caretakers" and "custodians" of life as such — a piece of crude biologism that defames woman's role in the making of a very human-oriented culture and its artifacts like pottery, woven cloth, and agriculture. In any case, many priestesses, witches, and shamanesses seem to have stood — and still stand — in a distinctly hierarchical relationship with their female congregants and acolytes.

TOWARD A GENERAL HUMAN INTEREST

The antirational, theistic, even antisecular impulses that are surfacing in the ecology and feminist movements raise an issue of very fundamental concern for our time. They are evidence of a sinister *anti*-Enlightenment tendency that is sweeping through much of contemporary Western society.

In America and Europe, nearly all the high ideals of the Enlightenment are being currently impugned: its goals of a rational society, its belief in progress, its high hopes for education, its demands for the human use of technology and science, its commitment to reason, and its ethical belief in humanity's power to attain a materially and culturally viable world. Not only have dark atavisms replaced these goals among certain tendencies within the ecology and feminist movements; they have branched outward in the world at large in the form of a Yuppie nihilism called postmodernism, in a mystification of wilderness as "true reality" (to quote one vulgarian), in a sociobiology that festers with racism, and in a crude neo–Malthusianism that lends itself to indifference to human suffering.

The eighteenth century Enlightenment, to be sure, had serious limitations — limitations of which many of its foremost spokespersons were fully aware. But the Enlightenment left society and the centuries that followed it with heroic ideals and values. It brought the human mind from heaven down to earth, from the realm of the supernatural to the natural. It fostered a clear-eyed secular view toward the dark mythic world that festered in feudalism, religion, and royal despotism. It challenged notions of political inequality, of aristocratic supremacy, of clerical hierarchy — a challenge that ultimately laid the basis for much of the antihierarchical sentiments of later generations.

Above all, the Enlightenment tried to formulate a general human interest over feudal parochialism and to establish the idea of a shared human nature that would rescue humanity as a whole from a folk-like, tribalistic, and nationalistic particularism.

The abuse of these ideals by industrial capitalism through the commodification and mechanization of the world does not negate these ideals by one whit. Indeed, the Enlightenment reconnoitred areas of reason, science, and technology that are by no means reflected by the present-day forms these achievements have taken. Reason, to thinkers like Hegel, meant a dialectic of eductive development, a process that is best expressed by organic growth, not simply the deductive inferences we find in geometry and other branches of mathematics. Science, in the thinking of Leibnitz, centred on the the study of the qualitative dimensions of phenomena, not simply on Cartesian models of a machine-like mathematical world. Technology was studied by Diderot primarily from an artisanal viewpoint, with a keen eye for craft skills as well as mass production. Indeed, Fourier, the true heir of this Enlightenment tradition, was to give technology a strongly ecological bias and stress the crucial importance of natural processes in the satisfaction of material needs.

That capitalism warped these goals, reducing reason to a harsh industrial rationalism focused on efficiency rather than a high-minded intellectuality; that it used science to quantify the world and dualize thought and being; that it used technology to exploit nature, including human nature — all of these distortions have their roots in society and in ideologies that seek to dominate humanity as well as the natural world.

The trends that denigrate reason, science, and technology, today, are perhaps understandable reactions to the bourgeois distortions of the Enlightenment's goals. They are understandable, too, in terms of the disempowerment that is felt by the individual in an era of ever-centralized and concentrated power in corporate and State hands, in the anonymity produced by urbanization, mass production, and mass consumption, and in the fragile condition of a human ego that is beset by incomprehensible and uncontrollable social forces.

But these trends, as understandable reactions, become profoundly reactionary when the substitutes they offer involve a dissolution of the general human interest advanced by the Enlightenment into gender parochialism, the substitution of a tribalistic folkdom for an emphatic humanism, and a "return to wilderness" for an ecological society.

They become crudely atavistic when they blame ecological dislocations on technics instead of the corporate and state institutions that employ them. And they retreat into the mythic darkness of a tribalistic past when they evoke a dread of the "outsider" —be it a male, an immigrant, or the member of a different ethnic group — as a threat to the integrity of the "insider's" group.

That groups of people may have unique cultural identities — claims that are justifiable as long as they are truly *cultural* and not "biological" — is not in dispute, especially if we acknowledge that their strongest commitment is to humanity as a whole in a free society, not to a special portion of it. Ecology's motifs of complementarity, mutualism, and nonhierarchical relationships are completely dishonoured by evocations of a racial, gender-oriented, or national particularism. If the Enlightenment left us any single legacy that we might prize above all others, it is the belief that humanity in a *free* society must be conceived as a unity, a "one" that is bathed in the light of reason and empathy.

Rarely in history have we been called upon to make a stronger stand for this legacy than today, when the sludge of irrationality, mindless growth, centralized power, ecological dislocation, and mystical retreats into quietism threaten to overwhelm the human achievements of past times. Rarely before have we been called upon not only to contain this sludge but to push it back into the depths of a demonic history from which it emerged.

I have tried to show that Western history has not been a unilinear advance from one stage to another and from one "precondition" to another in an untroubled ascent to ever-greater control over a "blind," "stingy," and intractable "first nature." Quite to the contrary: prehistory may have allowed for alternatives before the emergence of patricentric warrior societies — societies that might have seen a more benign social development than the one that formed our own history.

Possible alternatives were opened in the "age of cities," before the nation-state foreclosed the opportunities opened by urban confederations with their humanly scaled communities, artisanal technologies, and sensitive balance between town and country. As recently as two centuries ago, in the "age of democratic revolutions," the Western world with its mixed precapitalist society and economy seemed poised for an anarchic social dispensation.

Throughout, ever-expanding ideals of freedom based on the equality of unequals paralleled the more ancient "cry for justice" with its inequality of equals. To the extent that inherited custom was absorbed by a commandeering morality and both became part of a rational ethics, freedom began to develop a forward rather than a backward gaze and turn from a mere longing for a "golden age" to a fervent hope for a humanly created utopia.

The ideals of freedom became secular rather than heavenly, work-a-day rather than the fanciful bounty of nature or the largess of a privileged class. They became sensuous as well as intellectually sophisticated. Scientific and technological advances placed material security and the leisure time needed for a participatory democracy on the agenda of a radically new revolutionary project. From antinomies, or seemingly contradictory co-existents of these advances, particularly in the mixed economy that existed in Europe between the fourteenth and eighteenth centuries, various choices were possible between city and nation, commonwealth and state, artisanal production and mass production.

Anarchism, which came fully into its own in the "age of revolutions," stressed the importance of choice; Marxism stressed the inexorability of social laws. Anarchism remained sensitive to the spontaneity of social development, a spontaneity, to be sure, informed by consciousness and the need for a structured society. Marxism anchored itself deeply in an "embryonic" theory of society, a "science" based on "prerequisites" and "preconditions." Tragically, Marxism virtually silenced all earlier revolutionary voices for more than a century and held history itself in the icy grip of a remarkably bourgeois theory of development based on the domination of nature and the centralization of power.

We have noted that capitalism has yet to fully define itself. No "last stage" exists, as far as we can see, anymore than such a "stage," which was greeted with certainty by revolutionaries during the First World War and the Second, emerged in their time. If capitalism has any limits, they are neither internal, based on chronic crises, nor dependent upon the proletariat's pursuit of its particularistic interests. Proletarian socialism, or the Old Left foundered on these myths and now lies in debris.

The success of the revolutionary project must now rest on the emergence of a general human interest that cuts across the particularistic interests of class, nationality, ethnicity, and gender. The New Left, nourished by dazzling advances in the technologies of the post–World War II era and the gratification of the most trivial wants by unprecedented levels of production, thawed out the economistic grip of Marxism and returned the sixties, for a time, to the ethical, indeed sensuous, radicalism of the pre–Marxist era.

If a general interest can be reformulated today as a new libertarian agenda, it must be based on the most obvious limits capitalism faces: the ecological limits to growth imposed by the natural world. And if that general interest can be embodied in a nonhierarchical demand, it is the demand raised by women for a substantive equality of unequals — that is, the expansive ideal of freedom. The question we now face is whether the ecological and feminist movements can live up to this historical challenge. That is, whether these movements can be broadened into a sweeping *social movement;* indeed, into a libertarian New Left that will speak for a general human interest — or whether they will shatter into the particularized interests that centre around reformist parliamentarism, mysticism and theism in their various forms, and gender chauvinism.

Finally, whatever may have been the prospect of achieving a free, ecological society in the past, there is not the remotest chance that it can be achieved today unless humanity is free to reject bourgeois notions of abundance precisely because abundance is available to all. We no longer live in a world that treasures gift- giving over accumulation and moral constraints that limit growth. Capitalism has warped the values of that earlier world to a point where only the prospect of abundance can eliminate insensate consumption and a sense of scarcity that exists among all underprivileged people. No general human interest can emerge when the "haves" constitute a standing reproach to the material denial of the "have-nots" and when those who are idle mock, by their very existence, the lifetime of toil imposed on working classes. Nor will a participatory democracy ever be achieved by society as a whole as long as a public life is available only to those who have the free time to participate in it.

Insofar as humanity could make decisive choices about the social direction it should follow, its choices have been largely bad ones. The result has been that humanity has generally been less than human. Rarely has it fulfilled what it could be, given its potentialities for thought, feeling, ethical judgements, and rational social arrangements.

The ideals of freedom are now in place, as I have noted, and they can be described with reasonable clarity and coherence. We are confronted with the need not simply to improve society or alter it; we are confronted with the need to *remake* it. The ecological crises we face and the social conflicts that have torn us apart and have made our century the bloodiest in history, can be resolved only if we clearly recognize that our problems go to the heart of a domineering *civilization*, not simply to a badly structured ensemble of social relations.

Our present civilization is nothing if it is not Janus-faced and riddled with ambiguity. We cannot simply denounce it as male-oriented, exploitative, and domineering without recognizing that it also freed us, at least in part, from the parochial bonds of tribalism and an abject obedience to superstition, which ultimately made us vulnerable to domination. By the same token, we cannot simply praise it for its growing universality, the extent to which it fostered individual autonomy, and the rational secularism it brought to human affairs without recognizing that these achievements were generally purchased at the cost of human enslavement, mass degradation, class rule, and the establishment of the State. Only a dialectic that combines searching critique with social creativity can disassemble the best materials from our shattered world and bring them to the service of remaking a new one.

I have stressed that our foremost need is to create a general human interest that can unify humanity as a whole. Minimally, this interest centres around the establishment of a harmonious balance with nature. Our viability as a species depends upon our future relationship with the natural world. This problem cannot be settled by the invention of new technologies that will supplant natural processes without making society more technocratic, more centralized, and ultimately completely totalitarian. For technology to replace the natural cycles that determine the ratio of atmospheric carbon dioxide to oxygen, to provide a substitute for the decomposing ozone layer that protects all life from lethal solar radiation, to substitute hydroponic solutions for soil — all of this, if it were possible, would require a highly disciplined system of social management that is radically incompatible with democracy and political participation by the people.

Such an overwhelming, indeed global, reality raises questions about the future of humanity on a scale that no historical period in the past has ever been compelled to face. The message raised by an "ecological technocracy," if it can be called that, is for a degree of social coordination that beggars the most centralized despotisms of history. Even so, it remains very unclear that such an ecological technocracy can be achieved on scientific grounds, or that, in view of the delicate checks and balances involved, whether technological substitutes for natural processes can be so well adjusted that they will not be subject to catastrophic misjudgements.

If the life processes of the planet and those of our species are not to be administered by a totalitarian system, modern society must follow certain basic ecological precepts. I have argued in this book that the harmonization of nature cannot be achieved without the harmonization of human with human. This means that our very notion of what constitutes humanity must be clarified. If we remain merely conflicting class beings, genders, ethnic beings, and nationalities, it is obvious that any kind of harmony between human beings will be impossible. As members of classes, genders, ethnic groups, and nationalities, we will have narrowed our meaning of what it is to be human by means of particularistic interests that explicitly set us against each other.

Although ecology advances a message of diversity, it does so as *unity* in diversity. Ecological diversity, in addition, does not rest on conflict; it rests on differentiation, on the wholeness that is enhanced by the variety of its constituents. Socially, this view is expressed in the Greek ideal that the complete, many-sided person is the product of a complete, many-sided society. Class, gender, ethnic, and national interests are fearfully similar in their reduction of a widely expansive view of the world to a narrow one, of larger interests to smaller ones, of complementarity to conflict. To preach a message of reconciliation when class, gender, ethnic, and national interests are very real and objectively grounded in major conflicts, would be absurd, to be sure. Our Janus-faced civilization looks toward a long past that has seen mere differences in age, sex, and kinship reworked into domineering hierarchies, hierarchies into classes, and classes into state structures. The bases for conflicting interests in society must themselves be confronted and resolved in a revolutionary manner. The earth can no longer be owned; it must be shared. Its fruits, including those produced by technology and labour, can no longer be expropriated by the few; they must be rendered available to all on the basis of need. Power, no less that material things, must be freed from the control of the elites; it must be redistributed in a form that renders its use participatory. Until these basic problems are resolved, there can be no development of a general interest that will formulate a policy to resolve the growing ecological crisis and the inadequacy of this society to deal with it.

The point I wish to make, however, is that no general interest of this kind can be achieved by the particularistic means that marked earlier revolutionary movements. The present ecological crisis is potentially capable of mobilizing a degree of public support and involvement that is more transclass and wider than any issue that humanity has faced in the past. And with the passing of time, this crisis will become starker and more all-embracing than it is today. Its mystification by religious ideologists and corporate hirelings threatens to place the very future of the biosphere in the balance.

Nor can we ignore the recent history of the revolutionary project and the advances it scored over earlier ones. Past revolutions were largely struggles for justice, not for freedom. The ideals of liberty, equality, and fraternity, so generously advanced by the French Revolution, foundered on the faulty definition of the terms themselves. I will not belabour the fact that the crassly particularistic interests of the bourgeoisie interpreted liberty to mean free trade; equality to mean the right to contract labour; and fraternity to mean the obedience on an emerging proletariat to capitalist supremacy. Hidden more deeply in this slogan of classical republicanism was the fact that liberty meant little more than the right of the ego to pursue its own self interest; equality, the principle of justice; fraternity, taken literally, a male-centred society of "brothers," however much some men exploited others.

Taken at face value, the slogans of the revolution never ascended to the domain of freedom. On whatever level we examine the revolution, it was a project to achieve an inequality of equals, not to achieve an equality of unequals. The tragically aborted Spanish Revolution of 1936–1937 tried to go beyond this limited project but it was isolated. Its most revolutionary elements — the anarchists — never gained the popular support they needed in the country as a whole to realize their richly emancipatory goals.

Capitalism has changed in the decades that followed the era of proletarian socialism. Its impact on society and nature is perhaps more devastating than at any time since the Industrial Revolution. The modern revolutionary project, initiated by the New Left of the sixties, with its call for a participatory democracy, has gone far beyond the level of the classical revolutions and their particularistic aims. The idea of "the People," an illusory concept that informed the emergence of democratic movements in the eighteenth century just as society was beginning to differentiate itself into clearly definable classes, has now taken on a new meaning with the steady decomposition of traditional classes and with the emergence of transclass issues like ecology, feminism, and a sense of civic responsibility to neighbourhoods and communities. Movements like the Greens in Germany, and possibly other countries, or various citizens' initiative movements in a growing number of cities and towns are addressing larger human issues than increased wages and class conflicts at the point of production. With the rise of ecology, feminist, and citizens' movements, new possibilities exist for generalizing the ideals of freedom, for giving them a broadly human and truly populist dimension.

To talk vaguely of "the People," however, without examining the relationship of the ordinary citizen to populist-type goals, raises the danger of dealing with the kind of vague abstractions that characterized Marxism for more than a century. Over and beyond the need to share the earth, to distribute its fruits according to need, and to develop a general human interest that goes beyond the particularistic ones of the past, the revolutionary project must take its point of departure from a fundamental libertarian precept: every normal human being is *competent* to manage the affairs of society and, more specifically, the community in which he or she is a member.

This precept lays down a radical gauntlet to Jacobin abstractions like "the People" and Marxist abstractions like "the Proletariat" by demanding that society must be existentially "peopled" by real, living beings who are free to control their own destinies and that of their society. It challenges parliamentarism as a surrogate for an authentic democracy with Rousseau's classical observation:

> Sovereignty, for the same reason as it makes it inalienable, cannot be represented. It lies essentially in the general will, and will does not admit of representation: it is either the same, or other; there is no intermediate possibility. The deputies of the people, therefore, are not and cannot be its representatives: they are merely its stewards, and can carry through no definitive acts. Every law the people has not ratified in person is null and void — is, in fact, not a law. The people of England regards itself as free; but it is grossly mistaken: it is free only during the election of members of parliament. As soon as they are elected, slavery overtakes it, and it is nothing.[21]

Whatever interpretation one may give to Rousseau's "general will" and other formulations he advances, the statement's basic thrust forms an imperishable and unnegotiable ideal of human freedom. It implies that no substantive democracy is possible and no concept of self-administration is meaningful unless the people convene in open, face-to-face assemblies to formulate policies for society. No policy, in effect, is democratically legitimate unless it has been proposed, discussed, and decided upon by the people directly — not through representatives or surrogates of any kind. The *administration* of these policies can be left to boards, commissions, or collectives of qualified, even elected, individuals who, under close public purview and with full accountability to policy-making assemblies, may execute the popular mandate.

This distinction between policy and administration — one which Marx failed to make in his writings on the Paris Commune of 1871 — is crucial. Popular assemblies are the minds of a free society; the administrators of their policies are the hands. The former can always recall the latter and end their operations, depending upon need, dissatisfaction, and the like. The latter merely effects what the former decides and remains totally dependent upon their will.

This crucial distinction makes the popular assembly's existence a largely functional issue in democratic procedures, not a structural one. In principle, assemblies can function under any demographic and urban conditions — on the block, neighbourhood, or town levels. They have only to be coordinated by appropriately confederal sinews to become forms of self-governance. Given modern logistical conditions, there can be no emergency so great that assemblies cannot be rapidly convened to make important policy decisions by a majority vote and the appropriate boards convened to execute these decisions — irrespective of a community's size or the complexity of its problems. Experts will always be available to offer their solutions, hopefully competing ones that will foster discussion, to the more specialized problems a community may face.

Nor can populations be so large or the number of assemblies so numerous that they cannot be coordinated in a manner that perpetuates their integrity as face-to-face policy-making bodies. Delegates to town, city, and regional bodies, can be regarded simply as the walking mandates of the local assemblies. Furthermore, we must disabuse ourselves of the idea that consensus can always be attained in large groups. A minority does not have the right to abort a decision of a majority — be it within an assembly or between assemblies. If Rousseau's "general will" could, in fact, be transformed into a *generalized* will — that is to say, if it could be supposed that rational people who have no interests apart from those of the community at large will make shared rational decisions about transparently clear issues — it may well be that consensus can be achieved.

But by no means is this goal even desirable. It is a hidden tyranny based on unthinking custom, in fact, an atavistic throwback to times when *public opinion* was as coercive as outright violence (which, at least, existed in the open). A tyranny of consensus, like the famous "tyranny of structurelessness," demeans a free society. It tends to subvert individuality in the name of community and dissent in the name of solidarity. Neither true community nor solidarity are fostered when the individual's development is aborted by public disapproval and his or her deviant ideas are "normalized" by the pressure of public opinion.

Underlying the development of self-managing, face-to-face assemblies are a number of ethical, even educational problems that enter into developing competent individuals. The assembly reached its most sophisticated form of development in the Athenian *polis*, where, contrary to current criticisms of the Hellenic city as "patriarchal," most ancients viewed it as a huge "mobocracy." It retained this pejorative reputation well into modern times. That radicals in the twentieth century, who view it from the hindsight of more than two thousand years, can denounce it as a "tyranny" that oppressed women, slaves, and resident aliens, is not without a certain irony. Given the more morbid abuses of the ancient world, which was drenched in patriarchy, slavery, and despotism, the Athenian democracy stands out like a beacon of light. The view that Western democracy can be dismissed simply as a "male" tradition and that we should return to "tribal" traditions, whatever these may be, is atavistic to the core. In the *polis*, the Janus-faced nature of Western civilization — the East offers no notable improvements upon it, I may add — actually exhibits its better profile in the history of freedom.

All of this raises the question of what constitutes the ethical basis of the assembly and its time-honoured standards of competence. The first was the ideal of solidarity or friendship (*philia*), an ideal in which loyalty to the community was given flesh and blood by intimate relationships between its members. A lived, vital, and deeply felt consociation existed among many members of the Athenian *polis*, in the guilds of the medieval towns, and among an endless network of small societies in the towns and cities of the precapitalist world. The Greek symposium, in which knots of friends gathered to dine, drink, and discuss, was matched in part by the rich neighbourhood cafe life of French, Spanish, and Italian cities. The community was made up, in a sense, of smaller "communes." The counterculture of the sixties turned this literally into communal forms of living. The ideal of a Commune of communes was openly advanced in 1871 in the revolutionary proclamations of the Paris Commune during its brief lifespan. Popular societies clustered around the Parisian sections of 1793 and provided ways of associating that made the revolution an intimate exercise in civic affinity.

Still another ethical ideal was the importance that was attached to roundedness. The Greeks mistrusted specialists, despite Plato's favourable view of them, because excessive expertise seemed to involve a warping of one's character around a particular interest or skill. To know a little bit about everything and not too much about one thing was evidence of a rounded person who, as need arose, could form an intelligent view of an issue and advance a good case for his judgements. This emphasis on amateurism, an emphasis that did not prevent the Greeks from founding Western philosophy, science, mathematics, and drama, was to be an abiding ideal for centuries after the *polis* disappeared into history.

Roundedness also implied a measure of self-sufficiency. To be one's "own man" meant not only that one was competent but also independent. In earlier times, this rounded person was expected to be free of a client position. A special interest might render an individual vulnerable to and dependent upon the wishes of a master. The individual who could perform many different tasks, it was supposed, could understand a wide array of problems. If he was independent materially, say, like a farmer who owned the land he worked, and could meet most of his needs by his own efforts and skills, he was presumably capable of forming an objective judgement, free of undue influence by the opinions of others. The Greeks believed in owning property not because they were acquisitive; indeed, to give generously to one's friends and neighbours earned the highest esteem in Greek society. But a modest piece of land that could provide the farmer and his family with the basic means of life freed him from manipulation by landed aristocracies and merchants.

To give of one's free time and services to the *polis* was seen as another ideal that often led to agonistic efforts to gain public recognition, a Greek character trait that has been sharply reproached but often grossly misunderstood. The zeal with which the Greeks served their communities, in fact, was idealized as a form of civic dedication up to our own time. Civic recognition often required considerable personal sacrifices, and the zeal exhibited by leading Greeks stemmed from a desire for social immortality. Indeed, to destroy a Greek city meant to efface the memory and immortality of its more heroic figures as well as to destroy the very identity of its inhabitants.

If civic zealotry threatened to upset the relatively delicate balances of a class society that could easily plunge into insurrection, the Greeks formulated an ideal of "limit" — the "golden mean" which meant "nothing in excess" — that was to be carried deeply into Western ethics. The notion of limit was to appear in medieval towns and cities and even well into the Renaissance. Beneath the clamour that marked the Italian city-states of the late Middle Ages, there were unstated rules of civic behaviour that placed constraints on excessive zealotry and fractious behaviour, despite the ultimate emergence of oligarchies and one-man rule.

As M.I. Finley has pointed out, the Athenian *polis* — and, I would contend, many democratic towns that followed it in time — essentially established a system of civic etiquette that kept excessive ambition under a measure of control. Medieval Italian cities, for example, created remarkable checks and balances to prevent one interest in the city from gaining too much ascendancy over another, a balance that the Greek *polis* had established earlier in antiquity. Self-restraint, dignity, courtesy, and a strong commitment to civic decorum were part of the psychological attributes that many precapitalist cities, structured around assemblies, actually translated into institutions in a system of checks that fostered harmony, however tentative they may seem. Power was often divided and subdivided so that countervailing forces existed to prevent the ascendancy of any one institution, and the interests it represented, from becoming excessively powerful.

Taken together, this ethical ensemble was personified in a new kind of individual — a *citizen*. The citizen was neither a tribal person nor the member of a kin group, although strong family relationships existed in the precapitalist cities of the past and kinship ties played a major role in political conflicts. But to be a citizen in the traditional sense, one had to be more than a kinsman. The primary allegiances of the citizen were to the *polis*, town, or city — at least, before the nation-state turned citizenship into a parody of its original meaning.

Citizens, in turn, were created through training, a process of *character*-building that the Greeks called *paidaia*, which is not quite properly translated by the word "education." One had to learn civic responsibility, to reason out one's views with scrupulous care, to confront opposing arguments with clarity, and, hopefully, to advance tested principles that exhibited high ethical standards. Additionally, a citizen was expected to learn martial arts, to work together with fellow citizens in militia detachments; indeed, in many cases, to learn how to command properly during military engagements.

The citizen of a precapitalist democratic city, in short, was not the "constituent" of a parliamentary representative, or a mere "taxpayer," to use modern civic jargon. He was, in the best of cases, a knowledgeable, civically dedicated, active, and, above all, *self-governing* being who exercised considerable inner discipline and made the welfare of his community — its general interest — his primary interest to the exclusion of his own self-interest.

This constellation of ethical precepts formed a unified whole, without which civic democracy and popular assemblies would not have been possible. Rousseau's remarkable statement that citizens make cities, not merely buildings, cannot be restated often enough. Without citizens, viewed in this classical sense, cities were mere clusters of buildings which tended to degenerate into oligarchies or become absorbed into nation-states.

LIBERTARIAN MUNICIPALISM

From the foregoing, it should be obvious that the assembly of the people found its authentic home in the city — and in cities of a very special kind. The Janus-faced character of Western civilization obliges us to sift the unsavoury features of the city — the legitimation it gave to the private ownership of property, classes, patricentricity, and the State — from the great civilized advances it scored as a new terrain for a universal *humanitas*. Today, at a time when anti-city biases have cast the city in an ugly social light, it may be well to emphasize the major advance the city scored in providing a shared domain for people of different ethnic backgrounds, occupations, and status groups. "Civilization," a term that is derived from the Latin word for city, was not simply a "slaughter bench," to use Hegel's dramatic phrase. It was literally Janus-faced (as Hegel only too well appreciated) in its look toward the prospect of a common humanity as well as in its look toward barbarities that were to be justified in the name of progress and cultural advances.

Participatory democracies and popular assemblies, to be sure, originated in tribal and village communities. But they did not become *self-conscious* forms of consociation which people regarded as ends in themselves until the city emerged. There is some evidence that they existed as early as Sumerian times in the cities that appeared in Mesopotamia. But it was the Greek *polis* and later medieval towns that made these democracies and assemblies acutely aware of the fact that they were a *way of life*, not simply a technique for managing society, and that they should be constructed along *ethical* and *rational* lines that met certain ideals of justice and the good life, not merely institutions sanctified by custom. Cities comprised a decisive step forward in social life and, for all their limitations, gave us works like Plato's *Republic* and Aristotle's *Politics*, works that have been an abiding presence in the Western imagination for centuries.

The self-reflective nature of the city turned it into a remarkably unique and creative human institution. To Aristotle, the city — more properly, the *polis*, which was a highly self-conscious ethical entity — had to conform to certain structural standards if it was to fulfill its ethical functions. It had to be large enough so that its citizens could meet most of their material needs, yet not so large that they were unable to gain a familiarity with each other and make policy decisions in open, face-to-face discourse. Structure and ethics, function and ideals of freedom, were inseparable from each other. For all his faults, Aristotle tried — as did so many of the Athenians among whom he lived — to bring form into the service of content. He opposed any separation of the two, even in detailed discussions of city planning.

This approach became a cornerstone of the Western democratic tradition. It may have existed in the minds of figures like the Gracchi brothers in ancient Rome, Cola di Rienzi in medieval Rome, and Etienne Marcel in the Paris of the fourteenth century; men who led the urban masses in dramatic revolts to achieve city confederations and establish civic democracies. It was raised by Spanish cities that revolted against centralized rule in the sixteenth century and, again, in the French Revolution and the Paris Commune of 1871. It exists in our own time in New England town meetings, many of which still vigilantly guard their localist rights.

The city, in effect, opened a new terrain for social management that involves neither the use of state institutions — that is, statecraft — nor a strictly private domain that involves one's home, workplace, schools, religious institutions, and circles of friends. Taken literally from the Greek term in which it originates, the city created *politics*, a very unique world in which citizens gather together to rationally discuss their problems as a community and administer their affairs in a face-to-face manner.

Whether a municipality can be administered by all its citizens in a single assembly or has to be subdivided into several confederally related assemblies depends very much upon its size, hence Aristotle's injunction that a *polis* should not be so large that one could not hear a cry for help from the city walls. Although assemblies can function as networks on a block, neighbourhood, or town level, they fulfill traditional ideals of civic democracy when the cities in which they are located are decentralized. The anarchic vision of decentralized communities, united in free confederations or networks for coordinating the communities of a region, reflects the traditional ideals of a participatory democracy in a modern radical context.

Today, in the prevailing social condition that casts a dark shadow over the future of the present era, we are losing sight of the very *idea* of a city, of citizenship, and of politics as a domain of municipal self-management. Cities are being confused with huge urban belts that should properly be described as a seemingly unending process of "urbanization." Vast stretches of concrete and high-rise buildings are engulfing the definable, humanly scaled entities we once called cities and they are sweeping in the countryside as well.

By the same token, citizens are shrivelling to the status of anonymous "constituents" of elected representatives. Their principal function is to pay taxes, to do the onerous work-a-day job of maintaining the present society, to reproduce, and to decorously withdraw from all political life — a domain that is reserved for the State and its officialdom. Our warped discourse blurs the crucial distinctions between citification and urbanization, citizens and constituents, politics and statecraft.

The city, as a humanly scaled, self-governing municipality freely and confederally associated with other humanly scaled, self-governing municipalities, is dissolving into huge urban belts. The citizen, as an active formulator of policies, is being reduced to a passive taxpayer, the mere recipient of public services provided by bureaucratic agencies. Politics is being degraded into statecraft, an art practised by cynical, professional manipulators of power.

The entire ensemble is managed like a business. It is regarded as successful if it earns fiscal "surpluses" and provides needed services, or, it is a failure if it is burdened by fiscal "deficits" and operates inefficiently. The *ethical* content of city life as an arena for the inculcation of civic virtue, democratic ideals, and social responsibility is simply erased and its place is taken by an entrepreneurial mentality that emphasizes income, expenses, growth, and employment.

At the same time, power is thoroughly bureaucratized, centralized, and concentrated into fewer and fewer hands. The power that should be claimed by the people is pre-empted by the State and by semi-monopolistic economic entities. Democracy, far from acquiring a participatory character, becomes purely formal in character. Indeed, the New Left was an expression of a deeply felt desire for reempowerment that has continued unabatedly since the sixties — a desire to regain citizenship, to end the degradation of politics into statecraft: the need to revive public life.

These issues still remain at the top of the present social agenda. The rise of citizens' initiative movements in Germany, of municipal movements in the United States, of attempts to revive civic ideals in various

European countries, including France's recovery of words like *décentralization*, however much this term is honoured in the breach, are evidence of popular attempts to achieve reempowerment over social life. In many places, the State, with its extensive cutbacks of social services, has left a vacuum that cities are obliged to fill merely to remain functional. Transportation, housing, and welfare needs are being met more by localities than they have been in the past. Urban residents, obliged to fend for themselves, are learning the arts of teamwork and cooperation.

A gap, ideological as well as practical, is opening up between the nation-state, which is becoming more anonymous, bureaucratic, and remote, and the municipality, which is the one domain outside of personal life that the individual must deal with on a very direct basis. We do not go to the nation-state to find suitable schools for our children, for jobs, culture, and decent places in which to live. Like it or not, the city is still the most immediate environment which we encounter and with which we are obliged to deal, beyond the sphere of family and friends, in order to satisfy our needs as social beings.

Potentially, the sense of disempowerment that has become the popular malaise of our time could also become a source of dual power in the great nation-states of the Western world. Conscious movements have yet to arise that search for ways to get from a centralized, statist "here" to a civically decentralized and confederal "there," movements that can raise the demand for communal confederation as a popular alternative to the modern-day centralization of power. Unless we try — vainly, I believe — to revive myths of proletarian insurrections, of a feeble armed confrontation with the vast nuclear armamentarium of the modern nation-state, we are obliged to seek out counter-*institutions* that stand opposed to the power of the nation-state.

Communes, cooperatives, and various vocational collectives, to be sure, may be excellent schools for teaching people how to administer self-managed enterprises. But they are usually marginal projects, often very short-lived, and more useful as examples than as working institutions. No cooperative will ever replace a giant supermarket chain merely by competing with it, however much good will it may earn, nor will a Proudhonian "People's Bank" replace a major financial institution, however many supporters it may have.

We have other things we can learn from a Proudhon, who saw in the municipality an important arena of popular activity. I do not hesitate to use the word *politics*, here, if it is understood in its Hellenic meaning as the management of the community or *polis* by popular assemblies, not as statecraft and parliamentary activity. Every society contains vestiges of the past — of earlier, often more libertarian institutions that have been incorporated into present ones. The American Republic, for example, still has elements of a democracy like the town meeting, which Tocqueville described in his book, *Democracy in America.* Italian cities still have vital neighbourhoods that can form a basis for new community relationships. French towns still retain mainly humanly scaled features that can be organized into new political entities. Such observations can be made about communities throughout the world — communities whose solidarity opens the prospect of a new politics based on libertarian municipalism — which eventually could become a counterpower to the nation-state.

Let me emphasize that this approach presupposes that we are talking about a *movement*, not isolated instances where people in a single community assume control of their municipality and restructure it on the basis of neighbourhood assemblies. It presupposes that a movement will exist that alters one community after another and establishes a system of confederal relationships between municipalities; one that will form a regional power in its own right. How far we can take this libertarian municipalist approach is impossible to judge without knowing in detail the lived traditions of a region, the civic resources it possesses, and the problems it faces. Given this writer's experience with the issue of local control in the United States, this much can be said: no demand, when it has been raised, has been met with greater resistance by the State power. The nation-state knows, far better than its opponents in radical movements, how destabilizing to its authority demands for local control can be.

Yet the idea of libertarian municipalism has a pedigree that dates back to the American and French revolutions and to the Paris Commune, in which confederalism was a viable proposal to large masses of people. Dramatic as the changes have been since that time, there is no reason in principle to doubt why libertarian municipalism cannot be raised today, when squatters' movements, neighbourhood organizations, and community welfare groups have risen and fallen — only to rise again as evidence of a chronic impulse that the nation-state has never been able to exorcise.

DECENTRALIZATION AND TECHNOLOGY

Social ecology has added a unique, indeed urgent, dimension to the need for a libertarian municipalist movement and the issues it faces. The need to rescale communities to fit the natural carrying capacity of the regions in which they are located and to create a new balance between town and country — all traditional demands of the great utopian and anarchist thinkers of the last century — have become ecological imperatives today. Not only are they the seemingly utopian visions of yester-year, the dreams and desiderata of lonely thinkers; they have compelling necessities if we are to remain a viable species and live in harmony with a complex natural world that is threatened with destruction. Ecology, in effect, has essentially advanced the sharp alternatives: either we will turn to seemingly "utopian" solutions based on decentralization, a new equilibrium with nature, and the harmonization of social relations, or we face the very real subversion of the material and natural basis for human life on the planet.[*]

Urbanization threatens to efface not only the city but the countryside. The famous contradiction between town and country which figured so significantly in the history of social thought has now become meaningless. This contradiction is now being effaced by the spread of concrete over irredeemable areas of agricultural land and historically unique agrarian communities. The homogenization of rural

---

[*] I cannot help but make an observation about the massive ignorance that exists in the American and European ecology movements with respect to the long pedigree of these ideals. Anarchism, which has been pilfered repeatedly and scandalously by "neo–Marxists" of ideas like workers' control and decentralization, not to speak of the general strike — notions that Marx and Engels explicitly denigrated — are today common fare in self-styled "Marxist" movements. The same is true of Fourier, Owen, and particularly Kropotkin's ideas, not to mention views advanced by anarchists in the early sixties. Yet barely a word of acknowledgement is made by the ill-informed wags who, particularly in the shelter of the academy, have recycled so many eco-anarchist ideas in the name of "deep ecology" and "eco-feminism." Apparently, nothing exists in American and European thought until it has first been duly registered in an academic journal as a "paper" and, to be sure, by a professor or an aspiring one.

cultures by the mass media, urban lifestyles, and an all-pervasive consumerist mentality threatens to destroy not only regionally unique and colourful lifeways; it is totally degrading the natural landscape. What argibusiness has not already poisoned with its pesticides, chemical fertilizers, and heavy machines that compact the soil, acid rain and socially induced climatic changes are destroying in the form of deforestation and aridity. The urbanization of the planet is simplifying complex ecosystems, eliminating soil that was in the making for ages, reducing wilderness to fragile "reserves," and, whether directly or indirectly, profoundly altering regional climatic zones for the worst.

The technology we have inherited from earlier industrial revolutions, the insensate use of private motor vehicles, the concentration of massive industrial facilities near waterways, the massive use of fossil and nuclear fuels, and an economic system whose law of life is growth — all are producing in only a few decades a degree of environmental degradation that human habitation did not produce from its inception. Nearly all our waterways are odious sewers. "Dead seas" have been found in oceanic waters that extend over hundreds of miles in once thriving aquatic areas. I do not have to elaborate on this dark litany of widespread, possibly deadly, wounds that are being inflicted on every part of the planet. It is only too well-known what is being done to our atmosphere, to the ozone layer that protects life on the planet, even to more remote areas of the globe like the Arctic and, more recently, Antarctica, rain forests and, of course, temperate forests.

Our ultimate survival on the planet, not only our commitment to live fully human lives and fulfill our more libertarian visions, dictates that we re-asses our notions of urbanism and the relationship of cities to their ecological substrate. It also dictates that we re-assess our technologies and the goods they produce, indeed, our entire view toward nature.

We need smaller cities not only to realize cherished ideas of freedom but also to meet the most elementary needs to live in some kind of balance with nature. Giant cities, more precisely, sprawling urban belts, not only make for cultural homogeneity, individual anonymity, and centralized power; they place an impossible burden on local water resources, the air we breathe, and all the natural features of the areas which they occupy. Congestion, noise, and the stresses produced by modern urban living are becoming increasingly intolerable, psychically as well as physically. Cities which historically served to bring people of diverse background together, and made for communal solidarity, are now atomizing them. The city is the place in which to hide, as it were, not to seek human propinquity. Fear tends to replace sociality, rudeness eats away at solidarity, the herding of people into overcrowded dwellings, means of transportation, offices, and shopping centres subverts their sense of individuality and fosters indifference to the overall human condition.

Decentralization of large cities into humanly scaled communities is neither a romantic mystification of a nature-loving soloist nor is it a remote anarchic ideal. It has become *indispensable* to an ecologically sound society. What is now at stake in these seemingly "utopian" demands is a choice between a rapidly degrading environment and a society that will live in balance with nature in a viable and on a sustainable basis.

The same can be said for reconsidering the technological basis of modern society. Production can no longer be seen as a source of profit and the realization of one's self-interest. The finished goods human beings need to maintain their very lives as well as their cultural and physical well-being, are more hallowed than the mystified fetishes that have been used by various religions and superstitious cults to dazzle them. Bread, if you please, is more "sacred" than a priestly benediction; everyday clothing is more "holy" than clerical vestments; personal dwellings are more spiritually meaningful than churches and temples; the good life on earth is more sanctifying than the promised one in heaven. The means of life must be taken for what they literally are: *means without which life is impossible.* To deny them to people is more than "theft" (to use Proudhon's choice word for property); it is outright homicide.

No one has a right to own property on which the lives of others depend, — either morally, socially, or ecologically. Nor does anyone have a right to design, employ, or impose privately owned technological equipment on society that damages human health and the health of the planet.

Here, ecology completely dovetails with society to yield a *social* ecology that emphasizes the close interconnection between ecological social problems. Technology — the kind society uses to maintain human planetary life and the kind that undermines both — is one of the major points of contact between social values and ecological values. At a time of sweeping ecological degradation, we can no longer retain techniques that wantonly damage human beings and the planet alike — and it is hard to think that damage can be inflicted on the one without being inflicted on the other.

A major tragedy of our times is that we no longer look at technics as an ethical relationship. Greek thought maintained that to produce an object of high quality and artistry was a moral calling that involved a special relationship between an artisan and the object he or she produced. Indeed, to many tribal peoples, to craft a thing was to actualize the raw material's potentialities, to give soapstone, marble, bronze, and other materials, a "voice," as it were, an expression that realized its latent capacity for form.

Capitalism eliminated this outlook completely. Indeed, it severed the relationship of the producer to the consumer, eliminating any sense of ethical responsibility of the former to the latter, leaving all other ethical or moral responsibilities aside. If there was any moral dimension to capitalist production, it was the claim that self-interest was guided by an "invisible hand" — the interplay of market forces — so that production for profit and personal gain would ultimately serve the "general good."

But even this shabby apologia has all but disappeared today. Unabated greed, another example of the ethics of evil, has replaced any sense of the public good. A corporation is lauded simply because it is less greedy than another — not because its operations are intrinsically good. Although it is all too easy to blame on technics what is really the result of bourgeois interest, technics, when divested of any moral constraints, can also become demonic under capitalism. A nuclear power plant, for example, is intrinsically evil; it can have no justification for existence. That increased nuclear reactors will eventually turn the entire planet into a huge nuclear bomb if enough Chernobyl accidents occur — and with more plants, they cease to be a matter of mere accident and become one of probability — is no longer doubted by any informed person today.

Growing ecological dislocations are making what were once conventional industrial operations equally problematic. Agribusiness, at one time marginal to the family-type farm, has become so widespread in recent decades that its pesticides and synthetic fertilizers are becoming global problems. Smoke-belching installations and the wanton use of automobiles are changing the entire ecological balance of nature, particularly the earth's atmosphere, for the worse. If one surveys the landscape of modern technology, it is not hard to see a profound need to alter it enormously. Not only ecological interests, but human self-interest requires that we move toward ecological technologies and render our technological interaction with nature creative rather than destructive.

Let me emphasize again that such a change cannot be made without doing the same for our interaction with each other and formulating a general interest that outweighs the particularized interests of hierarchy, class, gender, ethnic backgrounds, and the State. The precondition for a harmonious relationship with nature is social: a harmonious relationship between human and human. This involves the abolition of hierarchy in all its forms — psychological and cultural as well as social — and of classes, private property, and the State.

The move from "here to there" will not be a sudden explosion of change without a long period of intellectual and ethical preparation. The world has to be educated as fully as possible if people are to change their lives, not merely have it changed for them by self-anointed elites who will eventually become self-seeking oligarchies. Sensibility, ethics, ways of viewing reality, and selfhood have to be changed by educational means, by a politics of reasoned discourse, experimentation, and the expectation of repeated failures from which we have to learn, if humanity is to achieve the self-consciousness it needs to finally engage in self-management.

No longer can radical movements afford to plunge unthinkingly into action for its own sake. We have never been in greater need of theoretical insight and study than we are today, when political illiteracy has reached appalling proportions and action has become a fetish as an end in itself. We are also in dire need of organization — not the nihilistic chaos of self-indulgent egotists in which structure of any kind is decried as "elitist" and "centralist." Patience, the hard work of responsible commitment in the day-to-day work of building a movement, is to be prized over the theatrics of prima donnas who are always willing to "die" on the barricades of a distant "revolution" but who are too high-minded to engage in the humdrum tasks of spreading ideas and maintaining an organization.

To move from "here to there" is a demanding *process*, not a dramatic gesture. It will always be marked by uncertainties, failures, digressions, and disputes before it finds its sense of direction. Nor is there any certainty that basic social change will succeed in one's lifetime. Revolutionaries today must draw their inspiration from the high idealists of the past like the great Russian and French revolutionaries of the last century who had little hope that they would witness the great upheavals that confronted later generations but to which they contributed the example of their lives, dedication, and convictions. Revolutionary commitment is not only a calling that seeks to change the world; it is also an inward imperative to save one's own identity and individuality from a corruptive society that degrades one's very personality with the lure of cheap emoluments and the promise of status in a totally meaningless world.

A new politics must be created that eschews the snares of parliamentarism and the immediate gratification of a media-contrived "forum," which is more self-aggrandizing than educational. Movements like the German Greens are already filled with self-serving stars who are undermining the integrity, ethical outlook, and elan of their more heroic days. New programs and a new politics must be structured around the immediate environment of the individual — his or her housing conditions, neighbourhood problems, transportation facilities, economic conditions, pollution issues, and workplace conditions. Power must be steadily shifted to neighbourhoods and municipalities in the form of community centres, cooperatives, occupational centres, and ultimately, citizens' assemblies.

Success cannot be measured by the immediate and constant support a movement of this kind gains. Only a relatively small number of people will initially work with such a movement and only a relatively few are likely to participate in neighbourhood assemblies and municipal confederations — except perhaps when very important issues emerge that command wide public attention. Old ideas and methods which have become routine in every day life die very slowly; new ones are likely to grow very slowly. Citizen initiatives' groups may spring up suddenly with fervour and elan when a community is confronted with, say, the siting of a nuclear power plant in its midst or the discovery of a toxic dump in its environs. An ecologically oriented municipalist movement must never delude itself that such mass activities are necessarily lasting ones. They can fade away as quickly as they emerge. One can only hope that they establish a tradition that can be invoked in the future and that the popular education they provide has not been lost on the community at large.

At the same time, truly committed members of such a movement must advance with a vision of what society *should* be like in the long run. They must go very far in their goals so that others increasingly go far enough in their activities. Such a core of people must advance historic solutions as well as immediately practical ones. The present society makes all the rules of the game by which even the most well-intentioned rebels play. If this all-important fact is not clearly seen, morally debilitating compromises will, in fact, become the rule that will lead to an ethics of evil based on lesser evils that eventually yield the worst of evils. No radical movement, in effect, can lose sight of its ultimate vision of an ecological society without losing, bit by bit, all the constituents that give it its own identity.

This vision must be stated clearly so that it can never be compromised. The vagueness of socialist and Marxist ends has done irreparable damage in degrading these ends by the exigencies of a "pragmatic" politics and by manipulative compromises — ultimately, the surrender of a movement's very reason for existing. A movement must give a visual character to its ideals so that it enters into the imagination of a new politics, not merely present its ideas in programmatic statements. Such attempts have been made with considerable success in the past by groups like People's Architecture, which took the pains to replan entire neighbourhoods in Berkeley, California, and visually demonstrate how they could become more habitable, communal, and aesthetically attractive.

AN ECOLOGICAL SOCIETY

Today, we have a magnificent repertoire of new ideas, plans, technological designs, and working data that can give us a graphic picture of an ecological community and a participatory democracy. Valuable as these materials may be in demonstrating that we can finally build sustainable communities based on renewable resources, they should not be seen simply as new systems of engineering society into a balanced relationship with a given natural environment.

They also have far-reaching *ethical* implications that can only be ignored by fostering an eco-technocratic mentality toward so-called appropriate technologies, a term that is too ambiguous to be used in a larger ecological context of ideas. That organic gardening can meet our basic requirements for chemically untreated food, provide us with a superior inventory of nutrients, and improve our soil rather than destroy it are the conventional arguments for shifting from agribusiness to ecological forms of food cultivation. But organic farming does much more than this. It brings us *into* the cultivation of food, not merely its consumption. We enter into the food chain itself that has its beginnings in the soil, a chain of which we are a living component and play a transformative role. It brings us closer to the natural world as a whole from which we have been alienated. We grow part or all of our food and use our bodies artfully to plant, weed, and harvest crops. We engage in an ecological "ballet," if you like, that greatly improves upon the current fad for jogging on asphalt roads and concrete sidewalks. As one occupation among many that the individual can practise in the course of a day (to follow Fourier's advice), organic gardening enriches the diversity of our everyday lives, sharpens our natural sensibilities to growth and decay, and attunes us to natural rhythms. Hence, organic gardening, to take only one case in point, would be seen in an ecological society as more than the solution to our nutritional problems. It would become part of our entire being as socially, culturally, and biologically aware beings.

The same is true if we engage in aqua-culture, particularly in monitoring self-sustaining systems developed at the pioneering Institute for Social Ecology in Vermont, where the very wastes of herbivorous fish were recycled by aquatic plants to provide food for the fish themselves, thus creating a fairly closed, self-sufficient ecological cycle in providing human communities with edible proteins. The use of solar power, a technology that has reached an extraordinarily high degree of sophistication and efficiency, can be regarded as ecological not only because it is based on a renewable energy resource, but also because it brings the sun, changing climatic conditions, indeed the heavens, as it were, into our everyday lives in a very palpable way. The same can be said for windpower, the presence of livestock in a community, mixed farming, composting techniques that recycle a community's wastes into soil nutrients; indeed, an entire ecological ensemble or pattern in which one component is used to interact with others to produce a humanly modified ecosystem that meets human needs while enriching the natural ecosystem as a whole. *

An ecological society, structured around a confederal Commune of communes, each of which is shaped to conform with the ecosystem and bioregion in which it located, would deploy this ensemble of technologies in an artistic way. It would make use of local resources, many of which have been abandoned because of mass production techniques.

How would property and the control of property be dealt with in such a society? Historically, modern radicalism has emphasized nationalization of land and industry or workers' control of these resources. A nationalized economy, as anarchists have been quick to point out, presupposes the existence of the State. This single fact would be enough to reject it outright. What is no less disquieting is that a nationalized economy is the breeding ground for parasitic economic bureaucracies that have left even the so-called socialist countries of the East in an economic, crisis-ridden limbo. We no longer have to question its operational validity on strictly theoretical grounds as a source of statism, even totalitarianism. Its own acolytes have been abandoning it, ironically, for a relatively "free-market" solution.

Workers' control, long favoured by syndicalist tendencies in opposition to nationalized economies, has serious limitations of its own. Except for Spain, where anarchist-influenced unions like the CNT

---

*   These views were advanced decades ago, in the author's essay, "Toward a Liberatory Technology" and have since percolated into the ecology movement. Acknowledged or not, they have since become part of our contemporary conventional wisdom in a technocratic rather than an ecological and ethical form.

maintained a tight grip on any wayward enterprises that might easily have turned into collective capitalist concerns, a collective enterprise is not necessarily a commune — nor is it necessarily communistic in its outlook. More than one workers' controlled enterprise has functioned in a capitalistic manner, competing with like concerns for resources, customers, privileges, and even profits. Publicly owned, or workers'-controlled cooperatives all too often turn into oligarchic corporations, a trend widely experienced in the United States and Scandinavia. What singles out many of these enterprises is the fact that they become a particularistic interest, more or less benign. But they are no different in kind from capitalistic enterprises and are subjected to the same social pressures by the market in which they must function. This particularism tends increasingly to encroach on their higher ethical goals — generally, in the name of "efficiency," the need to "grow" if they are to survive, and the overwhelming temptation to acquire larger earnings.

Libertarian municipalism advances a holistic approach to an ecologically oriented economy. Policies and concrete decisions that deal with agriculture and industrial production would be made by citizens in face-to-face assemblies — as *citizens*, not simply as workers, farmers, or professionals who, in any case, would themselves be involved in rotating productive activities, irrespective of their professional expertise. As citizens, they would function in such assemblies at their highest level — their *human* level — rather than as socially ghettoized beings. They would express their general human interests, not their particular status interests.

Instead of nationalizing and collectivizing land, factories, workshops, and distribution centres, an ecological community would *municipalize* its economy and join with other municipalities in integrating its resources into a regional confederal system. Land, factories, and workshops would be controlled by the popular assemblies of free communities, not by a nation-state or by worker-producers who might very well develop a proprietary interest in them. Everyone, in a sense, would function as a citizen, not as a self-interested ego, a class being, or part of a particularized "collective." The classical ideal of the rational citizen, engaged in a discursive, face-to-face relationship with other members of his or her community, would acquire *economic* underpinnings as well as pervade every aspect of public life. Such an individual, presumably free of a particularistic interest in a community where each contributes to the whole to the best of his or her ability and takes from the common fund of produce what he or she needs, would give citizenship a broad, indeed unprecedented, material solidity that goes beyond the private ownership of property.

It is not too fanciful to suppose that an ecological society would ultimately consist of moderately sized municipalities, each a commune of smaller household communes or private dwellings that would be delicately attuned to the natural ecosystem in which it is located. The wisdom of living communally or individually is an issue that can only be left to decisions made by future generations, individual by individual, just as it is made today.

Communal intimacy would be consciously fostered. No municipality would be so far from another that it would not be within reasonable walking distance from its neighbours. Transportation would be organized around the collective use of vehicles, be they monorails, railroads, bicycles, automobiles, and the like, not single drivers who clutter huge highway systems with their largely empty vehicles.

Work would be rotated between town and country and between everyday tasks. Fourier's ideal of a highly variegated workday might well be honoured in apportioning the working day into gardening, the crafting of objects, reading, recitations, and a fair portion of time for manufacturing installations. Land would be used ecologically such that forests would grow in areas that are most suitable for aboreal flora and widely mixed food plants in areas that are most suitable for crops. Orchards and hedges would abound to provide niches for a wide diversity of life-forms and thereby remove the need for pesticides through a system of biological checks and balances. Still other areas would be set aside, perhaps more extensively than they are today, for wildlife. The physical use of the body would be fostered as part of a diversified work process and greater athleticism. Solar and wind power would be used extensively and wastes would be collected, composted, and recycled. Production would emphasize quality over quantity: homes, furnishings, utensil, and clothing would be made to last for years, in some cases, for generations. The entire municipal pattern I have described would be planned with a deep sensitivity for a given region to preserve its natural features as much as possible with a concern for nonhuman life-forms and the balance of nature.

Industrial installations, based on small, multipurpose machines, the latest innovations in humanly scaled technologies, the production of quality goods, and a minimal expenditure of energy, would be placed within regions to serve as many communities as possible without the mindless duplication of the same facilities and products that occurs in a market economy.

Let me state flatly that a high premium would be placed on labour-saving devices — be they computers or automatic machinery — that would free human beings from needless toil and give them unstructured leisure time for their self- cultivation as individuals and citizens. The recent emphasis of the ecology movement, particularly in the United States, on labour-intensive technologies, presumably to "save" energy by exhausting the working classes of society, is a scandalous, often self-indulgent, middle-class affectation. The salad of academics, students, professionals, and their like, who have expressed these views are often people who have never been obliged to do a day of onerous toil in their lives in, say, a foundry or on an automobile assembly line. Their own labour-intensive activities have generally been centred around their "hobbies," which may include jogging, sports, and elevating hikes in national parks and forests. A few weeks during a hot summer in a steel foundry would quickly disabuse them of the virtues of labour-intensive industries and technologies.

Between a "here" that is totally irrational, wasteful, based on giant industrial and urban belts, a highly chemical agribusiness, centralized and bureaucratic power, a staggering armaments economy, massive pollution, and mindless labour on the one hand, and the ecological society I have tried to describe on the other, lies an indefinable zone of highly complex transitions, one that involves the development of a new sensibility as well as new politics. There is no substitute for the role of consciousness and the support of history to mediate this transition. No *deus ex machina* can be invoked to make the leap from "here to there," nor should we desire one. What people cannot shape for themselves, they will never control. It can be taken away from them as readily as it is bestowed upon them.

Ultimately, every revolutionary project rests on the hope that the people will develop a new consciousness if they are exposed to thoughtful ideas that patently meet their needs and if objective reality — be it history, nature, or both — renders them susceptible to the need for basic social change. Without the objective circumstances that favour a new consciousness and the organized means to advance it publicly, there will be no long-range change or even the measured steps needed to achieve it. Every revolutionary project is, above all, an *educational* one. The rest must come from the real world in which people live and the changes that occur in it.

An educational process that does not retain contact with that real world, its traditions as well as everyday realities, will perform only a part of its task. Every people has its own libertarian background, to repeat a claim I made earlier, and its own libertarian dreams, however much they may be confused with media-generated propaganda and the images that distort them.

The "American Dream," so much in fashion today, for example, has anarchistic components as well as bourgeois ones and has taken many different forms. One strand can be traced back to the revolutionary Puritans who crossed the Atlantic Ocean to establish a quasi-communistic "New Jerusalem." For all their failings, they produced coherent, basically egalitarian communities which governed themselves in directly democratic town-meetings. Another "American Dream" was shaped by the southwest cowboy culture in which the New England domestic hearth was replaced by the lonely campfire. Its heroes were fiercely individualistic gun-slingers that are celebrated in Sergio Leone's so-called spaghetti westerns such as the movie, "The Good, the Bad, and the Ugly." Still another that emerged at the turn of the century was the impoverished immigrant "American Dream," the myth that American streets are "paved of gold," in short, a dream of unlimited material possibilities for betterment and the notion that "everything is possible" in the United States.

I have adduced these quasi-utopian visions, each uniquely national when one tries to ferret out a variety of "dreams" in European countries, to emphasize that in one way or another, the revolutionary project must make contact with these popular longings and find ways to rework them into the contemporary ideals of freedom. Anarchism is not a product of the labours of a genius who spent most of his life in the London Museum and delivered a socialist "science" to the world of his time. Either it is a social product — sophisticated, to be sure, by able theorists, but one that stems from the deepest, most generous, and liberty loving aspirations of a people — or it is nothing. Such was the case with Spanish anarchism between the 1880s and the late 1930s or Italian and Russian anarchism before the rise of Mussolini and Stalin, when the writings of Bakunin, Kropotkin, and Malatesta gave theoretical expression to deeply felt aspirations of oppressed people. Wherever anarchism took root, it did so because it literally became a voice of freedom for a yearning people and spoke in their language — notably, their most cherished ideals, most fervent hopes, and in the idiom of their specific tongues. It is this deeply popular attribute, its rootedness in the social life of a people and their communities, that has made anarchist ideas profoundly ecological in nature and that has made anarchist theorists the authentic radical initiators of ecological ideas in our own day.

TOWARD A FREE NATURE

Anarchism and social ecology — that is, eco-anarchism — must count on the probability that normal people have the untapped power to reason on a level that does not differ from that of humanity's most brilliant individuals. Eco-anarchism must work with the supposition that humanity as a whole is highly distinctive. It occupies a very unique place in evolution, which, to be sure, does not justify the notion that it should, much less can, "dominate" nature. What makes human beings unique in contrast to all nonhuman forms of life is that they have extraordinary powers of conceptual thought, verbal communication structured around a formidable array of concepts, and sweeping powers to alter the natural world in ways that could be utterly destructive or magnificently creative.

Can we dismiss these remarkable powers as mere accidents or incidents in the evolution of life, indeed, of nature as a whole? There is no way to disprove Bertrand Russell's famous lament that human consciousness is the mere accidental product of unforeseeable circumstances, a short-lived spark of light in a black, meaningless, and lifeless cosmos that emerged out of the nothingness of reality and must eventually disappear into it without leaving a trace. Perhaps — but every philosophical approach that raises the question of the "meaning" of humanity must be derived from unprovable presuppositions. In the last century, physics made the all-important presupposition that motion is an "attribute" of matter and proceeded to erect a highly sophisticated body of tenable ideas on this unprovable notion. The ability of these presuppositions to clarify reality may well have been the best "proof" physics needed to validate the role of presuppositions as such.

Modern ecology, specifically social ecology, is also in need of presuppositions if it is to become a coherent outlook that tries to explain humanity's place in the natural world. A number of frivolous ecological theories have emerged that essentially deny humanity any unique place in nature, say, one that is different from the "intrinsic worth" of a snail. This view, as I have observed, has a name — "biocentricity" — and it advances the view that human beings are neither more nor less "worthy" than snails in the natural world (hence the myth of a "biocentric democracy"). In the natural scheme of things the two are merely "different." That they are "different" is a rather trite fact, but one that tells us nothing whatever about the *way* they are different and the *significance* of that difference in the natural world.

We are thus faced with an important question. What *is* humanity's place in nature? Looking back almost intuitively over the evolution of the universe, we can see — *as no other animal can* — an overall tendency of active, turbulent substance to develop from the simple to the complex, from the relatively homogeneous to the relatively heterogeneous, from the simple to the variegated and differentiated. The most striking attribute of substance — a term I believe we require to single out the dynamic and creative notion of a seemingly "dead," static "matter" — is a process of development. By development, I do not mean a mere change of place or location; rather I refer to an unfolding of the latent potentialities of a phenomenon, the actualization of possibility and undeveloped form in the fullness of being. Within substance at its most primal level is a germinal unfolding over varying gradations of development in which each whole is a potentiality for a more differentiated whole, of tendency toward ever-greater subjectivity and flexibility. I speak, here, not of a preordained teleology or a predetermined end that marks the completion of an inexorable development. Rather, what I am trying to explore is an inherent striving or nisus and tendency toward greater differentiation, complexity, increasing subjectivity (which is not yet intellectuality until we encounter it in human beings), and physical flexibility.

These are presuppositions, and basic ones. But apparently, at a certain point, the tendency of the inorganic development toward complexity does reach a visible and clear threshold at which point life emerges. The dividing line between the two domains consists of a phenomenon called *metabolism*, in which proteins, formed from amino acids, developed the property of *active* self-maintenance and, with it, a vague sense of self- identity. Rocks and the running water that erodes them are passive. Water simply erodes and dissolves the mineral material in rocks.

By contrast, a mere amoeba is intensely active. It is literally occupied with being itself by maintaining a dynamic equilibrium between the building-up and breaking-down process that determines its existence. It is not simply passive in its relationship to its environment: it is an incipient self, an identifiable being, that is engaged in immanently preserving its identity. Indeed, it exhibits a dim sense of self-directiveness, the germ of what eventually appears as purposiveness, will, and intentionality when we examine more complex and more subjectively developed life-forms at later periods of evolution.

The further differentiation of unicellular organisms like the amoeba into multicellular ones like the sponge and eventually high complex ones like mammals yields an ever-greater specialization of organs and organ-systems. A point arrives in this process where we begin to clearly witness the emergence of nerve networks, autonomic nervous systems, layered brains, and finally, self-conscious beings over a long evolutionary process.

This is simply evidence of a trend in nature itself that reaches back to the interactivity of atoms to form complex molecules, amino acids, and proteins. Life acquires greater flexibility with warm-bloodedness, a development that renders specific life-forms more adaptable to different climates. Species interact with each other and their environment, moreover, to produce increasingly more diversified ecosystems, many of which open new avenues for evolutionary development and greater subjectivity that leads to elementary choices in following, even developing, new evolutionary pathways. Life, at these levels of complexity, begins to play an increasingly active role in its own evolution. It is not the mere passive object of "natural selection"; it *participates* in its evolution so that we are obliged to change our terminology from Darwin's day and speak of "participatory evolution."

If we survey the evolutionary unfolding of this ever-cumulative process — in which life-forms reabsorb early developments into their own development, be it early nerve networks that cover skin, nerve ganglia that form our spinal cord, "reptile" brains, and the like — we can more than hypothesize that nature exhibits a tendency toward its own self-directive evolution, a drift toward a more conscious development in which *choice,* however dim, reveals that biotic evolution contains a potential for freedom. To speak of nature simply as a "realm of necessity" is to overlook its fecundity, trend toward diversity, matrix as a development of subjectivity, self- identity, rudimentary choice, and conscious intentionality, in short, a realm of potential freedom in which life, at least, emerges from its long evolution as the basis for genuine selfhood and self-directiveness. It is in the human species that we find this development fully actualized, at least within the limits created by social life and the application of reason to the conduct of human affairs. Humanity, in effect, becomes the potential voice of a nature rendered self-conscious and self-formative.

We can thus speak of prehuman nature as "first nature" in the sense that selfhood, consciousness, and the bases for freedom are still too dim and rudimentary to be regarded as fully self-directive. We may even encounter many approximations of self-consciousness, primarily in the primate world. But it is not until we reach humanity that this potentiality acquires a new social or "second nature" that lends itself to full realization: a product of evolution that has the fullness of mind, of extraordinary communicative abilities, of conscious association, and the ability to knowingly alter itself and the natural world. To deny these extraordinary human attributes which manifest themselves in real life, to submerge them in notions like a "biocentric democracy" that renders human beings and snails "equal" in terms of their "intrinsic worth" (whatever that phrase may mean) is simply frivolous.

Moreover — and very significantly — this "biocentric" approach is meant to dilute the most characteristic trait of humankind: its capacity to engage in purposeful *activity*. It denies humanity's power to *change* the world and, in great part, to change itself. Instead, disarmed by a deadening gospel of passivity and receptivity, the trend of this "biocentric" mode of thinking is largely adaptive and basically non-critical. One hears such quietistic tenets from Taoism and from Western philosophies of "Being" that range from the static views of Par-meniedes up to, Martin Heidegger, whose outlook, in my view, can be easily brought into conformity with the ideas of National Socialism, a movement to which he belonged for more than a decade.

The great precepts of early radicals, from Robert Owen, Charles Fourier, Michael Bakunin, and Karl Marx, among many others, to our own time, placed a crucial emphasis on the belief that humanity must be an *active* agent in the world. These precepts lie at the core of the revolutionary project and the ideals of freedom. That various schools of ecology have emerged that preach the need for a passive relationship between humanity and nature; indeed, for an abject obedience of human beings to the "laws of nature," which presumably produce famines as "checks on population," may well earn ecology a reputation even worse than that of economics. If economics once acquired a reputation as the "dismal science," ecology, in its more reactionary forms, may well deserve the sobriquet of the "cruel science."

Humanity, as I have noted, is still less than human. Given the present competitive, divided, and unfeeling society, it has a long way to go in order to fulfill its potentiality for reason, care, and sympathy. But that potentiality expresses itself in countless ways that have no equal in other life-forms and its actualization depends upon basic social changes that have yet to be made. The most heinous crime of certain ecologists in dealing with these social imperatives stems from the ease with which they have dropped the human social condition from the very discourse of their concerns. This treatment of people merely as a "species" brings all human beings into complicity with their own degradation by elites, classes, and the State, not only the degradation of nature by a grow-or-die society.

Viewed from the standpoint of what humanity *can* be, we have reason to speak of a relationship between human and human and between humanity and nature that will transcend the pristine "first nature" from which a social "second nature" emerges and will open the way to a radically new "free nature" in which an emancipated humanity will become the voice, indeed the expression, of a natural evolution rendered self-conscious, caring, and sympathetic to the pain, suffering, and incoherent aspects of an evolution left to its own, often wayward, unfolding. Nature, due to human rational intervention, will thence acquire the intentionality, power of developing more complex life-forms, and capacity to differentiate itself. We encounter at this point the far-reaching questions of developing an ecological ethics. Human intervention into the natural world is not a sick aberration of evolution. Human beings can no more be separated from nature and their own animality than lemmings can thrive without their skins. What makes the human animal a product of natural evolution is not only its physical primate characteristics; it is also the extent to which humanity actualizes a deep-seated nisus in evolution toward self-consciousness and freedom. Herein lies the grounding for a truly objective ethics, conceived in terms of a philosophy of potentiality and actuality, not a mechanical cause-and-effect relationship or the causal agnosticism of Hume and his modern-day positivist followers.

Reality is always formative. It is not a mere "here" and "now" that exists no further than what we can perceive with our eyes and noses. Conceived as formative, reality is always a process of actualization of potentialities. It is no less "real" or "objective" in terms of what it *could* be as well as what it is at any given moment.

Humanity, conceived from this dialectical notion of causality, is more than it is today; it is also what it *could* be — and perhaps *will* be tomorrow or generations from now. Insofar as we encounter a tendency, even a potentiality, that could yield freedom and self-consciousness, freedom and self-consciousness are no less real (or, in Hegel's more precise term, "actual") in society than they are as potentialities in nature.

What also makes the human animal a product of nature is not only the voice it gives to nature, but the fact that it can intervene into nature precisely as a *product* of natural evolution; indeed, that it has been organized over aeons of organic development to do precisely that, insofar as it has any place in the natural world. What is warped about the human condition is not that people actively intervene in nature and alter it, but that they intervene actively to destroy it because humanity's *social* development has been warped. To react mindlessly to the compelling fact that human social development is warped by demanding that human beings "minimize" their intervention in nature or perhaps even terminate it, as so many concerned ecologists have done, today, is as naïve as the behaviour of a child that furiously kicks the chair over which it has stumbled.

Social ecology advances a message that calls not only for a society free of hierarchy and hierarchical sensibilities, but for an ethics that places humanity in the natural world as an agent for rendering evolution — social and natural — fully self-conscious and as free as possible in its ability to make evolution as rational as possible in meeting non-human and human needs. I am not advancing a view that approves of "natural engineering." The natural world, as I have stressed repeatedly in earlier writings, is much too complex to be "controlled" by human ingenuity, science, and technology. My own anarchist proclivities have fostered in my thinking a love of spontaneity, be it in human behaviour or in natural development. The imagination has a major place beside the rational; the intuitive, aesthetic, and a sense of wonder for the marvelous, belong as much to the human spirit as does the intellectual. Natural evolution can not be denied its own spontaneity and fecundity any more than can social evolution.

But we cannot reject the place of rationality in life and the extent to which it is no less a product of natural development than it is of human development. We stand at a crossroads of conflicting pathways: either we will surrender to a mindless irrationalism that mystifies social evolution with myths, deities, and a crude particularism in the name of gender or hidden elites — one that renders social evolution aimless, with grim results for human and nonhuman life alike — or we will regain the activism, that is denigrated today, and turn the world into an ever-broader domain of freedom and rationality. This entails a new form of rationality, a new technology, a new science, a new sensibility and self — and, above all, a truly libertarian society.

NOTES

1. I have not penned this reference to viruses lightmindedly. The "unimpeachable right" of pathogenic viruses to exist is seriously discussed in David Ehrenfeld's *The Arrogance of Humanism,* (New York: Oxford University Press, 1978), 208–210.

2. See Bill Devall and George Sessions, *Deep Ecology,* (Salt Lake City: Peregrine Smith Books, 1985) for a comprehensive book-length account of the views expressed by the "deep ecology" movement. Much of the language used by "deep ecologists" — such as "biocentric equality" — will be found in this work.

3. *Ibid.,* 225.

4. Robert Briffault, "The Evolution of the Human Species" in *The Making of Man,* V.F. Calverton, ed. (New York: Modern Library, 1931), 765–766.

5. David Ehrenfeld, *op.cit.,* 207

6. Dorothy Lee, *Freedom and Culture* (Englewood Cliffs, NJ: Prentice Hall, Inc, 1959), 42.

7. Paul Radin, *The World of Primitive Man* (New York: Grove Press, 1960), 11.

8. I've examined this important, and largely neglected, aspect of magic in my book, *The Ecology of Freedom*, (Palo Alto: Cheshire Books, 1982). By no means do I think, however, that this noncoercive form of magic has any meaning for our time. I cite it merely as an example of *how* nonhierarchical communities viewed the natural world, not as another technique that should be recovered for use by modern mystics and theists. Early hunters were wrong, of course. Game did not obligingly expose themselves to spears and arrows any more than they were "forced" by more coercive magical practices to become food in a Paleolithic diet. To try to restore these rituals today (and no one quite knows what forms they took) would be naïve at best and cynical at worst. To the extent that ritual has any place in a free society, it should be new ones that foster a high regard for life and for human consociation — not descend into an atavism that is absurd and meaningless to the modern mind.

9. Janet Biehl, "What is Social Ecofeminism?" in *Green Perspectives*, No. 11.

10. Paul Radin, *op.cit.*, 212, 215.

11. To substitute words like "industrial society" for capitalism can thus be highly misleading. "Industrial" capitalism actually preceded the Industrial Revolution. In Venice's famous arsenal, a large labour force worked with very traditional tools, and in England's early factories the labour force was structured around simple machines and techniques. What these factories did was to intensify the labour process, not introduce particularly startling technical innovations. The innovations came later. To speak of an "industrial society" without clear reference to the new social relations introduced by capitalism, namely wage and labour and a dispossessed proletariat, often willfully endows technology with mystical powers and a degree of autonomy that it does not really have. It also creates the highly misleading notion that society can live with a market economy that is "green," "ecological," or "moral," even under conditions of wage labour, exchange, competition, and the like. This misuse of language imputes to technology — much of which may be very useful socially and ecologically — what should really be

directed against a very distinct body of social relationships, namely, capitalistic ones. One may gain greater "influence" with an unknowing public by using this expression, but often at the expense of miseducating people.

12. Ernst Bloch, *Man on His Own* (New York: Herder and Herder, 1970), 128.

13. H. and H.A. Frankfort, "The Emancipation of Thought From Myth," in *Before Philosophy*, H. and H.A. Frankfort, *et.al.* (Baltimore: Penguin Books, 1951), 242-243. The passages from Egyptian chronicles appear in the pages above.

14. Peter Kropotkin, *Mutual Aid* (Montreal: Black Rose Books, 1989), 195.

15. Marie Louise Berneri, *Journey Through Utopia* (London: Routledge and Kegan Paul, n.d.), 54.

16. Ronald Fraser, *Blood of Spain* (New York: Pantheon Books, 1979), 66.

17. For a fairly complete discussion of this mixed precapitalist economy, see my book, *The Rise of Urbanization and the Decline of Citizenship* (San Francisco: Sierra Club Books, 1987).

18. Karl Marx, "The Eighteenth Brumaire of Louis Napoleon," *Collected Works*, Vol. 11 (New York: International Publishers, 1979), 103.

19. Karl Marx, *Gründisse* (New York: Random House, 1973), 109-110.

20. *Ibid.*

21. Jean Jacques Rousseau, *The Social Contract* (New York: Modern Library, 1950), 94.

INDEX

anarchy and, 115-16, 119-20, 126
as bourgeois ideology, 128, 130
capitalist stabilization and, 128-31
determinism in, 130
ebbing of, 138
feminism and, 154
as floawed model, 133-36, 168-69
historic failure of, 129-30
nature and, 136, 154
revolutionary project and, 150
theoretical limits of, 130
ubanism and, 135-36
matriarchal law, 97
matricentric societies
historical possibiities of, 77
warlike elements in, 76
Maupertuis, Pierre, 109
May Days in Barcelona (1937), 132
May/June events (1968), 145, 148
mechanism, 111
medievalism, *see Middle Ages*
"mega-machine," 45
Meister Eckhart, 109
men
"big," 59-60, 63
civil sphere of, 58, 76
classes among, 60
domination among, 57
female subordination to, 56-57, 65-66,
77, 155-56, 157
feminism and, 76
in Greece, 69
in history, 76, 77
in tribal society, 52
in slave societies, 65
Middle Ages, 19
anarchistic ideas and, 118
city-states in, 70, 88, 179
Enlightenment reaction to, 166
social structure of, 87
millenarianism, 107-09
militia, Greek, 70
misanthropy, 22, 153
ecological, 15, 23
mixed economy, 87, 89, 112-13
modernity and anarchism, 120
monarchy, *see* kingships
Montesquieu, de, Charles de Secondat, 114
morality
Christian heretics and, 107
custom contrasted with, 99-100
freedom and, 113
nature of, *see* values
monastery as utopian model, 111
More, Thomas, 112, 113

Morelly, 114
Morris, William, 122, 123
Muir, John, 152
Mumford, Lewis, 45
municipal anarchism, 131
see also libertarian municipalism
municipalism, *see* libertarian municipalism
mutual aid
in counterculture, 146
Proudhon's, 131, 183
mysticism
dialectical tradition and, 108-09
ecology and, 12, 162-65
fallacies in, 76
in feminist movement, 12, 163-65
myths, 100-07
hierarchy and, 34-35
origins of freedom in, 101-03

Naess, Arne, 12
nation-state, 15, 114
anarchism and, 126
as fully developed state, 70-71
historical impact of, 85-87, 88
kingship and, 86
Marx and, 126
urban opposition to, 88
nationalization of industry, 128
natural selection, 201
naturalism, 162
nature
civilization versus, 21
damage inflicted on, 128-29
creativity of, 37
ethics and, 35
free, 198-204
humanity's place in, 35-36, 39, 42-43,
202-04
idea of dominating, 33-34, 44-46, 154-
55
liberalism and, 154
Marx's view of, 33, 136, 154
"Mother," 38
mystification of, 13
as passive, 101-02
revenge of, 128-29
restoring humanity's balance with, 171
revolutionary project and, 153-54
second, *see* second nature; society
social ecology and, 32, 153-54
as static, 103
as stingy, 32-33, 154
Nazism, 161
neanderthal communities, 98

Books by Murray Bookchin

The Modern Crisis

The Rise of Urbanization
and the Decline of Citizenship

The Limits of the City

The Ecology of Freedom

Toward an Ecological Society

The Spanish Anarchists

Post-Scarcity Anarchism

Crisis in Our Cities

Our Synthetic Environment

About South End Press

South End Presss is a nonprofit, collectively run book publisher with over 150 titles in print. Since our founding in 1977, we have tried to meet the needs of readers who are exploring or are already committed to the politics of fundamental social change. Our goal is to publish books that encourage critical thinking and constructive action on the key political, cultural, social, economic and ecological issues shaping life in the United States and the world. In this way, we hope to give expression to a wide diversity of democratic social movements and to provide an alternative to the products of corporate publishing.

If you would like to receive a free catalog of South End Press books or get information on our membership program—which, for $40, offers two free books of your choice and a 40% discount on all other titles—please write us at South End Press, 116 Saint Botolph Street, Boston, MA 02115.

Other Books of Interest Available from South End Press

Fighting For Hope
Petra Kelly

The Imagination of the New Left: A Global Analysis of 1968
George Katsiaficas

Architect Or Bee? The Human/Technology Relationship
Mike Cooley

Against The State Of Nuclear Terror
Joel Kovel

Liberating Theory
Michael Albert *et. al.*

Conversations In Maine: Exploring Our Nation's Future
James and Grace Lee Boggs, Freddy and Lyman Paine